Time of Remembering

The Outcast Series
Book Two

SUSAN ILEEN LEPPERT

Paperback ISBN: 978-1-956467-03-1
Hardback ISBN: 978-1-956467-04-8
E-book ISBN: 978-1-956467-05-5

Printed in the United States of America
1 3 5 7 9 10 8 6 4 2

DEDICATED TO:

Earl Leonard Colmus, Jr.
(Your laughter fills my heart with Joy!)
and
Eric Lee Colmus
(Your sense of humor fills my heart with delight!)
and
John Raymond Colmus
(Your depth of caring fills my heart with love!)

God Bless You.
Love Always,
Mom

WITH SPECIAL THANKS TO:

Laura Rickord--for all your time and effort. I appreciated the smiles and the tears.

Bryan Locey--for proofreading--again and again, and--hopefully again.

Jerry Ahrens--for taking time from his metal detecting to cheer me on-- ever encouraging.

Cathie Yager--for keeping me sane, with that special article, and all your prayers.

Carla Dick--for your many loving "threats," emails, and long distance calls!

John Bruce--for having lived: one "Courageous Outcast" to another.

Kelsey Colmus--for helping, again and again. You're my favorite "author's" helper!

Ronda Moore--for all her time, tremendous encouragement, and tireless "PR" work!

And, again, to Deb Diamond--for "sharing" her beautiful "Glory Horse."

God Bless You all,
Susan Ileen Leppert

AUTHOR'S NOTE

Life is not easy, Only God, and time, heals its wounds. Given enough time, We learn the value of these wounds...Some by kneeling and praying, Some by looking for a cardinal in flight. Thank you for being there for me, Dad. I love you.

TRANSLATIONS-
SCOTTISH/ENGLISH

du--do

dee--die

na'--not

ken--know

ain--own

nae--no

per'aps--perhaps

'tis--it is

du na'--do not

tha'-that

git--get

e'er--ever

aboot--about

ye've-you've

verra--very

grit--great

nuthin'--nothing

nae doobt--no doubt

me--my

aye--yes

bairn--baby

afore--before

wha'--what

wee--little, small

jist--just

mither--mother

auld--old

t'--to

wi'--with

doon--down

oot--out

o'--of

fer--for

whaur--where

thuar--there

whuare'er--where

anither--another

frae--from

CHAPTER 1

Word spread quickly of the woman in Indian dress standing at a grave in the cemetery west of Hastings. Tom Dawson, proprietor of Dawson's General Store, heard it from Johnathon Clark, the bank president, who heard it from Reverend Higgins, the minister from over in the valley, who heard it from his friend, Amanda Culpepper, who said her husband, Amos—ex-gunfighter turned deputy sheriff— yelled it, as he lit out on horseback to tell the sheriff, Moses Gentry.

It took Moses about two minutes, at a full gallop, to cover the distance between the schoolhouse east of town and the cemetery. He knew, even before he saw her, that it was Sarah. No one said her hair was auburn and shone in the autumn sunlight like the stand of red maples on the ridge beyond the cemetery. No one had to. He knew it in his heart, like a man knows in his bones when he's seriously ailing. He knew it was Sarah, as sure as he knew the sun was shining and the sky was blue. As sure as he felt the pounding of his heart as he reined in Midnight and jumped from the horse.

She stood at her father's grave—not wailing or weeping as most would have done—but calm and composed. A faraway look in her eyes as she gazed out across the field to a lone birch tree, its few remaining leaves fluttering in the breeze, a mixture of yellow and green. He watched her, not wanting to interrupt, entranced by the sight of her. Her hair hung down her back to her waist in two thick braids. Her buckskin dress was decorated with beads that formed a design across her breasts,

1

ending in a cascade of fringe. Moccasins rose to her knees—fringe also decorating their sides—and across the toes porcupine quills formed a design he could not see clearly from where he stood.

Standing there, outlined by the sun's brilliant rays, her back straight and head held high, she reminded him of the young woman he had so enjoyed teasing, years earlier. The young woman he had called "darlin'" back then, at first just to see her reaction, and later because it came naturally. He could tell this woman was stronger and more confident. He could sense that she had faced some trials and tribulations and yet her bearing gave evidence to the fact she had transcended adversity. She now had the elegant bearing of a mature woman.

"Sarah," he said, causing her to slowly turn her head toward him. He noticed the sadness in her eyes, the dampness of unshed tears upon her lashes.

"Moses," she said softly, "I knew you would come." She turned toward him but did not move closer. Time seemed to stand still as they stood there, the whisper of the wind the only sound.

Sarah had known he would come. Hoped he would not be put-off by the obvious changes that had taken place over the five long years she had been away. Hoped he would accept her, regardless of how she now dressed and more importantly, how she now thought. She thought of herself as an Indian now, though white of skin and tanned a honeyed shade of brown by the sun, unlike the pale skinned women of Hastings who covered themselves from its rays. Would he draw back, too, as had the couple whom she passed as she entered the cemetery? They had stared at her, backing away, nearly falling over each other in their rush to avoid her. She raised her chin without realizing it, her eyes looking steadily into his. She saw the tousled black hair and dark moustache now suffused with gray, the thinness of his body, and hollow-cheeked gauntness of his face that gave him a somewhat haggard look. She watched his face for a hint of what he was thinking. Then, just as she was about to speak, the slow, devilish grin began to spread across his face, the same grin she had seen in her mind whenever she thought of him over the past five years.

"I've missed you, darlin'," he said, the words booming from his lips.

She didn't remember later if he had closed the distance between them, or if she had walked to him. She only knew that, suddenly, she was in his arms and kissing him, her hands resting against his buckskin shirt, his arms encircling her in a warm embrace.

"Sarah, Sarah," he repeated between kisses, holding her tightly against him. She didn't pull away, as once she would have, but let him hold her as feelings of contentment and security filled her.

They stood there, bodies touching, her breath gentle against his ear and neck, his heart beating a fierce staccato in time with hers. Both felt deep contentment and neither made a move to distance themselves as they held each other and waited for their hearts to resume their normal rhythms.

"Oh, Moses," Sarah whispered, keeping her head against his shoulder, her voice feeling like a welcomed vibration inside him. "I've missed you so," she said, her words: music to his ears.

They stood there, unaware of the sun beating down upon them or the wind swirling leaves, hither and yon, around them. It had been five years since she had left with Gray Eagle, five long years. Moses stepped back away from her, studying the woman before him. She met his gaze, watching intently for even the slightest change in his features, for the slightest sign of disapproval.

"Welcome home," he said at last. "I'm sorry you had to find out about your father's death like this. I hoped to break the news when...*if*...you ever came back."

She smiled sadly, looking toward Samuel Justus' grave. "I already knew. Wolf Hunter...ah...Silas Haverty brought furs into town soon after and heard the news. He came and told me."

"Where's Gray Eagle?" Moses asked, adding, "I'm surprised he'd let you come into town alone—things being the way they are with most folks toward the Indians now."

Sarah looked out beyond the cemetery to the one lone birch before answering. "Gray Eagle's dead. He died four years ago."

He watched her closely, noticing how she shut her eyes as though to shut out the unbearable pain of her loss. Moses reached out slowly, touching her arm, wondering how she had managed in a strange land, among people who were so different from her own in language and customs. More importantly, he wondered why she hadn't come back to Hastings, to her cabin and to those who loved her, long before this.

"Have you come to stay?" He was sorry he asked, as she turned toward him, shaking her head, a look of immense sadness in her eyes.

"No," she answered. Then she looked once more at her father's grave. "No," she replied again, so softly he could barely hear her. He bent and picked up his hat where it had fallen when he embraced her, not knowing what else to say. He felt a deep sense of sadness fill him. He ached to hold her, to stop her from ever leaving again.

"Moses, I need to go back...to 'The People'...to Gray Eagle's people. I came for medicine. We have smallpox in our village, and none of the herbs have helped. Many are dying, many of them young children."

"Doc Valentine can help," Moses stated. "He's new here, but folks like him. Doc Pearson passed on last winter. Doc Valentine's young, but real smart. He came here right out of medical school in the east... Boston, I think it was. Planned on heading to California, but liked our little town. Him and his missus been here since last spring."

He knew he was talking too much, but couldn't seem to stop. It was as if by telling her of the Doc and his missus, he could somehow make Sarah a part of Hastings again, could make her want to stay. She smiled at him, knowingly.

"I need to rest before I head back," she said. "It's a long, tiring journey. And I need to eat something."

"You'll want to see your stepmother, Rosie, won't you?" Moses asked, watching her closely.

"Yes," she answered decisively. "Though I wish I could just go home to my cabin."

"You can, darlin'," he stated, his heart lifting with sudden hope.

"Probably been taken over by mice and other critters," she said, pensively.

He laughed then, making her look at him questioningly. "The only critter that took it over, darlin', is me. I...well, I got tired of staying on a cot in the spare room at the jail. Never was comfortable on that old cot and...well, I hope you don't mind, Sarah, but I felt sort o' close to you somehow, being out there."

She laughed then, the laugh he remembered so well. "Why, you old softie," she said, a look of tenderness shining deeply in her eyes. "You surprise me, my friend."

"Well, somebody had to take care of Pet," he stated. "Got yourself a right fine herd now. Pet's had a calf every year you've been gone, from a bull I had brought in. I had to put an addition on the barn to keep 'em all comfy in winter. The oldest O'Leary boy, Michael, helped me, and when I'm busy "sheriffin'" he sees to it that all the chores get done. Couldn't have done it without him, and that's a fact." They laughed together then, laughter that dispelled the fact that they had been apart the past five years, and temporarily eased the knowledge that she would soon leave again.

CHAPTER 2

Sarah had just begun to tie Glory to the hitching rail in front of Rosie's when the door flew open and Rosie, her hair now more white than red, hurried across the yard and wrapped her in a hearty welcoming embrace.

"Sarah!" Rosie exclaimed, her mixed-pronunciation of English and Irish, just as Sarah remembered. "Oh, dear, dear Sarah, how I hoped you'd come home." She squeezed Sarah tightly as her words tumbled over each other in her joy. "Let me look at ya'. Well, I do declare, you look like ya' haven't eaten in months!" Rosie smiled at her, giving her no time to reply. "Come on in, child. I've got some venison stew on the stove. You, too, Sheriff. Looks like you could use some fattenin' up, too."

She hurried Sarah toward the house, then stopped abruptly, looking questioningly at Sarah and then at Moses. "Oh, dear," she declared, raising a hand to her mouth, her eyes suddenly brimming with tears. She looked intently at Moses, a beseeching look upon her face.

"She knows, Rosie. She's known for awhile," Moses said, guessing what was on her mind.

"I found out that Father died, soon after," Sarah replied, assuming a stoic demeanor.

"Oh, dear," Rosie said. "I still can't believe it. Find myself settin' two places at the table, pourin' his monin' coffee. So many times a day I start to tell him something…" she grew silent, tears threatening to flow unchecked.

Sarah patted her arm. "I'm so sorry, Rosie. I know how much you must miss him. I remember how happy you made him. I miss him, too..." Her words drifted off.

Rosie smiled slightly, wiping her eyes with her hanky, then shoved it back into her apron pocket. "Well, come on," she ordered. "I've got to fatten you children up. Looks like you're both near starved to death."

They entered the house, which seemed strangely empty somehow. Rosie began dishing up heaping dishes of stew as Moses pulled out chairs for himself and Sarah. Sarah turned away, however, walking slowly into the parlor. She stood silently before her father's chair, then straightened the doily on one arm of it, running her hand slowly over the arm of the chair.

Rosie glanced toward the parlor, watching her, then shook her head sadly. "Poor child, she loved him so," she whispered.

Moses got up and walked into the parlor. "You all right?" he asked, watching the woman before him.

Sarah straightened—standing tall—then turned to face him. He noticed there were no tears upon her face, only an all ensuing look of sadness. "Yes," she replied, then walked over to him, reaching up to touch his arm with one hand. "Thank you," she said.

The stew was delicious, as were all the dishes Rosie ever cooked. They ate ravenously, following with tall glasses of milk and a piece of her special chocolate cake smothered in a creamy chocolate frosting. Little was said during the meal after Rosie said the blessing. She felt it best to see to the nourishment of these two people whom she cared so deeply about. There would be time for talking, later, she thought. But to her dismay, this was not to be. For as soon as Sarah finished eating, she announced that she would be leaving.

"Leavin'? Why ya' can't be serious! You've only just arrived!"

Sarah had expected her to be upset, and calmly tried to explain. "Children in my village are dying, Mother, of the pox. I only came to get medicine and...and...to pay my respects. They're counting on me." Determination filled her unwavering voice.

"But you've only just got here. Ya' *must* stay," Rosie pleaded, "at least for awhile."

"No," Sarah stated flatly as she stood up from the table. "I must return with medicine if the children are to live." She glanced at Moses, who had also risen.

Rosie got up quickly from the table and hurried to where Sarah stood. She had tears in her eyes as she reached out and hugged the younger woman to her. She had heard Sarah call her "Mother" and it warmed her heart immensely, not realizing it was an Indian term of endearment and respect for *all* older women. "You will come back, won't ya', daughter?" Rosie blurted out between fresh tears. "You tell that husband of yours he's welcome in my home. Tell him I miss ya', Sarah."

Sarah stiffened slightly at Rosie's words, glancing quickly at Moses, then back at Rosie.

"Gray Eagle died four years ago," Sarah replied, her eyes taking on a pained expression as she continued, "I miss you, too, Rosie, but...I don't know if I will return." She hesitated, adding, "I must go now." Then kissing Rosie on the cheek and giving her a quick hug, she turned and walked from the house, never looking back. Moses patted Rosie on the arm, then followed.

When they were outside, Sarah once again gathered herself together for the mission at hand. "Where is Doc Valentine?" she asked, leading Glory over beside Moses' great black horse.

"Same place...at old Doc Pearson's. Bought the whole shebang— house, office and all the medical supplies—from Mrs. Pearson. She went to stay with her younger sister back east—too old to stay alone any longer." He was rattling on again, much to his surprise.

"Let's go," Sarah said, grabbing a handhold of Glory's mane and swinging up onto the horse's silver-grey back. Her buckskin dress rode up, exposing her legs far above the knees, but she seemed unaware of it. Unaware, too, of the revulsion most folks in town would feel, it being extremely unladylike and highly improper. She was also totally unaware of the effect it was having on Moses. He couldn't seem to take his eyes off her. He devoured every inch of her, as a heat built within him that made him want to pull her into his arms and make love to her. She glanced at him, noticing the odd way he was looking at her, and spurred Glory into a trot ahead of him. She rode bareback, her shapely legs hanging down on either side of her horse, an Eagle feather hanging from her long auburn braids. Moses nudged Midnight, hurrying to get abreast of her, all the while attempting to get control of the feelings raging inside him.

At Doc Valentine's, Sarah threw a leg over Glory and slid off the horse, turning to look at Moses as he continued to sit in his saddle watching her.

"Well?" she said, impatiently. "Are you coming?"

A devilish grin burst across his features as he continued to sit there, looking at her.

"Well?" she repeated, slightly exasperated.

"You sure are a sight for sore eyes, darlin'," he said at last.

She laughed then, shaking her head in response. Even as a grown woman, once married and four years widowed, she had no idea how very beautiful she had become.

Judith Valentine ushered Moses and Sarah inside. Judith reminded Sarah of Rosie as she chatted happily, a ready smile brightening her lovely face. Her exuberance and joy-filled countenance complemented her husband's more serious 'doctor' side. She was shorter than Sarah, a wee bit on the plump side, with beautiful dark hair that she wore pulled back off her face in a loose bun. Her dark eyes seemed to dance and twinkle as she talked. Though Sarah guessed her to be in her mid-twenties, she could not help noticing the confidence with which she moved about her kitchen, preparing the noonday meal before her husband would leave to see his patients. Sarah liked her at once and was certain if she ever returned to Hastings, they would become steadfast friends.

Doc Valentine was in his mid-thirties, of medium height, with thinning brown hair. A quiet-spoken man who moved about his office with an ease and steadiness that exuded a solid measure of confidence. On his desk, his piano and piano stool, and even on a large crate in the corner of the room beside a tall, ceiling-high bookshelf, lay opened medical books. Here and there, they were scattered about as though he studied them every spare moment, between patients.

Sarah smiled, remembering old Doc Pearson had rarely consulted a book. He had seemed to carry all the information he needed inside his head. Of course, times were different, Sarah realized. Never was it more apparent as now, with her people, she thought. *Gray Eagle's people*, she corrected herself, as she remembered how difficult, even futile, it had seemed when both she and the medicine man had tried to heal 'The People' of the deadly scourge that had befallen them. She had tried in vain to heal them with herbal concoctions her mother had shown her. While the medicine man had chanted and prayed, invoking the help of Wakantanka, the Great Spirit. They had both failed miserably. Now, shaking herself from these painful memories, she marveled at the many powders, bottles and concoctions the doctor had at his disposal. The medicine man had argued vehemently when Sarah proposed going to Hastings to ask the doctor there for white man's medicine. But Sarah had stood firm, never wavering in her determination to get help. Finally the council had agreed, convinced by Chief Standing Elk—Gray Eagle's father—and here she was.

Sarah watched as Doc Valentine gathered up some dark vials and wrapped them carefully, placing them side by side in a small cloth bag. There was no medicine to cure folks of smallpox at that time, he told her, but he advised her to burn all the blankets and clothing that had come in contact with those who were ill, to help stop its spread. He also told her to keep those who were sick isolated from those who were well. The medicine he gave her, though not able to cure or heal the Indians, would ease the suffering, somewhat, of those who were stricken, he said.

Moses was having an animated conversation with Judith in the other room, laughing and slapping his knee in response to something she had said. Sarah enjoyed the sound of his laughter and wondered what it was that they were discussing. As she walked around the Doctor's office, she suddenly noticed the many beautiful paintings hanging on every wall. They were extremely beautiful. She went closer, squinting to see the name of the artist. To her surprise, they were signed simply "Val."

"Oh, my!" she exclaimed. "Did *you* paint these?"

Doc Valentine looked up from where he worked. "Yes," he replied, a shy smile upon his face. "Do you like them?"

"Yes!" Sarah replied. "They're beautiful!" He blushed slightly at her passionate response. "I like to paint," he said. "Wanted to be a full-time artist. *Was*, in fact, back in Boston, until my father insisted I get a more "sensible" profession. I tried to tell him a living could be procured from art, if you were indeed as good as I hoped I was, but you know how fathers can be." He shrugged, continuing, "No amount of talk could sway him, so...I chose to become a doctor."

"I'm sorry he didn't understand," Sarah replied, remembering her own father not being able to understand her choice of mate because of his intense hatred toward all Indians. Remembering too, how she had left with Gray Eagle, never seeing her father again and never really getting much chance to explain, except for the letter she had written. The letter Moses had taken to her father, for her, a week or so after she had left.

Doc Valentine interrupted her thoughts. "Well, actually, he did me a favor."

"What do you mean?" Sarah asked.

"Being a doctor brought Judith and me out here, where meadows stretch for miles and miles in a glorious profusion of colors, unlike in Boston. And tremendous flocks of birds and herds of wildlife surround us daily. I see the possibility of a great painting every second of every day here. In the sunrise and sunset, in the sky and clouds, and everywhere I travel over this beautiful land. Glorious, glorious scenes, all waiting for an artist to render them onto canvas!" His eyes sparkled with happiness as he talked, captivating Sarah with the scenes he spoke of and enthralling her with the sense of magic and beauty he felt so passionately.

"I'm glad you still have your painting," she said. "Someday I'd like to show you a place so beautiful...a place very special to me."

"I'd like that," he answered.

Moses paid for the medicines, insisting on it, though Sarah had intended to barter some richly elegant beadwork she had made during the long days of the previous winter.

Once outside, Moses asked the question that weighed so heavily on his mind. "You'll stay tonight, won't you, Sarah?"

She hesitated a moment, then looked off to the northwest in the direction of Gray Eagle's village. "Tonight," she answered decisively. "Come morning I must leave. Many were ill when I left, Moses. Every moment I delay, more will die." He smiled at her, feeling an abundance of pride fill him. He had never met a woman he respected more.

"Sarah?" Tommy Dawson called, rushing from Dawson's General Store. Two little boys followed him, pushing and shoving each other, their laughter and squeals proceeding them. They stopped just behind their father, peeking out at Sarah, shyly.

"Tommy..." she answered. "Are these little ones yours?"

Tommy smiled a proud smile. "Yes, they sure are. Danny's inside with Melinda Rose and the latest one, our first little girl." Sarah smiled, a tightening feeling closing over her heart, small protection from the pain that threatened to overwhelm her every time she saw other parents with their children. Moses noticed, but said nothing.

"Come see Melinda Rose," Tommy insisted, "and Polly, the new baby." Sarah smiled and followed him into the store.

"I'll be right back," Moses said. He knew this would be his only chance to make some arrangements with Amos to have the O'Leary boys look after Sarah's cabin and livestock, and to see if Amos would take his place as sheriff, for awhile. He excused himself and turned away, heading across the street toward the jail, determination in every step.

"Sarah!" Melinda Rose exclaimed, hurrying over to Sarah. A tiny pink-faced baby wrapped in a soft blanket was tucked within her arms. "Look at you," she said. "You look more Indian than...well, you know." Sarah couldn't help notice how she wrinkled her nose as she spoke, as if the mere word 'Indian' was repulsive. She smiled, overlooking the boisterous revelry in the background, going on between the two younger boys. Indian children were taught to be quiet, to listen, always on the alert for danger and out of respect for their elders.

"Sarah, did you hear me? Boys! Boys! Stop! Be quiet! Sarah, do you want to hold the baby?" Melinda Rose asked, depositing the baby into Sarah's arms before she could reply. Sarah looked down into the tiny pink face as little hands flailed the air and a loud burp issued forth from the infant. "I never seem to get a moment that I'm not hauling someone around, cleaning off one of the kids, or chasing after them," Melinda Rose whined.

"Now, Posey," Tommy replied, coming to stand beside her. "You love every minute of it. You know you do."

Melinda Rose smiled up at him. "I wouldn't be able to manage if it wasn't for you," she said, turning to tend to young Danny, who was pulling at her skirt and holding a broken carved horse in his hands.

"How are you doing?" Tommy asked. "Don't mind the ruckus. You know how young'ns are. Say, we were real sorry about your father...meant to get to the funeral, but with Posey so close to birthin' the youngest boy, and all, we just couldn't make it. Where's your husband? Is he afraid to come to town, with all the trouble that's been going on?"

"Gray Eagle's dead," Sarah solemnly replied. "Here. Take the baby. I have to go." She turned abruptly, walking outside to where Moses now stood, watching her closely, knowing she was upset without her telling him. "Let's go," Sarah said, grabbing Glory's mane and swinging up onto the horse's back with nary a backward glance. Moses mounted Midnight and hurried after her.

When they reached the cemetery at the edge of town, Sarah glanced quickly toward her father's resting place, then averted her gaze and nudged Glory on faster. A few people looked and pointed as she rode by, looks of surprise on their gaping faces. Sarah looked straight ahead, urging Glory into a full gallop. Moses spurred his horse on, not quite certain if she wanted to be alone. He couldn't help wondering if even *his* company upset her.

After a while, Sarah pulled up, wheeling Glory around to face him. "Well, why don't you say it? Why don't you just go back where you belong, Gentry? Spare yourself the embarrassment of being seen with this *white* Indian!" she exclaimed, lashing out at him with sentiments that he understood all too well. At that, she whirled her horse around and raced away from him, kicking Glory in the sides with her heels, urging the old horse on as fast as it could go.

Moses spurred his horse, cutting across a hill among some trees in pursuit. He understood, more than Sarah could ever guess, the pain she was feeling. How many years had he felt lost between two worlds: the world of his Indian mother and the world of his white father? He guided his horse through the trees, weaving to avoid the branches and brush, hoping he could catch her at the next rise.

As he cleared the woods, he saw her heading in his direction, bent low to Glory's neck as they thundered on, Glory's hooves pounding and muzzle beginning to spew foam. He pulled across her path, grabbing her reins, as she tried to pull up on them to avoid him. She was nearly unseated as Glory shied and came to an abrupt halt! Moses held tight to the reins as Glory circled Midnight, snorting and shaking her head, her eyes wide with excitement.

"Sarah!" Moses exclaimed. "What were you trying to do, kill Glory? Or yourself?" He bristled with anger as she slid off Glory and began to run.

Moses jumped off Midnight and raced after her, tackling her before she got very far. She lay beneath him, her teeth clenched, her eyes filled with fury, her breath coming in great gasps as both tried to catch their breath. He held her hands over her head until she stopped struggling. He was too darned old to be running across fields tackling pretty girls. Why hell, it would serve her right if he keeled over dead on top of her, he thought.

"Of all the lame-brain, fool things..." he began, then noticed—to his dismay—that she was crying. Crying as if all the grief of the world had landed on her slender shoulders.

"Ah, hell," he groaned. "Did I hurt you, darlin'?" he asked, rolling off of her. "Sarah, tell me, are you hurt? Don't cry, darlin'. I'll go get Doc. Just tell me where you're hurt. Did you break something when I tackled you?" He rubbed his chin with one hand and was beside himself with worry when she didn't answer, yet continued to cry. "Tell old Moses where you hurt. Damn! I just didn't want you to run Glory to death! I didn't mean to hurt you." He was relieved to see she no longer cried as hard and seemed to be listening. He pulled her hands away from her face. "Tell me where you hurt, Sarah! Do you hear me?" He was shouting, he realized, so great was his concern for her. She pulled her hands away from his and clamped them over her face again. Moses shifted his position, kneeling on his other knee, his head hanging down as he shook it back and forth, not certain what to do next. Then, suddenly, he became aware of a sound...a sound he could not believe. The sound of laughter! "What the hell...? Sarah...are you... have you...?" She opened her eyes, tears running from them, as gales of laughter filled the air. "Damn!" he exclaimed, standing. Then he paced beside where she lay, muttering and sputtering in anger and confusion. "Get up!" he ordered, still pacing. "Darn fool woman. Scared the pants off me. I thought you were hurt. Do you know that? I was just about to throw you over my saddle and take you back to town, so Doc could check you out." He felt foolish now, though relieved to hear her laughter and know she was all right. "Darn fool woman," he repeated. "Like to drive a man crazy with worry."

She got up as he stood there, his back to her, trying to get control of his emotions. He jumped as he felt her arms encircle his waist. She laid her head against his back, her arms still around him.

"You all right?" he asked, at last, calming somewhat.

"Yes," she answered. "You?" He shook his head in affirmation.

"I'm sorry," she said. "I was hurting. Feeling...like I didn't belong...I took it out on you...and Glory. I'm sorry, Moses."

He pulled away from her encircling arms, then turned to face her, eyeing her suspiciously, his anger gone. "You're sure you're not hurt?"

"Not a bit," she answered, smiling. "Let's go home, Gentry. I'm tired."

"Good idea," he replied. And hand in hand, they walked to their grazing horses, mounted, then turned in the direction of her cabin.

CHAPTER 3

At first glance, the homestead looked the same to Sarah as they rode into the yard. Glory began to prance and perked up her ears, recognizing the home she had been away from the past five, long years. Pet began to low, as soon as she heard Sarah's voice, ambling over to be petted by her old friend, her bag swaying as she walked.

A good-sized herd, similar in color to Pet and of various ages, gazed at the humans as the woman scratched Pet's ears and neck, then resumed their grazing.

"Quite a herd you've got here," she said, smiling at Moses. "Didn't know you were a cattleman."

"A lot you don't know about me, Sarah," he answered. "But these aren't mine. They're yours. I've just been tending them for you."

She looked out over the pasture, at the new fencing, mended rails and new addition to the barn, unable to change the image in her mind of Moses Gentry, sheriff and ladies man, to a man who now took on the persona of a homesteader.

"Why?" she asked, turning to look up at him, trying to read the answer in his face and eyes.

"Why?" he repeated, mesmerized by the golden flecks of color in her beautiful hazel green eyes. He pulled his attention away from her and back to her question. "Why not?"

"I just can't picture you as a...homesteader, Gentry. Or a farmer," she stated.

"Always thought I'd like a little farm," he said, his eyes taking on the faraway look of distancing she knew so well. "I almost bought a small place ...once." His voice trailed off and Sarah knew it was long ago, when he was with his wife, before she was killed.

"I'm impressed, Moses, with everything you've done. Thank you."

"No need to thank me. Had a lot of time on my hands, thought I'd give it a try," he said.

"Well, thank you, anyway," she said, and turned toward the cabin.

"Go on in. I'll turn our horses out, then be right in."

She nodded at him, wondering what state of disarray the cabin would be in. But, to her surprise, nothing was amiss. The dishes were all washed and in their place in the cupboard. Her father's bed looked made up just as she had left it. Even the vase of flowers looked the same. A bouquet of white daisies nodded their dainty heads as the breeze from the opened door reached them.

"Home," Sarah thought, surveying the cabin where she had lived for the larger part of her life. To her surprise, her thoughts turned to her latest home: her Indian tepee with its cozy bed of hides and colorful pots and her delicate, yet useful, hand-woven baskets. She had toiled over them many long hours until she got the knack of weaving them from the reeds along the stream by the encampment.

She thought, too, of her friend—Gray Eagle's father, Standing Elk— old and weather-worn, but wise beyond his years. She also thought of Running Deer: a young Indian maiden with dark, trusting eyes and gentle heart. She had taught Sarah so many things necessary for her to learn to fit in as Gray Eagle's wife—and later—as an accepted figure amongst 'The People'.

"Home," Sarah said aloud, as if in saying it she could somehow make herself feel it. But instead, she felt troubled, standing there where once she had felt so comfortable. She felt like a stranger now, as though she no longer belonged at the cabin, but did she belong amongst Gray Eagle's people? She had learned many of their ways and been accepted by them, but did she truly belong with them, now that Gray Eagle was dead? These thoughts assailed her.

"Sarah?" Moses spoke as he approached the cabin, noticing that she still stood by the door, as though uncertain of entering. He set a bucket of water by the door, then entered, walking over to the stove.

"I'll put on a pot of coffee. Are you hungry?"

"No," she replied, moving first to the table, then over to her small rocker. She stood beside it, a million memories flooding her mind.

Moses filled the coffeepot and put it on to boil, watching her, knowing in his heart what she felt. Long ago, when his wife, 'his Sarah' had died, he had tried to go back to their small home. Had tried to face the emptiness and pain of seeing her dresses hanging in the wardrobe, the dishes she had washed and put away so carefully, her apron hanging on the notch by the door to their room. Worst of all, had tried to get past the searing pain that filled his whole being as he had looked at the little cradle with its array of small colorful quilts, each one sewn with love for the baby that would never cuddle beneath them. The drastic change in his life had come when 'his Sarah' was gunned down while crossing the street to go to him, shot down for no reason. She had died in his arms, along with the baby inside her. No, I'm no stranger to change, he thought, more than a little aware of what *this* Sarah had to be feeling. She had fallen in love with the one person her father would never accept, choosing to marry him and live with him, far away from the world she had been raised in. The world where women did what was expected of them, where there were rules and restrictions, where women led lives filled with priorities and not lives filled with fanciful notions and farfetched dreams. Lives ordained by their parents, their churches, and society as a whole. Sarah had chosen another path. A path that few would or could have ever imagined. That she had *stayed* with that choice for four years *after* her husband died, spoke volumes. Moses admired her more than he could ever say, yet he knew what it had cost her to return to Hastings and to her cabin. Now she was torn between the two worlds: one she had been raised in, surrounded by those who loved her, one she had grown to love.

He cleared his throat, a lump filling his chest, as he thought again of the senseless murder of his wife and unborn child. He had felt lost in his home that day when he tried to go back to it. Felt raw with the pain of knowing his world had ended and nothing would ever be the same. He had stood at the door to his small home, feeling he no longer belonged there or wanted to. Feeling the emptiness and the end of *all* his hopes and dreams. Sometimes, there *was* no going back. Sometimes there was *nothing* to go back to. He wondered, momentarily, if Sarah had anything...or anyone...to go back to in Gray Eagle's village.

Taking two cups down from the shelf in the cupboard and filling them with coffee, he took them over to the table. "Coffee's ready, darlin'," he said. Sarah turned and walked to the table, quickly sitting down. She sipped the hot coffee, looking at him pensively, as she continued to study the room.

"I feel...so...as if I don't belong," she said, her voice soft, and eyes betraying the emotion she was feeling so strongly.

"I know," he answered. "I understand."

"You do, don't you?" she asked. "Oh, Moses, I didn't know it would be so hard to come back. I thought...well, I guess I thought everything would be the same. You know?" He nodded, saying nothing, hoping she would somehow "talk through" her upset. "My father's gone and people shy away from me, from my way of dressing...like an Indian. *Am* I so different? Have I changed *so much*? Do these clothes make me a *different* person?" She picked up her cup and took more sips of coffee, looking around the cabin between sips. "You kept the place up. Looks nice. Doesn't even look like you slept in the bed...my bed," she commented, smiling at him.

"I didn't," he answered, surprising her. "I sleep in the other bed, in the other room. Feel more comfortable in there."

She looked at him in disbelief. "But, why? The big bed is so much more comfortable. You should have slept in it."

"No. I figured if you ever came back, you'd want that bed, so I just settled in in the other room," he replied.

She finished her coffee, a yawn escaping her lips. *"If I* ever came back," she repeated his words, letting them drift off into silence. He waited, saying nothing, then she continued. "I never thought I'd come back. I missed Father and Rosie and you so much...*so much!* But I *never* thought I'd come back. I thought Gray Eagle and I would ride off into the sunset and live happily ever after...like in those books of my mother's that I used to read. I thought...Oh God! I don't know *what* I thought!" she exclaimed.

She reached up, covering her face with her hands. Moses longed to reach out and comfort her, to get up and walk to her side, to pull her up into his arms and hold her. Instead, he stayed where he was, wondering if she would break down and cry. But, instead, she continued to talk.

"I was so young and foolish, Moses. Oh, I know twenty-eight wasn't young, but I had no idea of life beyond these cabin walls. I only knew the lonely existence my Mother and Father shared, and the adventure and excitement in the lives of the people in those books." She looked at the vase of daisies by her rocker and got up and went over to it, pulling one of the daisies from the vase, cradling it within her hands.

"I wanted excitement, Moses. Excitement and adventure. I didn't want a life like my folks had...like my *mother's*. I wanted to experience life to its fullest..." she paused, tenderly touching the petals of the daisy she held. "When I saw Gray Eagle for the first time, Moses, my heart leapt with excitement. An Indian! A handsome, bronze-skinned, dark-haired Indian! I think I loved him right from the very first moment I saw him."

She yawned again, her eyes becoming more and more tired looking. "I loved him. I always knew that. I didn't know how difficult life would be as his wife. I had so very much to learn." She pulled the petals off the daisy, her eyes closed, obviously lost in her thoughts. "I didn't know that he'd die...so soon. I thought we'd grow old together."

"You did what you thought was right, Sarah. You followed your heart. I remember you saying that. We all do things we question later... especially when...we're...in love." He watched her closely, realizing she had no idea of the hidden meaning behind his words.

"Love," she replied, a deep yawn interrupting her. "Now that I've had love, where am I, Moses? *Who* am I? How do I find where I belong...*now*? As she spoke, she laid her head upon her arms on the table and soon was fast asleep.

Moses got up quietly and walked over to her. He brushed back the few unruly strands of auburn hair that escaped her long braids, then scooped her up into his strong arms and walked over to her father's large rocker. As gently as he could, he eased down into it. Sarah's head lay against his chest, her breathing soft and easy against his skin where his shirt lay open, the greying chest hairs warmed by her breath. She was sound asleep.

"Oh, darlin'" he said, his voice a deep whisper. "I've waited so long... hoping you'd come home." He rocked them as he spoke, her slim body cradled safely in his arms. "All the time I thought it was *my* Sarah I was still missing. It wasn't until you went away with Gray Eagle that I realized it was you." He lay his head against hers, smelling the sweet body-scent of her. "It wasn't until you left with Gray Eagle that I realized I loved you." He continued to rock them gently, placing a kiss against her auburn tresses. "I was a fool to ever let you go, Sarah. *I'm* where you belong, darlin'. *I'm* where you belong."

The daisy dropped from Sarah's hand as she shifted, snuggling her cheek against the hollow of his neck. Unaware that she was doing so, she slept peacefully within the arms of the man with the rogue's grin and dark devilish eyes: the man who loved her.

Just before sunset, Moses lifted Sarah, careful not to wake her. He carried her to the large bed that had been hers before she left with Gray Eagle and laid her down, gently pulling off her moccasins and untying the thin strips of buffalo sinew that held her hair. He unbraided her hair, enjoying the silky texture of it beneath his fingers as it fell loose upon the pillow. His eyes took in the leanness of her body and he felt concerned that she was so much thinner than he remembered. Her face looked serene and angelic as she lay there and he felt an immense urge to touch her. Watching her sleep, he controlled his feelings by concentrating on other thoughts. He wondered what she had been through the past five years, what hardships she had to endure in living with and losing Gray Eagle. He wondered how he had died and if they had been happy. Wondered, too, if she had been happy with his people. Obviously she had, he thought, or she would have come back to Hastings long before this.

"Oh, darlin', there's so much I'd like to ask you, but I guess it'll all come in time. At least you're here now, and safe, and I'm never losing you again," he whispered, then walked over to the stove to pour himself another cup of coffee.

Later that night—chores done and darkness surrounding the little cabin—he pulled the large rocker up beside the bed where she slept and sat down in it, stretching out his long legs in front of him. There was no need for a fire as the cabin was warm, but he placed a light quilt over Sarah, just the same. She stirred slightly, murmuring something he couldn't understand, then rolled over, curling her body away from him as she continued to sleep. Moses closed his eyes then and dozed, dreaming dreams that were unsettling.

In his dreams, his mother reached out to him as he rode away. His father lay on the ground—drunk or dead—he couldn't tell which, as there—in a dim, gray mist—Sarah stood, her back to him. The dream seemed to drag on and on, as if in slow motion. In it, he rode past his mother, ignoring her outstretched arms and pleading looks, only concerned with reaching Sarah. As he reached her side, she turned to face him and it was 'his Sarah' who stood there, the front of her dress covered with blood. Her eyes glazed and unseeing—as in death—yet open and staring at him, beseeching him to help her, to save her!

Moses jerked awake in the rocker, yelling out, nearly upsetting the small table beside it and the vase of daisies, upon it. His brow was covered in beads of sweat, his heart pounding fiercely within his chest. He wiped his brow with his sleeve, glad to see that Sarah still slept peacefully. He groaned, seeing in his mind the events and images of the dream, as he tried to decipher what they meant.

"I'll keep *this* Sarah safe," he whispered into the silence of the room. "Nobody will *ever* hurt her. I vow this on my life." Then he settled back into the rocker and watched the shadows of the night dance—ghostlike—across the floor and walls of the cabin. It was nearly morning when he finally drifted off to sleep.

CHAPTER 4

Moses woke with a stiffness in his neck and back from sleeping in the rocker and felt like he had about an hour of sleep, if that much. But, morning dawned bright and clear—with birds singing—and when he saw that Sarah still slept peacefully, he felt happy with the world. He slipped quietly out of the cabin, going to the pond to bathe, then dressed and brushed his hair. He enjoyed the sounds of morning, and whistled a tune as he watched a rabbit dash across the path to the cabin and back, ever alert for danger. A hawk drifted lazily across the yellow-tinged blue sky, beneath the few smoke-like puffs of cloud.

Moses sat on the bench he had made, beside the cabin door, pulling on his socks and boots. "I'd best quit dawdling," he said aloud. "Sarah will be anxious to leave. Best get breakfast cooking." He glanced around, surveying the land. "I thank you, Lord, for this day and for bringing Sarah home. I'm hoping we return here…together."

The hearty aroma of breakfast cooking woke Sarah. "I didn't know you could cook," she said, stretching contentedly, her voice husky from sleep.

"Lots you don't know about me," Moses answered, smiling at the sight of her. "Get washed up. Breakfast's 'bout ready."

"I'd forgotten how good a bed could feel," she said. "Slept so sound I thought I was home."

"You *are* home," he replied. *"This* is your home, darlin'. I kept it for you. Now hurry, so we have time to put some meat on your bones."

She laughed happily, feeling almost as if she had never left the place, and went out to the pond to wash.

When they finished eating, Sarah was surprised to see his horse saddled and waiting beside Glory. "Well, it was nice seeing you, Moses," she said. "Are you planning to ride a ways with me?"

"You got away once, darlin'. *This* time I'm going *with* you," he stated.

Sarah looked at him in surprise. "Don't suppose it would do any good to argue with you, Gentry. You always were a stubborn cuss."

"Woowie!" he exclaimed. "A long time ago, you called me a "pompous bag of wind," now I'm a "stubborn cuss." Sounds like you're starting to like me again," he teased.

She glanced over at him as she mounted Glory. "I'll like you better when you're riding, instead of talking, Gentry." Then she winked at him and nudged Glory into a trot. Moses grinned at her, then swung up onto Midnight, hurrying to catch her.

They rode until the sun was high in the sky, concentrating on the terrain. Sarah amazed Moses. He couldn't help notice her skill in riding and her diligence, as she pressed on relentlessly, in spite of the sun beating down on them or the roughness of the trail. Beads of sweat stood out on his forehead and his shirt felt damp with sweat across his back, yet Sarah rode on, looking fresh and energetic.

Much later, they came to a grassy knoll that edged a fast-moving stream. Moses drew up, calling to Sarah to stop. He dismounted and lay on his stomach at the water's edge, scooping up handfuls of the cool refreshing water. Sarah joined him, and they cupped the water into their hands and drank to refresh themselves, and wet their faces to wash away the dust and dirt of the trail.

"Ready to go?" Sarah asked, rising and heading back toward Glory.

"Gonna take a short walk," Moses answered. "And maybe we should eat a bite or two."

Sarah snorted in response. "White men travel on their stomachs, I've heard tell. Guess it must be true."

Moses looked at her, his ire rising. "Some people get "sharp-tongued" when they're hungry," he remarked, then he walked off into the bushes. Sarah patted Glory's neck as the horse drank next to Moses' great black horse, Midnight. Then she walked away in the opposite direction he had gone.

When she returned, he was mounted and ready to go. She knew by the stern expression on his face that he was not happy with her ungracious 'white man' remark. She grasped Glory's mane and flung herself up onto the horse. Moses watched her, still trying to figure a fitting response. Should he tell her he was not the white man she thought him to be? Should he tell her he was as much Indian as her husband, Gray Eagle, had been? *More* Indian than she was, for all her Indian ways and dress?

"Best not," he grumbled, urging his horse past Glory and into a gallop. Sarah dug her heels into Glory's side, hurrying to catch him.

"Maybe I should have held my tongue," she thought. "Maybe a bite or two wouldn't have been such a bad idea, after all." But Moses continued to rush on and she had to hurry to keep up, her attention diverted by the many tree branches that jutted out along the way and the unevenness of the ground.

The next time they stopped, it was dusk. Sarah's backside hurt and her legs felt stiff as she dismounted. She longed for a hot bath, wondering how long it had been since she had enjoyed a real tub bath.

"I'm caught between two worlds," she said aloud.

"What?" Moses asked, as he approached her.

"Nothing. Just talking to myself," she replied. She noticed the many gray hairs that showed at the neck of his shirt, remembering that they had once been all black. She noticed, too, the hollows of his cheeks. I should have been more considerate earlier, she reckoned. After all, maybe he had needed something to eat. No wonder he got cross.

"Moses," she said, speaking softly, "I'm sorry about before. I wasn't considering your needs. All I kept thinking about was the children in my village, and getting the medicine to them as soon as possible. I'm sorry."

He was surprised at the contriteness in her voice and how remorseful she looked. He felt ashamed of the way he had acted, too, but simply said, "You're forgiven" and began unsaddling his horse and setting up their camp for the night. Sarah felt worse as he went about busying himself and didn't tease her as he normally would have.

"Moses?" she said, walking to where he was spreading out a blanket beside the small fire he had built. "I really am sorry. Please don't be angry with me."

He turned toward her, his voice a deep drawl as he replied, "There's a lot you don't know about me, Sarah—and the time's not right for the tellin'—but, you're not the only one who's sorry, okay?" She was surprised by his words and wondered what he meant, but was glad he seemed no longer angry with her.

"Moses, I sure could use a hug," she said, her voice barely a whisper. To her delight, the devilish grin she remembered so well burst across his face.

"You're not the only one, darlin'," he replied, and in a mere instant she found herself wrapped securely within his strong arms. In response, she tightened her arms around him, his body's warmth sending shivers of feeling through her from head to toe. How long had it been since a man had held her and comforted her? How long had it been since her body had responded to a man's embrace? Unbidden, tears began to run down her cheeks.

"It's okay, darlin'," he crooned into her silky auburn tresses. "Sh-h-h, darlin', it's gonna be all right. Old Moses is right here. You don't have to worry, I'm not gonna leave you."

Until her last tear was shed, Moses held Sarah close, realizing now—more than ever—how very much he loved her.

CHAPTER 5

The next morning, Sarah had breakfast cooking when Moses awoke. "About time you woke up," she teased, smiling at him.

"Had a nice dream," he replied, stretching. "Dreamt I was holding a sweet young gal in my arms," he added, grinning. "She had a buckskin dress on just like yours."

"Lucky girl," she commented. "Anyone I know?"

"Could be," he said, his dark eyes twinkling.

"Thank you," she said, looking up at him tenderly.

He reached out, gently squeezing her shoulder. "No need for thanks. My pleasure, darlin'. Wouldn't mind holding you again, sometime."

Sarah smiled, noticing the tenderness in his voice and the cute way his hair fell across his forehead, all tousled from sleep. She had the strongest desire to run her fingers through it.

"Breakfast," she said, turning away, concentrating on pouring them each a cup of coffee. What nonsense, she thought, laughing inwardly at herself. Moses Gentry was her friend. A *special* friend, yes, but a friend. She had missed him so much, after she left Hastings, but she was Gray Eagle's woman…she caught herself, realizing the devastating truth… that she hadn't been Gray Eagle's woman for a long time. Not since he had died four long years before. She stood there, suddenly realizing that she was pouring coffee over the sides of Moses' cup.

Moses saw it, too, wondering what was bothering her. "Sarah?" he questioned. "Are you all right?"

"Yes," she answered, her face blushing a deep red. "Eat up, Gentry. We've got a long way to go. I want to make it to the Havertys before dark."

"Yes, ma'am," he answered, taking the last bite of his sourdough biscuit into his mouth.

Sarah smiled at his antics. "You're something else," she stated, smiling at him.

"You've got that right," he replied, glad to see her smile again. He winked at her and went to saddle Midnight.

The day dawned cool and overcast and the terrain spread out before them. No longer were they in woods and dense brush. As far as the eye could see, they were surrounded by gently rolling hills and valleys that abounded with wildflowers. It reminded Sarah of the meadow she used to run across near Hastings. She spurred her horse on, trying not to think about those days, so long ago, when she ran across the meadow on her way to the cave where she had met Gray Eagle. Where he would often be waiting for her.

They rode all day, making good time, stopping only to water the horses and relieve themselves. At one point, Sarah caught up to Moses, handing him two pieces of pemmican and two biscuits from her pack, and getting out two for herself.

"Want to stop?" she asked, being more considerate of him than she had been the day before.

"Not unless you need to," he replied. "You said you wanted to stop for the night at Silas and Nancy's. We'd better keep going if we're to make their place by nightfall."

Sarah smiled, happy at the idea of seeing Nancy and the little girl she had helped deliver on the day of her marriage to Gray Eagle. Nancy had named the child Sarah—after her—and Sarah wondered how she was doing. She would be nearly five years old. Nearly a year older than...She spurred her horse on, passing Moses, who pulled back in surprise as she raced by.

"Sarah! What is it? Sarah, *wait*..." Moses yelled, racing after her, concern showing on his face.

In a short while, Sarah stopped, covering her face with her hands as Moses rode up beside her. He was surprised to see that she seemed about to cry.

"Sarah, what is it? What's wrong?" he asked, reaching across the space between them to touch her arm.

"Memories," she answered softly, looking at him with unspeakable sadness in her eyes. "Just memories," she repeated, moving away from him, putting an end to any further discussion.

Moses drew back, wondering what it was that caused her such pain. It must be she's grieving the loss of Gray Eagle, he thought, a knot of discomfort tightening in his belly. She still must have feelings for him, even after all this time. He frowned, as he watched her canter on ahead. Maybe she has no room in her heart for loving anyone else, yet...anyone *new*. He remembered how long he had grieved the loss of his wife, and his heart felt heavy.

He rode on, remembering then, the evening before, when he had held her in his arms. He had held her close, comforting her. It was she who had first mentioned needing a hug. Hadn't that meant anything? He smiled as he remembered how she had held him, too. It had seemed so right, holding her like that, comforting her. Which one of us were you holding, darlin', me ... or the memory of your dead husband? With those thoughts in mind, he spurred Midnight on, angry inside at the possibility that he had no chance of a future with her.

"Sarah, pull up a minute," he ordered gruffly, coming up alongside of her. "We need to talk."

Her eyes widened in surprise at his tone. "What is it?" she asked, as he dismounted and walked toward her. She slid off Glory's back, looking questioningly at him.

He stopped a few feet from her, glowering at her, his scowling look penetrating her whole being. He turned then, pacing away from her, then turned back, clenching his hands as he continued to pace, choosing his words as he tried to control his mounting anger.

"What is it?" she asked, wondering what it was that was bothering him so. He scowled at her again, stopping before her, obviously more than a little upset. "Moses?" she questioned, her voice soft. He kept looking at her, trying to find the right words, his dark eyes flashing.

"Damn it, woman! You just don't get it, do you?" he shouted. "Why do you think I'm here? Do you think I *like* riding all day with little rest and little to eat? Do you think I like riding along, watching your cute bottom bouncing along in front of me all day? Damn it, Sarah, I'm a *man!* Not some good-hearted *friend* out for a ride with you!"

He stopped talking and stood looking at her. Her mouth had dropped open at his words, surprise showing upon her face. He shook his head, looking down at the ground, trying to control the emotions that still threatened to overwhelm him. "I know you have memories," he said, looking at her, his voice softening. "It's obvious you still miss Gray Eagle...still love him." He paused, looking deep into her eyes. "But, damn it, Sarah, I love you! I'm *not* Gray Eagle. I never will be. But I love you, darlin'. Knew it ever since the day you left with him. Knew I should never have let you go!" His voice was getting louder, but he was unable to control his feelings any longer. "You have to let him go, Sarah. You can't keep crying over a...a *dead man!* He can't come back and love you. I carried the memory of my wife in my heart for years. *Years!* And because of it, I let *you* go off and marry another! Well, Gray Eagle's dead, Sarah, and *I'm* not! You can cry over your memories everyday, honey, or you can open your heart to a *living* man. A man who loves you with all his heart!"

Sarah stared at him, shocked by his words, even more shocked to realize he thought her tears were for Gray Eagle. Having run out of words, Moses stood before her, silent at last, except for the pounding of his heart. He waited for her to turn away or to slap him, after his outburst and the cruelty of some of the things he had said. The silence between them seemed to go on forever. Then, just as he was about to apologize for his outburst, Sarah walked into his arms, her hands reaching up on either side of his face, her eyes brimming with fresh tears.

"I'm sorry, darlin'. I shouldn't have let you have it like that. I...I was out of line," he began, then realized she was speaking so softly he could barely hear her. He bent closer, listening.

"My memories weren't of Gray Eagle," she whispered. "They were of our baby." And she began to cry softly against his chest, her shoulders shaking with the grief she had carried inside for so many years.

When at last she quieted, Moses continued to hold her. She seemed as thin and fragile as a sapling and he kept his arms firmly around her a long while after her tears had abated. She dried her face, noticing the wet area where her tears had fallen on the front of his shirt. She felt as though a tremendous weight had been lifted off her shoulders and it was a welcomed relief. For nearly five years, she had kept her emotions inside, hiding her grief and sorrow, willing herself to show only strength and fortitude. She had carried on, in spite of all the sadness and hardships, persevering where a lesser person would have given up and fallen by the wayside.

She gently pulled back from him, looking at him with a look he would always remember. "So you think you love me," she remarked, watching him closely.

"Don't think it, I *know* it," he stated. She smiled at him, wondering what to reply, wondering how she could not have realized the depth of his feelings.

"I'm glad," she said, at last, placing a finger on his lips as he was about to speak. "There's a lot we need to talk about, Moses. A lot that I need to tell you before…before…"

He interrupted her then, kissing the finger that lay across his lips, then gently pushed it aside. "I know this was a surprise, Sarah, one you aren't really ready for. It's okay. I'm not gonna rush you. We'll talk later. There's things I need to tell you, too. I just want you to know that I meant what I said, darlin'. That I love you. I have for a long time. If you feel the same, someday, we'll take it from there."

She looked at him, a sweet smile upon her face. "You talk too much, Gentry. Kiss me." And he bent quickly, delivering a kiss like none he had ever given her before. A kiss that sent fire coursing through their bodies, from head to toe, making them *both* tremble with desire.

CHAPTER 6

It was dark when they reached the Havertys. "Hello there," Moses called out as he dismounted and tied his horse to the hitching rail in front of the cabin. Sarah was glad when he walked around Glory and gently lifted her down. She was bone-tired and would welcome a good night's sleep after two days in the saddle.

The door opened and Silas Haverty spoke. "Who goes there?" then he added, "Sarah...? Moses...is that you?"

"It is," Moses answered. "Tired and trail-weary."

"Well, come on in. Nancy's putting on some coffee, as we speak," Silas said, holding up a lantern so they could see their way to the door.

Nancy rushed around Silas to embrace Sarah. She had seen no other women since Sarah's last visit, five years earlier, except for a couple of Indian women who had been traveling with some trappers. But those women were sullen—not friendly—and stayed a distance from the cabin when the trappers stopped to ask Silas for directions to Buffalo Creek, to the south of them.

"Sarah!" Nancy exclaimed. "I'm so happy to see you!" The women hugged and Sarah couldn't help noticing Nancy was, again, with child.

"Am I going to have to deliver this one, too?" Sarah asked, nodding toward Nancy's stomach.

"No, not unless you'll be back here in the early spring."

"Afraid not," Sarah replied. The women laughed and Sarah noticed a small blonde haired little girl watching her from behind her mother's rocker in the corner. "Hello, are you Sarah?" Sarah asked, and the child laughed and ran to stand behind Nancy.

"She knows my name, Mama," the girl said, her hair bobbing as she peeked around at Sarah.

"Yes, honey, that's because her name is Sarah, too. You were named after her."

"Oh," the child replied, giggling and clapping her small hands together.

Moses and Silas entered the cabin then, having settled the horses for the night.

"Did you get any medicine, Sarah?" Silas asked. She had met him on the trail when on her way to Hastings, and had told him of the smallpox in the Indian village. Also, that she would stop at his place on her way back to the tribe, to say a quick hello to Nancy and little Sarah.

"Yes," she replied. "I got a couple different medicines, but the doctor said the most I could hope for was to ease their suffering. The stronger ones might survive, I suppose, but it doesn't look good. He did say that burning the bedding and clothes of those who are ill and those who have died would help stop the spread of the pox. Looks like I've got my work cutout for me when I get back."

Silas shook his head sadly. "It's a dam shame. I wish I knew of something to help."

Nancy walked over to Moses, placing her hand on his arm. "Welcome to our home, Sheriff Gentry. We don't get many visitors. It's good to see you again."

"Good to see you, too, Nancy. But, call me Moses."

"All right, Moses it is. Would you like something to eat? I've got some bear stew and biscuits on the stove."

"Sounds good," he replied.

"Sarah, you'll have some, too, won't you?" Nancy asked.

"A little, please," she answered and covered her mouth as she yawned.

Nancy bustled about setting the table and heating the stew. Moses and Silas talked at the table, each drinking a cup of coffee. Sarah walked over to Nancy's rocker and sat down, watching young Sarah, who sat on a rug by the window playing with a rag doll Nancy had sewn for her. For only an instant, the thought of her own child crossed Sarah's mind as she watched the little girl play. Then her head eased slowly to one side and she slept.

Moses looked up a short time later, noticing that she was asleep and walked over to her. "Sarah?" he called quietly. She did not reply. "Can you show me where she's to sleep?" he asked, looking at Silas and Nancy.

"In there," Nancy said, pointing to a small room just off the main room. "There's fresh bedding on the bed and it's real comfortable."

Moses bent, sliding his hands beneath Sarah's legs and back, then lifted her up into his arms. She stirred and murmured something. "Sh-h-h, darlin', go back to sleep. I'm right here," he whispered and carried her into the other room.

Nancy hurried in before him, pulling back the covers on the bed. "Can you manage?" Moses asked her, laying Sarah gently down upon the bed and pulling first one moccasin, then the other, off her feet.

"Yes," Nancy whispered, smiling at the man who so obviously loved her friend. "Go eat, Moses, while the food is hot. Sarah can eat later, after she's rested awhile."

He smiled at her, knowing she was aware of what he felt in his heart. "She's had a rough time of it," he explained, gently covering Sarah's feet with the patchwork quilt that graced the bed.

"I know," Nancy replied, her face showing a gentle understanding. "I know."

Moses left the room, shutting the door quietly behind him, then sat down to eat the delicious bear stew and biscuits. Silas smoked his pipe and reminisced about the years that had passed since they had last seen each other at his wedding to Nancy.

Silas told of the upsurge of trappers that had come to the area of late, depleting the number of animals he had always relied on each year to make his living, exchanging furs for supplies. He also told of the trappers and the two Indian women who had come through some weeks before. He said the women had suffered badly at the hands of the trappers.

Moses listened, enjoying the other man's company and the delicious food, but talk of the trappers and the Indian women turned his thoughts back to his own lovely Indian mother and how she had been won in a game of cards. It sickened him to remember the ill-treatment she also had received, made worse because it came from his own father. Moses thought of Sarah, in her buckskin dress and beaded moccasins. What a prize she would be to men such as those. Men with no compassion or caring. Men totally lacking in morals. His hands drew up into fists as he thought these thoughts, causing an anger to quickly build within him. He would die before men such as those ever got near her! In his heart she was his now, and no one would ever hurt or threaten her, as long as he lived.

"Moses?" Silas said, startling him. "I asked if you wanted more stew?"

"Sorry," Moses replied. "I was lost in thought. Yes, just a little, please." He ate heartily, then, more than he had intended, commenting on what a good cook Nancy was.

"Yes," Silas replied, "I'm a lucky man to have found her. Is her father still alive?" he asked, lowering his voice.

"Yes," Moses answered, also lowering his, "but he hasn't changed any. Still drinks heavy."

"A shame," Silas remarked. "Nancy misses him, sometimes, regardless of how he treated her. I promised her I would take her with me—for a visit—when I take furs into Hastings next spring. Depends on how healthy she and the new baby are then, though. He looked at his daughter, sitting in her mother's rocker, rocking her dolly. Moses saw the expression of love on his friend's face and felt admiration for the man he was sharing good food and pleasant conversation with.

Silas Haverty was a good honest man—as decent as they came—and Moses was proud to call him 'friend'. He knew Silas was called "Wolf Hunter" by the Indians and had gained their respect and friendship in his many years of living as a trapper. He also knew that many years earlier, Silas had been married to Gray Eagle's sister and had been grief-stricken when she died in childbirth along with their baby. He was a man who immensely enjoyed the peace and serenity of the wilderness. Yet, he had come into Hastings then, to drink and cry, unable to find solace at his home where they had died. He had been overwhelmed with grief. Staggering in his drunkenness, unshaven, smelling of the pelts he usually carried. Moses had talked to him then, trying to give him counsel and comfort.

A lot like me, Moses thought, thinking of his own drunken, unaccounted-for days, after his wife and baby had died. He sipped his coffee, his thoughts going to happier times. How different Silas had been, the day he married Nancy Pearly. He had gotten his feet back under him again, had cleaned up and gradually learned to accept his loss. Like me, Moses thought, again. He learned to keep busy to assuage his loneliness. Then, awhile later, he had met Nancy and had grown to love her, soon marrying her and finding love and happiness again, it seemed, after those earlier days of grief.

Nancy came out of the small adjoining room, just then, shutting the door quietly behind her. "I believe she'll sleep all night," she said, smiling at her husband and Moses. "Time for bed," she said to her daughter. "Bring your dolly and tell your Paw and Sheriff Gentry goodnight."

Young Sarah grabbed her doll and ran to Silas, hugging his neck and kissing him a loud smack on the cheek. "Night, Paw," she said. Then, to Moses' surprise, she turned to him and reached up quickly, hugging his neck and gave him a resounding kiss solidly on his cheek, her eyes sparkling with merriment. "Night, Sheriff Gently," she whispered excitedly, then ran to her mother.

Moses couldn't help laughing. "I've been called a lot of things, Silas, but never 'Sheriff Gently' before." Both men chuckled at that, enjoying the sweet words of the child. "Well, I'd better be heading for your barn and get some shut-eye before I fall on my face," Moses said.

"We've got a lot of blankets," Silas replied. "You can bunk down right here by the fireplace, if you want, or in the other room," he stated, nodding toward the room where Sarah slept.

"Out here will be just fine," Moses said, "not sure she'd want to see my ugly face first thing in the morning."

The men spread a quantity of blankets on the rug in front of the fireplace and Moses said goodnight to his hosts. Nancy and Silas said goodnight and went into an adjoining room at the back of the cabin. Moses sat down, pulling off first one boot and then the other. He pulled off his socks, laying them over the boots, wiggling his toes, enjoying the feel of fresh air on his feet. He sat there in the silence then, looking around the comfortable home, thinking of Sarah asleep in the other room. Someday—if things went as he hoped they would—he'd add more rooms onto her cabin and make it similar to this one...for Sarah and the child she had mentioned earlier. He hadn't even asked if it was a boy or a girl. He stretched and yawned, his mind filled with thoughts.

He had never thought of himself as a father before. Not since the death of the child his wife had been carrying. It wouldn't be so bad… raising Gray Eagle's young'n. He wondered what she or he was named. Wondered if the child looked Indian like Gray Eagle or red-haired and green-eyed like Sarah. He got up and walked across the room to the window. A child, he thought. If Gray Eagle died four years ago, that would make the child about four…or so. "Well, I'd better start thinking like a man with a family," he said aloud, smiling into the darkness. "Looks like there'll be three of us to consider." For just a moment as he crossed to the blankets and crawled between them, his holstered gun and knife in its sheath hung by the door, and his shirt draped over the back of Nancy's rocker, his thoughts flashed to the room his wife had scrubbed and decorated for their baby. "I'll build a room or two on Sarah's cabin. Be plenty of room for all of us," he said, speaking softly into the silence. "All *three* of us…and more."

As his eyes closed in sleep, he saw himself sitting in the large rocker in Sarah's cabin. Sarah sat near him in her smaller rocker, sewing one of his shirts. As he looked around the room, he saw a small form lying on the bed, covered completely, head to toe, with a heavy woolen blanket. He jumped from the rocker and raced to the bed, pulling frantically at the blanket, trying to uncover the child's head. To his dismay, the more he pulled, the larger and heavier the blanket became. He called out in alarm, "Sarah! Sarah! Help me! Help me!" But she continued to sew, oblivious to his cries. Then he gave one great tug and the quilt slipped from the infant onto the floor. To his horror, only a small white skeleton lay upon the bed!

Moses woke with a start, his heart hammering in his chest like a drum, his brow wet with sweat. "Dear God!" he exclaimed into the darkness of the room. "Dear, dear God!" He rose up on one elbow, staring into the darkness, distressing thoughts tormenting him. It was a long time before he finally drifted off to sleep.

CHAPTER 7

Upon waking the next morning, Moses was surprised to find the cabin empty. He had not heard the others get up or leave. He got up and folded the blankets, placing them in a pile on the rocker. Then he walked to the window, glad to see the sun was beginning to shine through the trees. It looked like it was going to be a nice day. He still felt uneasy about the dream he had had, wondering what on earth could have prompted it. But this was a new day and the sun was coming up, lighting up the sky with rays of golden yellow that promised warmth, and he was not going to dwell on the dream. He picked up his shirt and walked outside to wash in the stream that ran across the far side of the clearing.

He went to the barn first, to get a clean shirt from his saddlebag and a bar of soap and towel, then walked to the stream. He washed the dust and sweat from his face, neck and upper body, glad for the refreshing feeling that he experienced. Then he washed his hair, drying himself on the well-worn towel and pulling on his clean shirt. It was the shirt he had purchased over at Dawson's General Store, just in case Sarah ever returned to Hastings, giving him a good excuse to get all 'gussied-up'. It was made of a soft, woven fabric and felt good against his skin, not as heavy or coarse as the buckskin shirts he usually wore.

He walked back to the barn, placed the bar of soap and towel back in his saddlebag, then folded the buckskin shirt he had worn earlier and slipped it into the saddlebag. He was barefoot, enjoying the feel of the grass beneath his feet, and he stretched, feeling at peace with the world. "Guess I'll go in and see if there's any coffee," he said aloud, starting for the cabin.

He was halfway to the cabin when he heard the first gunshot! It came from his left, about two or three hundred yards into the woods, he judged. His heart nearly stopped when it was followed by a woman's voice, screaming or squealing, he couldn't tell which.

He raced to the cabin, crashing through the door, skidding to a stop, grabbing his gun belt from the hook just inside the front door. Then he ran outside just as a second shot sounded, followed by a second outpouring of squeals or screams!

Running across the yard, he vaulted over the fence beside the barn, trying frantically to fasten his gun belt around his waist as he ran. Stones and brush tore at the soles of his feet, making him wince with pain as he raced on. By the time he entered the woods, he had all he could do not to cry out as sticks and pine needles jabbed the bottom of his feet. He was hobbling now, nearly bent double, breathing so hard his heart felt as if it might burst in his chest. He stepped on a sharp stick, yelping in pain, hopping on his other foot as his momentum carried him on.

He stopped running, leaning against a tree to listen and catch his breath. Sweat stung his eyes and he was certain people a mile away could hear his tortured breathing. Then he heard it... a strangled bunch of cries, as though someone was being throttled! He began to move again in the direction of the sounds, his gun in hand, stepping on only the heel of the foot the sharp stick had jabbed.

"Damn!" he cursed between breaths, trying to hobble faster. "I'll kill 'em if they've hurt Sarah," he vowed, his face red from exertion. He hobbled up the tree-covered hill in front of him, certain he was going to die from lack of air, his breath coming in short, sharp gasps. Then he stopped, not believing his eyes! Sarah and Nancy sat on the ground, aiming their guns at an old stump, firing at small cloth targets resting against it, then bursting into giggles and shrieks of laughter as they tried to out-shoot each other. "Damn!" The word exploded from Moses, surprising the two women, who looked up quickly at his unexpected arrival and outburst.

"That's a naughty word, Sheriff Gently," little Sarah said, from where she sat next to her mother. Moses bent double, trying to breathe, his vision blurred by the mixture of relief and upset he was experiencing.

"Oh, you're awake, Moses. Nancy was showing me how good a shot she's become," Sarah said, smiling at him.

He looked up at her, glaring at her, wanting to cry from joy because she was safe and cuss a blue streak because of the fear she had caused him. He was panting like an old dog and his feet hurt like hell. No doubt I'll die before I get back to the cabin, he thought, his heart quieting slightly as he stood there, bent double, his hands on his knees.

"Damn fool women," he said, his heart pounding in his ears.

"Mama, he said that bad word again," young Sarah said, much to her mother's and the grown Sarah's delight. Then young Sarah walked over to Moses, looking directly into his face, which was at eye-level with her own. She eyed him closely, trying to understand why he was acting so silly and saying such a bad word. Moses squinted, trying to squeeze the salty sweat from his eyes, so he could see her better.

Then, to everyone's surprise, young Sarah bent forward and kissed him right on his forehead. "I love you, Sheriff Gently. Now be good and don't say that naughty word *no* more, okay?" she scolded.

Moses scowled at her and then began to laugh. Sarah and Nancy also began to laugh, the woods resounding with their laughter.

After they returned to the cabin, they quickly prepared breakfast, chatting with Silas, who had been out looking for a calf that had gotten separated from its mother. He asked why Moses was hobbling and frowning so, but Moses only scowled and the women began to laugh.

After awhile, Moses hobbled out to the stream, carrying his socks and boots and a clean towel Nancy had handed him. He sat on the ground, his aching feet submerged in the stream. The icy water felt soothing and he wiggled his toes, enjoying the sensation.

Shortly, Sarah approached, a plate in one hand and a cup of coffee in the other. "How's your foot?" she asked, suppressing a smile.

"Humph!" he replied, not looking at her.

"Brought you some breakfast," she said, standing patiently at his side until, at last, he turned in her direction. She smiled then, offering him the cup of coffee. He reached up, taking it, then reached for the plate. She sat down on the ground beside him, pointing her bare toes, easing them into the cold water. He couldn't help noticing that her skirt had risen up to her knees. He gulped a large swallow of the coffee, not realizing till too late that it was so hot, then coughed and nearly choked, spitting it out on the ground on his other side. He cursed just under his breath and touched his sore mouth.

"Pull your skirt down!" he ordered, surprising her. She did as he said, not saying anything in reply, her chin raising defiantly.

"Well!" Moses exclaimed loudly, gulping a bite of eggs, his motions brusque.

"Well, what?" she asked, keeping her voice level and looking directly into his eyes.

"Well, nothing!" he answered, shoving a second bite into his mouth. "A man can't even eat a meal in peace," he grumbled just loud enough for her to hear.

She pulled her feet out of the water, turning toward him. "Do you want me to go?"

"Go *where?*" he asked. "Out in the woods shooting targets again, so I can break my fool neck going to rescue you?"

"I didn't need rescuing," she replied, softly.

"Well, *I* didn't know that!" he shouted, his eyes blazing. "Made a *jackass* out of myself and there you were, shooting targets! And squealing like a stuck pig!"

Sarah rose, brushing off the back of her dress. "I see there's no talking to you, Moses, so I guess I'll go say my goodbyes to Nancy and Silas and get ready to leave." He snorted in reply and jammed a large bite of food into his mouth. Sarah turned toward the cabin and walked away, her temper beginning to get the best of her. She was halfway to the cabin when he caught her. She hadn't heard him coming, so she gasped when his hand closed over her arm.

"I'm glad you didn't need rescuing...okay? *Darned glad"* She saw the look of relief in his eyes.

"Okay," she said, but couldn't help adding, "but when the time comes that I *do* need rescuing, Gentry, I just hope you've got your boots on!" He scowled at her, shaking his head, then he began to grin and did the only thing he could think of to erase the smile on her face. He took her into his arms and kissed her, a kiss that tasted better than his breakfast had, and lasted a whole lot longer!

Inside the cabin, Nancy and Silas stood by the window, watching their two friends and smiling. "Looks like the old "love bug" has bitten the sheriff," Silas said, standing behind Nancy, pulling her close and wrapping his arms around her, above her extended stomach.

"She loves him, too, I'm sure of it," Nancy whispered, leaning her head back against her husband's cheek.

"Don't know about that," Silas replied, "but it's pretty obvious how he feels. Only one problem, as I see it," he continued. "As I told you before, I ran into her on the trail when she was heading to town to get the medicine, and that seemed to be her main concern: the Indian children, I mean. I'm not sure Sarah would want to leave them. Call it love that she feels for them—or just loyalty to Gray Eagle's memory—I don't think Sarah will *ever* leave Gray Eagle's people."

Nancy lifted her head, looking out the window, once more. "Judging by the kiss being shared out there, I'd say you're wrong, dear husband," she said, then went to finish packing the food she was sending with Sarah and Moses.

CHAPTER 8

They rode all day, refreshed by the time spent at Nancy and Silas Haverty's. Moses had to laugh every time he thought of how their little girl had called him 'Sheriff Gently' and had admonished him not to say 'naughty words'.

That night when they made camp, they lay under the stars, talking quietly until sleep beckoned. Sarah told Moses how she had delivered young Sarah.

"That makes two deliveries for you," he commented. "Melinda Rose's boy and Nancy's girl. I'll have to hurry if I'm going to catch up with you." She laughed softly, happy that he was no longer angry with her.

The night sounds surrounded them as they lay there: the hooting of an owl nearby and the rumbling of distant thunder. Now and then, coyotes could also be heard in the distance.

"Sarah?" Moses spoke, breaking the silence.

"Yes," she replied, turning on her side to face him across the campfire. The embers were dying down and she could barely make out his form in the surrounding darkness.

"Tell me about your life with Gray Eagle. Were you happy?"

She lay still so long that he wondered if she had fallen asleep. Then she began to speak. "Yes. Yes, I was happy. He was a good husband. Kind and... a good provider. A proud man who was looked up to and respected by all 'The People'." She paused a long time, then continued, choosing her words carefully. Moses could tell she was not comfortable talking about those days, but was pleased when she continued. "We stopped at Wolf Hunter's...ah...Silas,' two days after we left Hastings. Nancy was close to birthin', though we didn't realize just how close until the next day. Gray Eagle and Silas had been staunch friends for many years. He was called 'Wolf Hunter' by Gray Eagle's people, after he saved a young Indian girl from a pack of wolves, many years before. Not long after, he married Gray Eagle's sister and they moved to his cabin. Gray Eagle was often at the cabin and learned English from Silas. Sadly, his sister, Bending Willow, died giving birth to their baby, and the baby with her."

"I know," Moses said, surprising Sarah.

She continued..."Eventually, Silas met and married Nancy. Anyways, when Gray Eagle and I stopped there, Nancy was heavy with child and delighted to see me. Little did we suspect that the next evening she would begin to have their baby, young Sarah. At dawn she had still not delivered and Silas was wild with worry, having lost his first wife and child under very similar circumstances. We all knew it was too far to Hastings to get Doc Pearson, though Gray Eagle did offer. Nancy was becoming so drained of strength! I was so afraid for her, Moses, and for the child. All I could think of was the troubles we had encountered when Danny was born. It so happened that a traveling preacher came by about that time. Silas told him what was going on and asked him to stay—believing he would be needed to bury Nancy or the child—or *both.*"

She was quiet a long time, remembering back to the events of that day, and Moses shifted around to get in a more comfortable position, wishing he was nearer to her.

"By afternoon, the preacher looked as upset as Silas, and Gray Eagle paced across the porch as if *he* was the worried father," she laughed softly at the memory. Moses smiled in the darkness. "I was so tired I was afraid I'd drop where I stood, trying to assure Nancy that all was well and make her as comfortable as possible. Well, the preacher, a Reverend Woods, began to pray. Not quiet—like you tend to expect from a preacher—but shouting up to God and waving his arms and stomping his feet! I could see through the bedroom window that Silas was getting even more upset and had gone outside to pace with Gray Eagle." She shook her head, laughing aloud. "Oh, Moses, it was so funny...old Reverend Woods kept shouting; one minute pleading with God to spare Nancy and the baby, and the next, praising Him... all at the top of his lungs! I finally had all I could stand of his noise and decided to go out in the other room and tell him to stop all that caterwauling *immediately*! But, just as I started for the bedroom door, Nancy gave a horrible scream! Why it nearly tore my heart out with fear! Even Reverend Woods quit all his shouting, and there came the baby, as sure as I'm living and breathing! A healthy, red-faced infant with fuzzy blonde hair and dark-blue eyes. The prettiest little child you ever saw, Moses...once I got her all cleaned up, that is. And strong! Right from the moment she was born, she cried almost louder than the reverend had been shouting."

Sarah was silent for a moment, then she continued. "Silas came into the room with tears in his eyes and a look of pure joy on his face. He held the baby, carrying her over to Nancy, thanking her over and over for the beautiful little girl," Sarah sniffled, and Moses realized she was crying. "Nancy named her Sarah—after me—and Silas agreed to it. Before he left, Reverend Woods...her voice grew softer, "married Gray Eagle and me, right there in the bedroom with Nancy and Silas as witnesses, and baby Sarah asleep in her mama's arms." Moses lay still, listening to the emotion in Sarah's voice. He wished he was closer to her and could put his arms around her to comfort her, but she continued to speak. "We left the next day for Gray Eagle's village," then she paused a bit, adding, "we have a long ride ahead of us, Moses. We'd better get some sleep."

"Okay, darlin'," he answered into the silence of the night. As he lay there in the stillness, he realized she had not said much in answer to his question. She had said that she was happy, but mostly she had talked of Silas and Nancy and the birth of their little girl. He heard her sniffle again as he rolled onto his back, trying to find a more comfortable position. Stars shone above them and the rustling sound of some small critter drew his attention, momentarily. Then he closed his eyes and lay there a long time, wondering what it was that she was hiding.

CHAPTER 9

The next morning the sky was overcast with heavy grey clouds that threatened rain at any moment. Sarah was quiet as she poured Moses a cup of coffee. He was glad she had told him of the events surrounding young Sarah's birth, yet felt as if he had intruded, somehow.

When they finished eating and he was saddling Midnight, Sarah approached him, looking at him as though unsure of what she was about to say. "Moses?" she said, "you asked me last night if I was happy... with Gray Eagle."

He stopped what he was doing, giving her his undivided attention.

"Yes, I *was* happy. I..." she struggled to find the words, "I questioned myself...later...often asking myself if I had been wrong to leave as I did. To leave Hastings...and especially to hurt my father as I did. I thought God was punishing me when Gray Eagle died...and later, when..." she stopped talking as her voice broke and tears filled her eyes. Moses started to reach out to her, but she held her hand up, stopping him. She bit her bottom lip, straightening her shoulders and lifting her chin up as he had seen her do so many times before when she felt threatened.

"I blamed myself for Gray Eagle's death, blamed myself for other losses, too. But after, when I had gathered myself together, I realized that my *whole life*...seemed somehow to be leading, all along, to where I was ...and even *here*, to where I am now.

That all I went through was *necessary*." She paused, looking at him questioningly. "Do you understand?"

Moses nodded, remembering how, after his wife's death, he had finally sobered up and found a direction in life again and had felt—in quiet moments—that something or someone had actually led him to where *he* was in life, too. "I *do* understand," he replied.

"I knew you would," she said, and she smiled, reaching out to touch his arm. "We better ride now," she said, "or we'll never get there." And she turned and quickly walked to her horse.

The prairie spread out before them as far as the eye could see. Prairie grasses waved in the shadowed rays of the sun amidst the grey of the few clouds. Moses and Sarah rode for quite a few hours, before—off in the distance—the rains began. Billowing clouds of grey and black hung in the sky ahead of them and brilliant flashes of lightening slammed into the earth. Storms always made Sarah uneasy and she pulled up, tension showing on her face. Moses knew she was worried and tried to assure her the storm would pass ahead of them, but he could see it was useless to try to dispel her anxiety. He asked if she wanted to stop for while.

"Are you hungry?" she asked.

"I could use a bite," he answered. She looked anxiously at the billowing clouds, then slid from Glory's back. Moses dismounted, taking the pouch of food from his saddlebag that Nancy had prepared for them. They ate together, enjoying the chance to stretch their legs and limber up, after so many hours in the saddle. Moses wondered if Sarah would be able to keep up the pace, knowing they had at least four more days of riding ahead of them before they reached the Sioux village. He admired the fact that she had had the courage and stamina to come such a long distance alone, in spite of the possible perils that might have befallen her. Then, so soon after, to endure the return journey. None of the other women he had ever known would have been so courageous or possessed such strength and fortitude. He watched her as she sat down near him, chewing a biscuit, her expression more relaxed.

As if reading his thoughts, she asked, "We've got four or five more days journey, Moses, are you up to it?"

"I am, if you are, darlin'," he answered, smiling at her.

"I have no choice," she replied. "I *have to* get there with the medicine." She gazed off toward the west, relieved to see that he had been right about the storm passing them by. "There's an abandoned settler's cabin ahead. We should reach it just before dark, I think, if we hurry. Only the cabin still standing, and a ramshackle shed for the horses. But there's a pond near it and also an adequate corral. I stayed there on my way to Hastings. If nothing else, it'll be shelter if another storm threatens," she added.

"Sounds good," he answered, pleased to think of a roof over their heads for the night.

Just after dusk they reached the cabin. They approached cautiously, though caution was unnecessary. No one was around, not man or animal. Moses saw that though it was in dire need of repair, it would, indeed, provide more than adequate shelter for them and the horses. They quickly dismounted, and he unsaddled Midnight, then turned both horses into the corral, while Sarah carried their blankets into the cabin. A few mice scattered as she entered, but she was not one to be upset by a few rodents, though their gnawing in the middle of the night had infuriated her the last time she stayed there.

She looked out the window, noticing the streak of moonlight shining across the pond. At once she knew what she would do. Grabbing up one of the blankets, she quickly stepped out of her clothes and moccasins and wrapped the blanket around her. Glancing around, seeing that Moses still stood by the corral watching the horses, his back to her, she walked quickly across the clearing and over the crest of a low hill to the pond beyond. She looked once more for any sign of intruders, then dropped the blanket and eased into the cool water. She swam toward the center of the pond with ease, feeling refreshed and cleansed. When she got to the middle, she felt the aches and pains leaving her body and ducked under the water, enjoying the sense of vitality awakening within her. She surfaced, then ducked beneath the water again, an almost playful mood coming over her.

Moses heard the sound of movement in the water and quickly reached for his gun, easing it out of the holster. There was no time to warn Sarah that they had intruders, only time to act! He bent low, running toward the pond. His eyes searched the tall grasses along the water's edge as the slight splashing sounds continued, far out in the center of the pond. He didn't know if their 'visitor' was man or animal, but he could not take a chance where Sarah's safety was concerned. Quietly, he lowered himself to the ground, pressing against the dirt and grasses, listening to the pounding of his heart as he tried to tell how many intruders he must deal with.

When the slight splashing noises stopped, Moses lifted his head, cautiously peering out into the darkness, unable to see anything in the inky blackness. He wished the moon would break through the clouds so he could see better, but it didn't. Once again his attention focused on the sounds of someone or something swimming. He strained to hear, barely able to make out the sound, yet knew it was coming closer. He settled back down in the tall grass, tension building within him.

Then he knew by the sound that someone or something had stopped swimming and was coming through the shallow water straight toward where he lay. He felt the hair stand up at the back of his neck as the sounds ceased, suddenly, mere inches from him. He held his breath, his heart thundering in his chest, as he tried to tell if there was more than one intruder to deal with. He realized it had to be a person and not an animal that had come out of the water. An animal would have smelled the scent of a man long before now, and known he was there.

The silence, though lasting only a few seconds, seemed to go on forever. Then he heard the footfalls turn along the pond's edge, heading away from him. At the same time, a sliver of silver moonlight broke through the clouds, enabling him to make out the faint outline of his foe. He moved quickly, jumping up and lunging at the figure with all the force he could muster! A scream resounded, splitting the silence, as the two figures—carried by the force of his attack—hit the water!

He was surprised when his opponent did not fight back, but lay still beneath him in the water. "Knocked you out," he said, reaching under the water for a fistful of hair. To his horror, he realized suddenly that his opponent was not as he thought "him" to be. He felt shock tear through him as his hands felt the inert body—not of a male—but the smaller, smoother body of a woman. "Dear God!" he exclaimed, getting to his feet and lifting the unconscious form up into his trembling arms. "Sarah! Oh, God…Sarah! Wake up, darlin'," he pleaded. "I'm sorry, Sarah."

A cough, followed by retching, gave Moses little comfort. At least she's alive, he thought. I just hope I haven't hurt her. He held her in his arms, talking softly, his emotions awry. She continued to cough and gag, then suddenly her whole body stiffened.

"Sarah?" he questioned. But before he could say more, a scream tore from her lips and she began to pummel his chest with her fists! She fought to be free of his hold on her, her nails raking his cheek, as she kicked and bucked in his arms. She seemed to have the strength of ten women, and he had all he could do to ward off her blows. He put her down and drew back, too stunned to believe what was happening. "Sarah! It's *me*, Moses!" he shouted as she backed away from him, her hands held out in front of her, as if to protect herself from any moves he might make.

The moon pierced the clouds, lighting the area around them and Moses was able to make out her facial features. Her eyes wild! Her teeth bared! He had never seen her like this, had never seen *any* woman in such a state! Her eyes blazed and her breath came in staccato bursts as she screamed at him, again and again, "Get away from me! I'll *kill* you for this! Get away from me!"

Moses stood there, feeling helpless, unsure of what to do. It was obvious that she was hysterical. But, why? Had he frightened her that badly? Or had he hurt her when he tackled her? As brave as she was, had he frightened her so badly that she had lost her senses? He didn't know what to think. He took a step forward, reaching out toward her, asking softly, "Sarah, what is it?"

"Gray Eagle will *kill* you for this," she hissed, in a tone so venomous that Moses drew back in shocked disbelief.

"Sarah, Sarah, it's me, Moses. Gray Eagle's dead..it's *me*, Moses."

She stared at him, growing silent, a bewildered look upon her face.

"Sarah," he repeated, "it's me ... Moses."

She looked around in the partial darkness that surrounded them, as though completely confused. Then, in a voice so soft he could barely hear her, she whispered, "Moses?" And before he could answer, she swayed and her knees buckled. He caught her before she could hit the ground, lifting her up into his arms.

As he began to walk toward the dimly outlined cabin, he realized that the body he cradled in his arms was naked and he averted his eyes as best he could. Her head rested against his chest and she moaned softly, now and then, as they made their way to the cabin. He wondered if the pounding heart he felt was his own, or hers, as he reached the doorway.

Once inside, he laid her on the old bed in the corner, covering her with the blanket that was upon it. Sarah lay as though dead. He felt for a pulse in her neck to make sure she was alive, then hurried outside, glad to see a full moon now brightened the area. He had dropped his gun before plummeting into the pond and hoped he'd be able to locate it in the tall grasses surrounding the water. He felt sick at heart about what had happened, and could still feel the painful cuts where her fingernails had raked across one side of his face.

"I wonder just what happened to you," he said aloud. "Whatever it was, it won't *ever* happen again!" He spotted the blanket near the edge of the water then and knew she had used it to cover herself as she went down to the pond. "I'm a darn fool," he said. "I should have called out. Should have checked to see if it was her in the water." A glint of silver caught his eye just then and he knew it was the barrel of the gun that he had dropped when he tackled her. He bent, picking it up, glad to see it had not gotten wet. Then he turned and headed back to the cabin, shaking out her blanket, as he went.

Sarah lay where he had left her, her face serene, though her skin looked frightfully pale in the light from the moon that shone through the one lone window. She moved her arm then and one breast—small and firm as a ripe peach—was exposed. Moses felt heat well up in his body, spreading like wildfire. He walked to where she lay, looking down at her with intense longing, barely able to control the feelings that raged inside him. It'd been a long time since he had bedded a woman—too darned long—and his needs were great.

"You're a louse, Moses Gentry," he said to himself, reaching down to cover her. His hand lingered just above her so sweetly enticing breast as he fought to control the raging fire that nearly threatened to consume him. Then he covered her and quickly turned away, going outside to cool off and to think, disturbed by the words she had screamed at him.

When he returned, he was once again in control of himself. "Moses?" Sarah called, as he entered, sounding weak and still somewhat confused.

"I'm right here, darlin'," he answered, relieved that she had regained her senses.

"I...what happened? I remember I...went for a swim and then..." she paused, trying to reconstruct the events that had occurred when she went to the pond. "How did I get in bed?"

He walked over to where she lay, slowly sitting down on the edge of the bed, beside her.

"Something happened..." he began, not sure of what he should say.

"What?" she asked, totally unaware, it seemed, of the recent events that had occurred.

"I heard you swimming," he began, looking down at the floor, a feeling of shame passing over him. "I didn't know it was you. I thought we had an intruder. Someone up to no good—an Indian or trapper or some scoundrel—trying to sneak up on us. I got to the water's edge just as the moon went under the clouds and it was as pitch-black as Midnight's hide. I tackled you as you came out of the water, nearly drowning you." He shook his head, not looking at her. "I'm so darned sorry, darlin'. I'd never forgive myself if I hurt you. *Are* you all right? Do you hurt anywhere?"

She moved a bit, checking to see if she had any aches or pains. "I'm fine, I guess," she said, at long last, placing a hand upon his arm. "I'm fine," she repeated, smiling tenderly up at him.

He watched her face, studying it as best he could in the shadowy light, not sure if he should broach the subject of the words she had screamed at him. "Sarah...there's...ah...something I need to ask you..." he hesitated, his voice noticeably softer.

She looked at him curiously, as he took her hand in his, rubbing her skin gently. "What is it?" she asked, when he continued to remain silent.

"When you came to...afterwards...you went wild. You kept screaming, 'Get away from me! Get away from me or I'll kill you!'" He saw her expression change. Saw the overwhelming look of sorrow that filled her eyes. "You said 'Gray Eagle would kill me for what I had done'." He paused, watching her closely. "For *what,* Sarah? What happened to you after you left with Gray Eagle?" Her only answer, her fingers gripping his arm so tightly that it hurt. "Sarah, you can tell me... *anything.* I love you, darlin', but we have to talk about this."

She began to whimper then, her body trembling, as the pain she had carried for so long began to surface. Soon, deep shudders wracked her small body, her sobs filling the night air. Moses pulled her to him, wrapping her tightly within his arms, rocking her gently. The blanket had fallen down to her waist and her small breasts pressed against his shirt, though he was aware only of her need for comforting.

"It's all right, darlin'. It's all right," he crooned into her hair, as he rocked her, his heart welling up with sorrow for her because she hurt so. Sarah sobbed and sobbed, unable to stop the barrage of tears that had lain buried deep within her for the past five years. Moses continued to rock-long after his back had begun to hurt—and still she cried, as though a long pent-up dam had suddenly burst within her and she now had no recourse but to let it flow until it was spent.

When at last she quieted, she still trembled every so often and he continued to hold her, hoping she would explain what had happened, when she was able.

His eyes had begun to grow heavy from lack of sleep when she finally spoke. "Moses, I...I know this isn't fair to you, but I wish you would hold me."

"I *am* holding you, darlin'," he replied, confused by her request.

"No, I mean *really* hold me...here...in bed. Would you just lie beside me and hold me?" She trembled then, her body moving slightly, against his, as she did so. "Would you...could you just lie here beside me and hold me in your arms?"

"Oh, darlin'," he whispered, his voice deepening with desire.

"Please?" she pleaded.

Moses' heart pounded like he'd just run a race—and won—and there was nothing he wanted more than to lie beside her in the bed. But what did she think he was made of? As these thoughts ran through his mind, he took his arms from around her. His hand brushed her bare back, as he did so, and his body responded—a fire coursing through him from head to toe. She covered her breasts with her arms and lay back upon the bed, looking up at him so appealingly that he had to struggle for control.

"Sarah..." he said, his voice raw with desire. "I'm not sure I *can* just lie beside you. I want you, darlin'." His voice was hoarse with need and longing. "I *need* you, Sarah. If I hold you...I can't guarantee I can stop there." He was trembling now, so great was his desire to make love to her.

Sarah looked at him, filled with a fear that nearly paralyzed her. If only he would hold me now, she thought, maybe everything would be all right again. Maybe I could go on pretending, as before. Pretending that I'm still good enough to be the wife of a decent man, a decent white man like Moses.

"I *can't*" Moses said. "Go to sleep, Sarah. We'll talk in the morning." He rose and walked across the room, sitting down on an old wooden bench. He groaned, his body aching with pent-up desire. "Call out, if you need me, Sarah, all right?"

He assumed she was asleep already when she didn't answer and figured the tremendous bout of crying must have completely tuckered her out. He got up and walked outside to get a dry change of clothes out of his saddlebags. He changed into them, then reentered the cabin.

Sarah pulled the covers up around her neck and rolled onto her side, facing away from him. Tears threatened to flow again, as she lay there, devastated by his rejection. She had only wanted him to hold her. Was that so much to ask? She hadn't offered anything further, yet even her dear friend who had spoken so sweetly, proclaiming his love for her only a few days before, had now refused to so much as lie beside her.

I must have said something while I was out of my head, she thought. He knows what happened to me and now he wants no more to do with me. She squeezed her eyes tightly shut to stem the flow of tears that threatened. Very well, my dear Moses, you can go back to your saloon girls! I won't ask you to dirty your hands on *me* ever again! And with those thoughts heavy upon her heart, she eventually fell asleep.

CHAPTER 10

The remaining four days of their journey Sarah spoke only when spoken to, refusing to discuss what had taken place at the pond. Moses could not understand her sullenness and the pained expression that she wore. He tried to question her, to reason with her, to assure her of his love for her, but all his attempts fell on deaf ears. The fourth day, when they stopped to rest the horses and eat, he finally figured out what it was that was causing her forlorn demeanor.

"Sarah," he said, as she prepared food for them. "I know what's bothering you and we need to talk about it." She stiffened as he placed his hand upon her arm, making him all the more certain his assumption was correct. "Apparently you're upset because I…I carried you into the old cabin…naked." He paused, feeling somewhat embarrassed. Sarah watched his reaction as he spoke, and suffered all the more, realizing he had seen her naked and had still refused to hold her when she had asked him to that night. She looked down at the ground, hoping she would not cry.

"I put you to bed and covered you, Sarah, I…I never took advantage of you, never would. You know that, don't you?"

She continued to look at the ground, nodding her head to affirm his words, knowing just how true they were. She knew now, without a doubt, that he would never lower himself to lie with her. Hadn't he just said as much? She looked up into his face, raising her chin defiantly. "Yes, I understand," she replied, her voice a mere whisper.

He saw the look of sadness fill her eyes and also a look he didn't understand. A look of annoyed resignation. "I hope you understand," he said, unsure if he should explain more. Unsure if she *did* understand.

"You owe me no explanation," she said, turning away from him abruptly.

"Damn it!" he said, his voice rising as she began to walk away from him. He reached out and grabbed her by the arm, turning her toward him. "Sarah, I *didn't* touch you. I wouldn't do that! Don't you understand? I *can't*".

"I understand!" she snarled. "You *didn't* touch me! You *wouldn't!* You *can't*! I think you've made that *real clear*, Gentry!" She whirled away from him, furious with him for the pain he was causing her. Grabbing Glory's mane, she swung up onto the old horse's back and started off at a gallop.

Moses gathered up their things, muttering to himself angrily the whole time, then he mounted Midnight and raced off in pursuit of her. "Darn ornery woman," he sputtered. "Doesn't matter what I say or do, she's always mad." He raced along, following the trail she had left, wondering why she was so angry and upset. Any other woman would have been pleased he had been a gentleman. Any other woman would have been pleased that he loved her enough to hold himself in check, regardless of how temptingly beautiful and vulnerable she had been. He cleared the next small hill and saw her just up ahead, her hair glistening so appealingly in the sunshine, a ravishing shade of red-gold. "Darn ornery woman," he muttered, wishing he could take her into his arms and settle, once and for all, whatever it was that was stirring her up.

Just then he saw Sarah pull up hard on Glory, nearly unseating herself as she did so. She slid from the horse's back and began running. Moses couldn't see what had caused her to do so and he spurred Midnight on, filled with a sense of trepidation.

As he reached her side, he saw her kneeling in the grass, her body rocking back and forth, one hand covering her mouth. He jumped from his horse, rushing to her side. "Sarah, what is it?" Then he saw the body laying on the ground. It was the body of an Indian woman about the same age as Sarah. Flies buzzed around the body, giving credence to the fact that she had been dead only a short while. Sarah shooed them away, her hand trembling as she did so. "Do you know her?" he asked, placing a hand on Sarah's shoulder. She continued to rock back and forth, staring at the body before her.

"She was my friend...Running Deer is...*was* her name. She taught me the ways of 'The People' when I first came to the village. We were the best of friends," she replied, her voice as lifeless as the corpse before them.

"I'm sorry," he said, wishing he could say something more to comfort her. Sarah reached down to roll Running Deer onto her back and close the eyes of the dead woman. Moses put out a hand to stop her. "Here, let me," he offered, seeing the pustules that covered the woman's face and arms. There were a deluge of pockmarks upon her skin. "Smallpox," he stated, shaking his head.

"That's not what killed her," Sarah stated, sadly. "Look at her hands." He glanced down to where the woman's hands had begun to stiffen around the deer-horn handle of a knife, the blade buried to the hilt just below her ribs, her dress stained brown from her dried blood.

Sarah looked away, her shoulders slumping as she quickly squeezed her eyes shut to stifle her tears. "I left her to care for the children," she said, her voice barely more than a whisper. "She wouldn't have done this. Even though she had this horrible sickness, she wouldn't have done this! She knew I'd come back with medicine. It's all my fault...I shouldn't have left. I should have stayed and taken care of her... of all of them."

"Don't go blaming yourself," Moses said, turning her toward him. "You hear me? You *aren't* to blame."

"Not directly," she replied, surprising him, "but I left and *I'm* alive. If I had come right back and not stayed at the cabin...or stopped at Nancy's...if only I had returned sooner..."

"Sarah," he began, but she swung up onto Glory and sat there, her face pale, though she did not cry. "Is your village nearby?" he asked and she nodded, sadness filling her eyes. They mounted, and continued on their way.

As the village came into view, Moses drew up, calling to her. "I need to stop," he said, surprising her. She took his reins as he dismounted and pulled a small pouch from his saddlebag.

Turning his back to her, he slipped something over his head, tucked it inside his shirt, then took his reins from her and again mounted.

Sarah could not get the image of her friend, Running Deer, out of her mind, however, and sat with her eyes closed, remembering back to the enjoyable and warm friendship they had shared. "Are you okay?" Moses asked. She opened her eyes, shuddering slightly before replying. He knew what she was thinking before she spoke.

"We were such good friends. She taught me the ways of 'The People' and was there whenever I needed her. She was so kind, stood by me when...when...I loved her like a sister. I don't know how I would have managed without her friendship."

"We don't always know why things happen as they do, darlin', but I'm sure she's in a much better place now," he said, hoping to comfort her. Then his thoughts turned—for just a moment—to his wife and baby, and he hoped so much that what he had just said was true.

CHAPTER 11

The keening sound of those who were grieving was heard long before they reached the village. At one end of the camp they could not help but see the many tall burial scaffolds, the bodies upon them wrapped in burial robes. Long eagle-feather staffs, lances, bows and arrows and buffalo-hide shields stood beside some of them—symbols of the dead warriors' accomplishments and bravery. The stench of death filled the air.

The camp consisted of many tepees—about twenty—Moses figured as they rode in. Only a few adults approached as they rode through the camp and nowhere were there children running, laughing, or playing. Moses saw that Sarah held herself erect, her head held high, giving the impression of strength to those who watched their arrival. He felt proud of her. They dismounted before one of the tepees just as an elderly Indian emerged from it.

"Chief Standing Elk, I am glad to see you are well. I bring medicine," Sarah stated, respectfully.

"Red Bird, I thank the Great Spirit for your safe return. Many are ill. Still many more have died." Sarah was saddened by his words, suddenly remembering Moses, who stood patiently off to one side.

"This is my friend, Moses Gentry. He rode with me to make sure the medicine arrived here safely. Moses, this is Standing Elk, the great Sioux Chief, and father of Gray Eagle."

Moses smiled at the elderly Indian. "I am honored to be in the presence of Standing Elk. I have heard many times of your great wisdom and of your bravery as a warrior."

"You are welcome in our village, Moses. Come, we will smoke the pipe, in thanks for your safe journey."

"I must go to the ones who are ill," Sarah said. "The medicine will ease their suffering, though it is not strong enough to heal them."

"Go then, Red Bird. I will smoke the pipe, asking that Wakantanka keep you well." Sarah nodded toward Standing Elk and glanced quickly at Moses, then hurried away, leading Glory.

Moses watched her go, realizing how different she was amongst Gray Eagle's people. She carried herself proudly, her bearing similar to that of a warrior, it seemed, and he wondered at the change in her. The chief watched Moses, reading in his expression that he loved Sarah.

"Chief Standing Elk, before we smoke the pipe, I must tell you something that Sarah does not yet know," Moses said. "I am known as Black Hawk, son of Singing Raven, daughter of Red Fox, chief of the Blackfoot and friend of Gray Eagle." As he said this, Moses pulled from his shirt the round bone medallion with Blackfoot symbols on it.

Standing Elk looked into Moses eyes, already aware that he was a man of honor. "You are welcome, Black Hawk, in the village of 'The People'. I saw your arrival in a vision—two moons ago—and have expected you. Come. We will smoke and talk of many things."

Moses followed the elderly Indian into his tepee, remembering the many times he had heard his mother speak of her home in her father's village. He smiled at the memory. She had only spoken of such things when *his* father was in town, and the two of them were alone. It surprised him how comfortable the dwelling was with its bed of hides and baskets of many sizes sitting near the far wall. He saw buffalo horn cups, bow and arrows, and fine buffalo robes. He was pleased to be there, feeling strangely 'at home' in the dwelling of Standing Elk. He also felt a twinge of longing, remembering how lovely his mother had looked in her white dress of smoothest elk hide, her hair glistening dark as a raven's wing in the afternoon sun as he sat at her feet, when young. It wasn't until years later that he had realized how sad she must have been, remembering the sorrow in her eyes. He also remembered the wistful smile that always played across her lips as she spoke of her home and her people. He had asked her once why she had never tried to return. Why she had not run away from his father's cruelty and mistreatment. She had looked at him, a long time, then closed her eyes, not answering. Later, when he was older, he realized that she had been pregnant with one of his younger siblings, and apparently lacked the strength to do so.

He sat down across from Standing Elk. "It is good to be here," he said.

A short time later, Moses told of finding Sarah's friend, Running Deer, not far from the encampment and two braves were sent to tend to her. A hushed silence followed, as they smoked and spoke of many things: of Moses' friendship with Gray Eagle and of the wars between the whites and the tribes to the west, of the stories both had heard of the many wagons of whites that were starting to come, seeking the gold where the earth meets the water in the west. Great numbers of them who were killing the buffalo and, in doing so, destroying the Indian's hunting grounds that were so necessary to their survival.

Sarah rushed from person to person administering the medicine Doc Valentine had given her. She crooned softly in their native tongue as she tended them, adults and children alike. Almost every dwelling had at least one sick child or adult and she hoped she would not run out of the medicine that could give them some relief from their suffering. Bear That Walks, Snake Dancer, Little Fox, Three Feathers, Many Horses ... all gone, plus so many others. The sense of loss staggered her. Everywhere she went she encountered friends who lay ill and close to dying, their faces and bodies covered as Running Deer's had been, with pus-filled sores and drying pockmarks, and there was nothing she could do to save them. She had to steel her heart to both their death and suffering, in order to stand it, forcing herself to keep believing that her God or theirs would stop the scourge afflicting them.

She worked relentlessly, never once faltering, in her determination to stave off the illness and misery that had overcome so many of 'The People.' She would later wonder why so many had to die. Wonder where Wakantanka was when Running Deer breathed her last, and *why*, if the God of *her* people was so invincible, He had not heard *her* prayers for the Indians.

She pushed herself to go on, in spite of the extreme tiredness that threatened to engulf her, feeling weak from exhaustion. She longed to crawl into her bed of soft hides and sleep, no longer seeing the frightened looks and ravaged faces of so many of the friends she had come to know and had grown to love.

As night fell, she administered one last dose of medicine, too tired to do anymore. She stumbled from the tepee, wondering for the first time since she had left him, where Moses was.

"Sarah?" He spoke, as she came out into the darkness.

"Moses?" she answered, surprised and pleased that he was waiting for her.

"Is there anything I can do?" he asked, as he walked along beside her.

"There's so little that *can* be done," she said. "I've given everyone some of the medicine. Now all we can do is pray...and wait."

He cleared his throat, seeing her profile in the light from the moon. "I'm proud of you," he said, reaching out to take her arm. Cautiously, he turned her toward him, not certain if she would appreciate him doing so. She stood still, facing him, not saying anything, a sigh coming from her. "I'm really proud of you," he said again and bent toward her, kissing her tenderly, as an owl hooted off in the distance and another sliver of moonlight broke through the clouds, lighting the ground around them.

Sarah welcomed his kiss, too tired to fight it if she wanted to, which she didn't. She could not remember when she had been so tired and wished she could curl up in his arms and sleep. She realized now that her feelings for him had grown beyond those of a friend. Though the stark reality that he no longer felt her worthy of being his wife, came crashing back to her and she felt sorely ashamed.

He held her close, seeking another kiss, his lips feather soft upon hers and she groaned as he moved closer, his body pressing against hers and arms encircling her. She felt herself grow weak, both from exhaustion and the desire that began to build within her. He felt her body relax against his, realizing how tired she was, and scooped her up into his arms.

"Poor darlin'," he whispered, walking to the tepee she had pointed out to him as hers as they had ridden into the camp hours before. He entered, laying her on her bed of hides, then pulled off her moccasins and covered her. It was then he noticed the small child on the other side of the dwelling. She was a pretty child with dark hair and eyes, and a ready smile. He smiled at her and in response she giggled at him, then scurried further down under her bedding. Moses looked over at Sarah, seeing she already slept, then turned and walked out into the night. Spreading his bedroll just outside, he found he was smiling happily.

"So Sarah and Gray Eagle had a little girl," he thought, and he wondered why Sarah had never mentioned her all during the long journey they had shared. She had said something, he remembered— about a baby—then other things had come up and nothing more had been said about the child. A girl, he thought, a daughter. It didn't matter to him that she was another man's child.

Gray Eagle had been his friend and he vowed to be the best father he could be in his place. He would love her as his own, making certain she knew the kind of man her father had been, would teach her to revere his memory. That was the least he could do.

He lay down, his thoughts still on the child. He wondered what her name was, and if she would be happy—if and when—they left the village and moved back to Hastings.

Smiling contentedly, he pulled his hat down over his eyes and soon fell asleep. A tired sentinel, guarding the woman he loved, and her child.

CHAPTER 12

When he awoke the next morning, he saw that Sarah was already up and had fixed them something to eat. She looked tired, he noticed, yet seemed happy for his company. As he drank the cup of coffee she poured for him, he told her that he had seen the child and thought her very pretty. Sarah smiled, but seemed uninterested. She changed the subject abruptly, to his surprise, saying she had to go and check on those who were ill. He asked what the little girl was named and was more than a little surprised when Sarah replied, "Laughing Water." Then she again began to talk about the needs of those who were ill and those who had died during the night. He let her go on talking, wondering how she could be so worried about the Indians who were sick, and seem to care so little about her own daughter.

"Does she have another name?" he asked, turning the subject back to the little girl.

"Does *who* have another name?" Sarah asked, looking at him questioningly.

"Laughing Water," he explained. "I thought perhaps you call her by another name ... your mother's, maybe, or possibly Rosies?"

She looked at him, a perplexed look upon her face. "Why would I do that?" she asked.

"Why not?" he replied, his voice raising slightly. Was the woman daft? He was beginning to wonder. How could she have so much compassion for those who were sick or dying, and not seem to care at all about her child? He shook his head in disbelief.

One of the elders approached then, speaking to Sarah in his native tongue. She answered him and then rose. "I have to go. I'm needed," she said and turned, hurrying away.

Moses poured himself another coffee and finished his meal, looking off into the distance. He just could not understand her indifference to the child. He walked over to the tepee and poked his head inside. The little girl sat on her bed of hides, playing with a small doll, whispering happily. She looked up at him, a smile crossing her face at his presence.

"Hi, Laughing Water, I'm Moses...do you understand what I'm saying?" he asked, speaking softly. She giggled and crawled further back against the wall of the tepee. Moses straightened, afraid his presence might be frightening her. He told her goodbye, and for just a moment, thought of the baby his wife had been carrying the day she was gunned down. He wondered if that baby would have been a girl, too, not so unlike this one. He felt sadness fill him at these thoughts and turned away, going to see if he could find Sarah.

She was just leaving one of the tepees, heading for another, when he spotted her. "Sarah, do you have time to talk?"

"No, not now," she answered, remembering the way he had kissed her and held her the night before. If only ...she thought, knowing it was foolish to hope for anything more than a friendship with him now.

"I thought I'd tell you I'm going with the men to scout for buffalo," he said, surprised by the look of fear that suddenly crossed her face.

"No!" she exclaimed, before she could think.

"What's wrong?" he asked. "It'll be winter soon and with so many sick, they need every able-bodied man they can get to help scout, and hunt: to provide meat and hides for the winter ahead."

"I know," she said, a worried look still upon her face. "Just be careful...please."

"I will, don't you worry," he replied, pleased that she was concerned for his safety.

"Just be careful, Moses, please," she repeated, turning quickly away.

He saddled Midnight and checked his gun, bothered by the look of fear that had crossed her face. I don't know what you're afraid of, darlin', he thought, but I intend to keep my vow to never let *anything* happen to you or hurt you again, and I can't do that if something happens to me. He mounted his horse and hurried to join the scouts as they left the village.

It was a long and dusty ride before they came upon the buffalo herd. As far as the eye could see, buffalo grazed, a herd the size of which Moses had never imagined. If the hunt was good, he knew that there would be enough meat to last the Indians all through the winter and into the early spring. There would also be enough hides, horns and bones, for all the necessary things—hides for bedding, winter robes and tepee coverings, horns for cups, spoons and ladles, hair to be twisted into ropes, bones to be carved into knives and scraping tools, and hooves to be boiled to make glue. Nothing would be wasted. Everything would be used.

When they rode back into camp, two days later, dogs barked and ran alongside the men. Moses saw Sarah and the little girl sitting outside Sarah's dwelling. He waved and Sarah waved back, then she said something to the child and she waved, too. Moses was grinning as he dismounted.

"Got any food for a hungry traveler," he joked.

Sarah smiled at his words. "Yes," she replied. "Sit down. I'll fix you something."

Moses saw the little girl watching him. "You're sure pretty," he said, as the child giggled and ran into the tepee without answering, the small cloth doll clutched in her hand. "She's a shy one," he said to Sarah.

"Yes, until she gets to know you," she replied.

"I thought she'd look more like you," he said, thinking this would please Sarah. "Would have your auburn hair, maybe."

Sarah stared at him, her chin lifting. "Why would you think that? She's not *my* child," she said, tension entering her voice.

"Not yours?" Moses asked, stunned to learn this.

"No. She was orphaned when her mother died of the pox; one of the first to get it. Her father was killed on a buffalo hunt the year before. She has no one, so she stays with me on occasion, and is looked after by everyone in our village."

He was surprised by her words and blurted out without thinking, "But, on our journey here you said…well, where is *your* child? Yours and Gray Eagle's?"

She turned away from him and stared off into the distance as though searching for the answer. "Our child is dead," she said, and rose, holding up one hand to silence him. "I can't talk about it," she added, her eyes filling with tears, "someday perhaps, but not now... please."

He saw the tears glistening beneath her lashes and reached out, touching her arm, wishing with all his heart that he had not asked. "I'm sorry, darlin'. I'm real sorry," he said.

The camp was alive with activity as the women prepared for the trip to the buffalo hunting grounds. They quickly took down the tepees and loaded each onto a travois. Dogs ran barking as the men rode through camp on their specially trained buffalo-hunting horses. They were much faster than their war ponies and had been taught to overcome their fear of buffalo. It was common knowledge that a well-trained, buffalo-hunting horse not only meant the difference between a good hunt or a bad one, but often meant the difference between life and death to their rider. Moses was glad for the loan of just such a horse from Howling Wolf and rode through the camp with the other men, learning how his horse responded to his commands with just the touch of a knee or slight movement of his leg.

Moses wondered if the child, Laughing Water, would ride with Sarah. Soon this question was answered when he saw the little girl walking along beside one of the other young women. He waved at the child when she happened to look his way, but she held on tightly to her doll and only smiled at him. Just then, Sarah rode up to him on Glory, her auburn braids shining in the early morning sun.

"Be careful, Gentry. Have you ever been on a hunt before?" she asked, the look of worry once again on her face.

"Nope, can't say that I have, darlin,'" he answered, "but I'm gonna' do the best I can, you can count on that," he boasted. "Wish me luck, pretty lady."

"Just be careful, please...*please* ," she repeated, her tone imploring him to be.

"I'll be fine, don't you worry," he said, noticing how uneasy she was. He wondered just what it was that was bothering her so. "I'll be careful, love," he said, and before she had a chance to reply, he galloped off in pursuit of Howling Wolf and the other men.

Sarah watched him go, wishing with all her heart that he *did* love her, not just as an old friend, but as a woman worthy of being his wife.

Sadly, she turned Glory toward the other women and hurried to catch up with Little Moon, a woman her age who had been her friend for as long as she had lived among 'The People'. Thanks to Sarah's teachings, Little Moon spoke English almost as well as she did.

"Is it all right if I ride with you?" Sarah asked, as she approached her friend.

"Yes, I welcome your company," Little Moon answered, in perfect English. Over the years, she had eagerly sat many hours learning the white man's tongue, along with many of the Indian children. Sarah was a good teacher: patient and understanding, always encouraging them, applauding and rewarding their efforts with a hug or pat on the back, or both. Now, nearly all the children had at least the rudimentary skills needed to speak and understand some English, and many had even learned to write it. Sarah was proud of these accomplishments, knowing how difficult it was for the white adults she had known in Hastings who could not read or write. To her great surprise, even Standing Elk, and many of the elders, had asked her to teach them, giving her life purpose in the years following Gray Eagle's death. She especially enjoyed the many evenings she had sat with Gray Eagle's father in the quiet peacefulness of his lodge, teaching him word after word. He was a very wise man, highly intelligent, and learned quickly, though he was never one to boast of an accomplishment. Few knew he could speak and understand the white man's language. Even fewer knew that he could write it. He had explained to Sarah that he had long ago had a vision, and in this vision it was made clear to him that he must learn not only the *ways* of those white men who would come in great numbers—like the great buffalo herds—to the land of 'The People,' but also must learn their tongue, because often their words would be lacking in truth and honor. Having lived with both—whites and Indians—Sarah hoped he was wrong, as she had seen the respect the Indians had for the land and everything in it. No white man she had ever known, except maybe John Bruce, had ever seemed as respectful. No white man she had ever known had offered thanks for the animal that had given its life to feed or clothe him and his family. No white man she had ever known had shared a oneness with the earth or appreciated each precious gift they were given: a gift, for example, as small as the sweet song of a tiny bird.

Sarah had often wondered, when she was younger, if Indians

were a religious people and if they went to church as good white folks did. Living with Gray Eagle's people had answered these questions, and then some! They were *not* religious like the white folks. Their beliefs went *deeper* than mere religion, deeper than prayers on Sunday morning or in times of trouble. It was not something they "turned to," as even she had often done in times of trouble, danger or worry. It was an innate part of them, it seemed to her, as a people. True, not all were good or compassionate and decent. How well aware she was of that! Each had those who chose war and caused pain and suffering. Each had those who were evil. But, as a whole, she had lived with both the whites and with the Indians, and knew firsthand that the Indians lived every moment of every day with a reverence for the land and all things in it. Their "church" was the land and sky and waters, not a building to gather in on Sunday mornings.

The longer Sarah lived amongst the Indian people, the more she had come to respect them and find comfort in their simple beliefs. Even their family ties seemed deeper, somehow, than any she had ever seen amongst her own people, and she had often wished that she would have had the chance to tell her father about them. Especially the fact that what she treasured most about her life with them was the kind regard they showed her, often going out of their way to help her.

She thought then of Spotted Dog and a shiver ran through her, chasing away her feeling of peace and contentment. Why was it, she wondered, that in all people—red and white alike—there were those who followed no rules but their own? Who held no beliefs sacred? Why were there always some who caused grief and suffering and seemed to revel in it?

"Wakantanka, it is Sarah...Red Bird," she said softly, glancing up at the sky. "I ask that you provide many buffalo for 'The People' and watch over those who hunt, especially my dear friend, Moses. Bring healing to those who are ill, also." Then she hurried Glory along, to catch up with her friend, Little Moon, once again.

CHAPTER 13

As they reached the buffalo hunting grounds, the women immediately set about their work, setting up camp a safe distance from the herd. Buffalo were skittish animals—very easily frightened—and it didn't take much to stampede the herd. A stampede was greatly feared because they would run wild, trampling everything and everyone in their path. Looking like an endless brown blanket of dust spreading across the earth as far as the eye could see, they ran, their hooves pounding the earth, shaking it, their direction changing repeatedly as they advanced.

An Indian had to be an accomplished horseman to ride with the herd and not be thrown or trampled as he raced along on his buffalo-hunting horse, his bow raised, his arrow ready to fly. No reins did he use to direct his horse. Only the pressure of his body could he count on to guide the animal. Many hours of training had gone into each buffalo-hunting horse. His rider's life was dependent on him. To stumble or fall before even one of the large animals would mean certain death, often for both horse and rider.

Moses raced along at breakneck speed, not far from Howling Wolf. His horse was a good one—faster than some of the others—and he knew he would soon outdistance some of them. Being inexperienced, he watched Howling Wolf, as the earth reverberated with the sound of pounding hooves. The buffalo turned—as one—heading away from the men. Then they veered back, to his dismay, toward the closest riders: Howling Wolf, Laughing Fox, and himself. Moses took aim at one of the leading bulls, hoping to turn the herd before they were overtaken. He fired and the great animal dropped—hitting the ground—and the herd turned away in a single movement, running headlong toward the braves opposite them. Howling Wolf pulled back on his bow, his shot quickly dropping a large bull. Moses fired again and another great animal fell. Over and over again, they hit their target, dropping the great beasts in their tracks!

Moses was exhilarated by the thrill of the hunt and the possibility of danger! He had not enjoyed himself as much since the day he had shot an angry grizzly that had definite intentions of having him for its noonday meal! He had been only fourteen then, but he remembered the thrill of that encounter as if it was just yesterday! How proud he had felt when he had taken the meat to his mother. There was more meat than they had ever had—before or after—and her eyes had sparkled with pride, at his accomplishment. She had scraped and dried the hide and later, put it on his bed to keep him warm during the winter, he remembered. She had also made him a necklace of the bear's claws— in recognition of his bravery and success—thanking the bear for its generosity in the giving of its life to provide meat for them, and warmth from the bearskin.

His father had ruined the occasion, however, when he returned from town—drunk—and had grabbed the bear claw necklace from his mother's hands, shouting that no son of his would wear a necklace, like a girl. Moses had never seen it again.

When the hunt was over, they had enough meat and hides for all 'The People,' yet had taken no more than was necessary. The women rushed to butcher the buffalo, cutting the meat into strips, so they could hang it to dry. There would be enough to last through the long winter ahead.

Moses had downed many of the animals, and felt enlivened by all he had experienced. He pulled up to the carcass that Sarah and Little Moon were working on, his eyes showing the excitement he felt. Seeing the expression on his face, Sarah could not help smiling. "Big hunter home from the hunt," she teased, laughing softly. Moses laughed too, then turned to survey the day's kill. The hills were dotted with the bodies of the dead buffalo. Braves sang out with pride at their accomplishments, knowing the winter ahead would be easier with such a bounty. Moses felt a distinct connection with the Indians and wished he could tell his mother. He was sweating and yanked off his shirt, enjoying the refreshing coolness of the air against his skin.

"Moses?" Sarah questioned, looking curiously at him.

"What, darlin'?" he asked, smiling down at her from his mount.

"What is that?" she asked, pointing to the carved and painted bone medallion he wore on a narrow strip of buffalo sinew around his neck.

He had forgotten about it when he removed his shirt, and now bit his lip as he tried to think of the best answer. Out on the prairie in the middle of a buffalo hunt—while she was wrist-deep in buffalo entrails—was *not* the perfect time to tell her of his "mixed-blood" heritage. He cleared his throat, then knew the perfect answer. One that *was* the truth, though short on truth. "It was a gift from my mother," he said. "I'd like to tell you about it, darlin', but this isn't the best time."

"It looks Indian," she said, noticing the symbols on it, her curiosity peaked.

"I have to go help Howling Wolf," he replied, quickly changing the subject. "We'll talk later."

When they returned to the village, however, they saw each other only in passing. Sarah was busy—along with the other women—making pemmican, hanging strips of meat to dry, and treating the hides. They had to be soaked, to loosen the hair, and later stretched on frames to dry. Then, the hair and fat had to be scraped off. Next, they were rubbed with a mixture of fat and brains, and then washed. To Sarah, the most difficult task came next: pulling them through a rope loop to soften them. After that, they were again stretched on wooden frames to dry. It was hard work, and Sarah had little time to think of Moses, concentrating solely on the job at hand.

Moses spent most of his time with Standing Elk and the elders, or with the friends he had made among the braves. He was enjoying their companionship and learning many things from them, often joining them in their activities.

He wore a leather strip around his head to hold his hair back—as it had grown quite long—and two hawk feathers hung down one side. He had still not told Sarah that he was Indian on his mother's side, or that his Indian name was Black Hawk. His skin hid the fact, too, though he had tanned—from long days spent in the sun—and no longer looked as light-skinned, like his father. Truth was, for the first time in his life, he *felt* Indian and it made him proud—not ashamed— as he had always been before. He felt pride in himself—in the many things that he was learning—and it was a good feeling. He held his head high, and felt confident, and more at peace with himself, and it pleased him greatly.

Sarah noticed the change in him, and liked it. She caught herself watching for him, hoping to catch just a glimpse of him as she went about her daily tasks. She saw that he now wore his buckskins and moccasins and never the white man's shirts he had worn in Hastings. She also noticed that he always wore the medallion at his neck, but she had not seen it up close as yet. She was becoming more and more curious about it, however, but had not found any time to sit down and talk with him so she might ask him about it. There was much work to be done to prepare for the winter that would soon be upon them, and try as she did, she just never seemed able to find any time. Worse yet, he now had a tepee of his own on the far side of the camp and that made it even more difficult to see him. She had not realized, until he moved into it, how great a sense of security she had felt when he was near.

One evening as she sat by her fire, Moses approached. She had not heard him coming and was startled when he spoke. "Sarah, are you busy?"

"No," she replied, feeling a slight blush spread across her cheeks as she quickly gathered up the heavy buffalo robe she was sewing for him. Though it was a difficult task, she had fashioned it into a long coat, with sleeves and collar, using an awl and buffalo sinew. She had left the hair on it, so it would provide him warm protection against the coming cold weather.

"How are you?" he asked, a contented smile upon his face as he looked down at her.

"I'm fine," she replied. "Do you want some coffee?"

"Sure," he said, noticing how glad she seemed, to see him.

"Oh, I have to go get more water," she said, apologetically.

"I'll go get it," he offered.

"I'll go with you," she said, happy for the chance to spend some time with him. She rose, picking up the empty coffeepot, and they walked along, side by side, their breath visible in the air. The moon had come out from behind a cloud, lighting their path and crowning the rushing water with silver accents as they neared the narrow stream not far from the village.

"You look pretty," Moses stated, unable to help himself.

"I was just about to say the same to you," she said, "that you look handsome, I mean, not pretty." She blushed, adding, "You've changed. You look like an Indian now. I…like the change. Are those Eagle feathers?"

"No, they're from a Hawk…" he hesitated, knowing the time was right to tell her what he had wanted to tell her for such a long time. "There's something I need to tell you, Sarah," he began, just as a scream tore through the air! Pounding hooves shattered the silence as a horse and rider splashed across the stream straight at the startled couple! The horse side-swiped Moses, knocking him to the ground. The moon had once again gone under the clouds, and they could not see their attacker in the dark, only his outline. Sarah screamed and stumbled, landing on her side, her hip striking a large rock that jutted up out of the ground! Moses regained his feet, pulled his knife from its sheath and bent forward in a crouch as the rider whirled his mount around and again charged across the water. Sarah rolled to one side to avoid being stepped on as the horse neared, hoping Moses was out of the way and would not be hurt or killed! More sounds filled the air, sending shivers through her as she realized some were from Moses.

"Be careful!" she called out, seeing only confusing outlines of the men and horse. To her dismay, Moses didn't answer. Then, the horse reared, and the rider fell or jumped from it, cries of anger filling the air. Sarah crept a short distance away, trying to stay out of harm's way and still see the combatants. The air was filled with the sounds of the men as they fought both to win—and to stay alive! Sarah remained crouched where she was, her heart beating wildly within her breast with fear for Moses. She listened intently, realizing the men had rolled down to the water's edge now. Soon she heard them hit the water with a splash, followed by many loud groans and curses.

Then, suddenly, a high scream of victory sounded from their attacker, and he jumped to his feet, bolted across the stream, jumped on his horse and was gone! Sarah's heart froze in fear!

"Moses? Moses? Where are you?" she cried out, as she made her way down to the water. Behind her she heard the voice of Howling Wolf and some of the other braves. She knew they had heard the commotion and come running to see what was wrong.

"Moses…" she called again, then stumbled over something in the dark, knowing in her heart it was him. She fell to her knees, feeling his arm, chest, and face in the dark. Howling Wolf quickly knelt by her side, as the other braves ran for their horses, intent on finding whomever it was who had attacked them.

Just then Moses groaned and reached out, grasping her shoulder, believing her to be his attacker. "Moses, it's me…it's Sarah," she said, wincing in pain. He loosened his grip and began to sit up.

Seeing that he was conscious, and hearing the other braves returning on horseback—his horse with them—Howling Wolf left to join them in their search for the attacker.

Moses groaned, then pushed himself up to a sitting position, feeling his chest for any wounds. "I'm fine, darlin'," he said, rubbing the back of his head. "Hit my head, that's all. Got a nasty bump." He eased to his feet then, feeling a bit dizzy, and steadied himself till it went away.

"Who was it, do you know?" he asked her, rubbing his head where it hurt.

"I don't know," she answered, relieved that he was alive, even though he had been hurt.

"Seems strange that a lone brave would attack us this close to Standing Elk's village," he said. "He didn't hurt you, did he?"

"No," she said, moving closer to him, putting her arm around his waist.

"I think we've got us an enemy, darlin'," he said. "Maybe one of the braves is jealous of our closeness."

"Spotted Dog," Sarah whispered, surprising him.

Moses stiffened, turning her toward him. "Who is this Spotted Dog?" he asked. "Why would he want to attack us?" His voice was deadly serious now and Sarah wished she had kept quiet. She felt sick to her stomach at the mere mention of her long-time enemy's name.

The moon slid from behind the clouds just then and Moses looked at her, lifting her chin so he could look into her eyes. "Who is he, Sarah.

Why would he attack us?" he demanded, his voice rising.

She shut her eyes, afraid of the anger he would feel if she told him the truth. Afraid of the sadness *she* would once again have to face with the telling!

Moses waited, getting more and more upset the longer she hesitated. Someone had tried to kill them and she remained silent, obviously knowing the truth, yet afraid to tell him, or...could it be that she was protecting their attacker?

"Sarah, tell me who Spotted Dog is...*who* is he, Sarah!" he demanded, shaking her by her shoulders without realizing it, in his determination to find out. She remained silent, unable to lie to him, yet knowing the danger he would be in if he knew the truth and went after Spotted Dog. And he *would* go after him if he knew, she had no doubt about that!

"You're hurting me," she said, at last, as his fingers dug into her shoulders. Moses was surprised by her words, having not realized he was squeezing her shoulders so tightly. But, *why* wouldn't she answer him?

Just then the braves returned, led by Howling Wolf, saying the attacker had gotten away in the dark and they would resume their hunt for him in the morning, when it would be easy to pick up his tracks. Howling Wolf asked if Moses was all right and hearing that he was, bid them both goodnight and rode back toward the village.

Sarah walked to the waters' edge, bending to cup a drink of water into her hands. Moses noticed then that she was limping, and his concern for her grew, renewing his anger.

"He hurt you, Sarah! Tell me who he is!" he demanded.

She turned to face him, her face in full shadow, as the moon was now behind her. "I...I can't!" she exclaimed, and ran past him in the partial darkness, her eyes filling with tears as she hurried back to her tepee.

Moses walked over to the water, crouching down to get a drink. He sipped the cold water, noticing the headache that had begun to build across his forehead. As he reached for a second scoop of water, his hand touched the edge of Sarah's coffeepot and he fished it out of the water, intent on throwing it as far as he could across the stream and into the tall grass on the other side. But he thought better of it, and walked along the path toward the camp, all the while trying to figure out why she would not tell him who this Spotted Dog was. He stumbled up the path, no answer making sense but one. So that's it, he thought, that's why she won't tell me. That's also why she didn't come back to Hastings after Gray Eagle died. He shook his head, groaning at the pain he felt all through it. So that's why she's so hesitant about leaving here ... she has a young brave interested in her, and obviously has enough feelings for him to want to protect him from me. Well, I should have known. Four years without a husband, pretty as she is, I should have figured there'd be someone she had feelings for by now. His anger turned to a feeling of overwhelming sadness at these realizations and again he shook his head, a splitting pain nearly dropping him in his tracks. He paused, a bit off balance, then again began to walk, his steps slow and his heart heavy. "What a fool I've been," he muttered aloud, "to think she could have loved me."

Sarah saw him coming, saw the look on his face, knowing there was no way she could tell him about Spotted Dog. She knew beyond a doubt that Moses would not rest until he had killed him, if he ever found out. She knew, too, how little chance Moses would have in a fight with him.

Moses watched her expression as he stopped before her. "I'm sorry... about everything," he said, the words catching in his throat. "Here's your coffeepot. I'd better turn in," he added, at a loss for words.

"Moses..." she began as he slowly turned away, "I...don't go."

"I understand, Sarah," he replied, looking back at her. "It's all right... I wish you all the best."

Sarah stood there, stunned at his words, her mouth open, not understanding why he was wishing her well. "No, you don't understand,"she said, noticing the look of hurt in his eyes.

"I *do* understand," he replied. "I thought things would be different. Thought I could..." he hesitated, "I should have known better. I'm an old man who had a foolish notion that...just be happy, Sarah. What I thought doesn't matter. Just be happy." And he turned and walked away, never looking back.

Sarah ran inside, throwing herself down upon the buffalo robe she was sewing for him. Her heart felt raw with pain as she remembered the words he had spoken—'I thought things would be different. Thought I could'—"You thought you could love a woman who was raped by an Indian," she whispered into the dark. "Thought you could...but you can't," she said, tears running down her face. "You said you're an old man with foolish notions. Was it so foolish, Moses, to love me? I'm still the woman you knew in Hastings, still the woman you delivered Melinda Rose's baby with, before I married Gray Eagle. You said it doesn't matter what you think, but it *does* matter, so much more than you know. It matters because I love you, Moses Gentry, with all my heart!" and she rolled into a fetal position, covering herself with the buffalo robe coat she was sewing for him, and cried herself to sleep, certain she would never be happy again.

CHAPTER 14

Moses woke with a sour taste in his mouth and a sick feeling in his stomach. He opened one eye, then the other, dreading to face the day. An empty whiskey bottle lay beside him and he groaned as he remembered the events of the night before.

"Damn!" he exclaimed, as he tried to stand and the tepee rocked precariously. He tried to get his balance, steadying himself, as a shooting pain slammed through his head. He thought of the fight by the waters' edge, rubbing his head, surprised at the size of the lump he felt. "Ow!" he cried out, seeing the walls of the tepee begin to wave before his eyes. Suddenly he found himself flat on the ground, the spinning room making him sick to his stomach. He clenched his eyes shut, hoping that would make the spinning stop, a comforting black his last awareness.

Sometime later, the sound of soft laughter broke through his consciousness and he turned his head, slowly opening first one eye and then the other. The tepee had stopped spinning, he realized, though now Howling Wolf stood within his line of sight with two heads and four eyes! He shut his eyes again, willing his stomach to remain intact.

"Firewater strong," Howling Wolf said, smiling.

Moses tried to grin, but felt his stomach lurch in protest. He groaned and rolled onto his side, feeling certain if he wasn't dying, he wanted to. His stomach burned and bubbled and his breath smelled rank, even to him. He wondered if he had thrown up in his drunkenness and was certain he must have. He felt too sick to look. Very slowly, he rolled back onto his back, glancing to where Howling Wolf had been. He was alone. He lay still, certain that death was close-by. "Oh, God," he moaned, reaching up to cover his eyes in a vain attempt to erase the memories that now engulfed him. "Sarah," he said, the word nearly gagging him. He squeezed his eyes shut, trying not to remember her words. 'I can't,' she had said, and it kept repeating in his head, over and over, till he felt like weeping. He should have known she would have someone new in her life. Someone she loved. What kind of fool was he, anyways, to think she could love him? He bit his hand as a wave of nausea overtook him and as he did, a single tear rolled down his cheek. "I'm a darned old fool," he whispered, his voice filled with regret.

Suddenly, soft hands touched his face, brushing the tear away with great tenderness. He smiled, keeping his eyes tightly shut to stop the throbbing pain in his head. Sarah, oh, Sarah, he thought, you *have* come. You *do* care. You *must*, or you wouldn't be here. He reached out to touch her cheek, enjoying the softness of it against his hand. He groaned as a feeling of relief filled him. If she's here, he thought, perhaps I still have a chance of winning her heart. Reaching up, his eyes still closed, he cupped the face above him, pulling her closer. "Oh, Sarah," he crooned, forcing his eyes open. He was shocked to find it was *not* Sarah he was holding close, but Dancing Fawn, sister of Howling Wolf! Moses jerked back, trying to roll away from her and stand, all at the same time. In doing so, his foot landed on the empty whiskey bottle and skidded out from under him, sending him crashing to the ground, no longer conscious of his surroundings, or caring if he lived or died.

Sarah woke late, having cried most of the night. She felt as though her world no longer had any meaning and sat outside, a forlorn expression upon her face. The sun was just coming up over Moses' tepee and she looked in that direction, hoping to catch sight of him. If only I could tell him about Spotted Dog, she thought, and she rose, wondering if it would do any good to go over and talk to him. It was at that moment that Dancing Fawn walked from his dwelling. Sarah gasped in shocked surprise, chills running through her. So that's how it is, she thought, anger mixing with the sadness that consumed her. She hurried inside, her thoughts a jumble of grief and fury! Once a ladies' man, she thought, always a ladies' man! Well, what a fool I was, Moses Gentry, to think I ever loved you! And she threw herself down on her bed of hides and once more began to cry.

CHAPTER 15

Moses woke as the sun began its descent that evening. His stomach hurt only a slight bit less than his head. Rolling over carefully, he eased up to a sitting position. He got to his feet—more than a little unsteady—rubbing a hand over his face, feeling as though he had been trampled by a thousand stampeding buffalo and hoped he wouldn't be sick. What the hell was I thinking? I haven't had a drink in years, and then I go and finish off that bottle of whiskey. Well, so much for 'medicinal purposes' for that bottle, he thought. I'm surprised it didn't kill me. No wonder my stomach hurts so bad! He reached up and felt the lump on the back of his head, not at all surprised to find it still there. Groaning aloud, he rubbed the sleep out of his eyes, and took a deep breath. His head felt as if it was going to burst and the taste in his mouth was awfully similar to horse dung. He was upright, however, and that was an improvement!

Slowly he looked around. The empty whiskey bottle lay to one side of where he slept. His shirt lay on the ground beside it and his knife was nowhere to be seen, the sheath laying empty near one of his boots. It was then he thought of the attack by the waters' edge and wondered if his knife was still there. Opening the flap of the tepee, he stepped out into the dusk, careful not to jar his aching head anymore than was necessary.

There were some children playing off to his right, he noticed, and some older boys were practicing their skill with bow and arrows off to his left. He looked across the camp toward Sarah's, and wished he could talk to her, could tell her how much she meant to him. There was no sign of her, though. He turned—walking slowly—his balance off, somewhat, as he headed for the creek. Once he got cleaned up and washed the foul smell of the whiskey off him, he was sure he would feel much better. As he arrived at the stream, he remembered how the Indian had come out of nowhere, it seemed, the night before. He hoped he wouldn't return now. I'm no match for you tonight, he thought, if you come now, I'll be "toe-up" before dawn. He stopped then, seeing Sarah farther on down the creek, her head bent forward, washing her face. His heart did a happy skip upon seeing her and he walked over to her. "Sarah...I didn't expect to see you here," he said, his voice a bit slurred from the whiskey he had consumed.

She turned toward him, her eyes filled with anger, to his complete surprise. "Oh! Am I *intruding*?" she asked, her eyes blazing.

He was dumbstruck and said nothing, trying to figure out what she was talking about and why she was so riled!

"Here! I found this on the ground!" she said, thrusting her hand out toward him. He saw the medallion his mother had given him. "Your "mother" wouldn't want you to lose this," she said, her voice rising, and his head pounding with each word she spoke.

"What's wrong with you? What are you so fired-up about?" he asked, reaching out to take his medallion.

"You think you can just go around stompin' on women's hearts, Gentry? Well, I've got news for you...I may not be worthy to be your..." she caught herself just before she said the word 'wife', then continued, "I may not measure up in your "esteemed estimation," but that gives you no right to..."

"Wait just a minute!" Moses shouted. "I don't know what you're so darned mad about, Sarah. Would you just calm down one dog-gone minute and tell me what in tarnation's gotten into you?"

"You just don't get it, do you?"she yelled back at him. "Well, that's fine! From now on you can just go your own way, Gentry, and I'll go mine! We won't *intrude* on each others' lives...do I make myself clear?"

So that was it, he thought, her Indian fella had been angry about last night and she was afraid of losing him, that's what had her so darned upset. "You've made yourself clear," he said. "I told you last night to 'be happy' and I meant it, all right?"

She felt the lump in her throat tighten. He had told her to 'be happy,' but she just could not believe it had been his way of saying goodbye. Tears threatened, filling her eyes, nearly choking her. She looked at him, a plaintive look upon her face, then ran past him and back to camp.

Moses stood there, not sure why she had suddenly looked so sad, not sure of anything that had just taken place between them. He rubbed his hand across his eyes and forehead as he began walking along the creek. "Well, darlin', I won't intrude anymore, you can be sure of that," he said, and he knelt beside the stream in hopes that the cold water would wash away every trace of the previous night. As he knelt there, he spotted his knife, and picked it up, and wiped it off.

Sarah plunged headlong into activities that kept her busy, in the days that followed. She worked diligently, giving reading and writing lessons to the children and any adults who wanted them. In between, she worked on making herself some fur-lined winter garments. The buffalo robe coat she was making for Moses she continued to work on, too, knowing he would need it, though it made her heart grow heavier with each stitch, it seemed. Common sense told her she needed to finish it, regardless of the way things were now between them. She caught herself looking in the direction of his tepee often, hoping to catch a glimpse of him. Obviously he was busy though, she thought, with Dancing Fawn, no doubt, and her heart was filled with sadness.

Day after day passed as Moses acclimated himself to life in the village. He enjoyed the companionship he shared with the other men, especially Howling Wolf and Standing Elk. His talks with Standing Elk filled him with a sense of communion. He marveled at the wisdom of the older man and felt a quietness and contentedness deep in his soul after their talks. Talks which often lasted long into the night. He felt a kinship with both men that made him aware of how different his life would have been if his father had been an Indian. At the same time, he also felt sadness for the cruel treatment his mother had experienced at his father's hands. He had never realized the immense change his mother had to endure in going from the peaceful, simple life of her people, to the tumultuous, unsettled life with his father, and amongst the whites, many of whom had never accepted her or had shown her even the smallest sign of friendship. It was bad enough that she had been taken from her people by some trappers, worked like a slave, and ultimately won in a card game by Frank Gentry. He wondered how she had endured the sadness, shame, and sorrow of life with his father, never once whining or complaining. Always trying to make the best life she could for him—her firstborn—and his brothers, and above all, to instill in them the beliefs and values of her people. The bond he now shared with Gray Eagle's father, Chief Standing Elk, filled him with pride in his Indian heritage, and with even more admiration for his mother. In quiet moments when he went off by himself, he would give thanks for her teachings, and for his friends among the Indians. Howling Wolf taught him the skills he needed to hunt in the way of the Indians and other skills necessary for survival. Often they ventured far from the village in search of game. Moses' skill with a bow and arrow now closely equaled that of his friend, and they would often have contests, challenging each other. In the evening, as they sat listening to Standing Elk's wise counsel, Moses would glance over at Howling Wolf, only to discover him smiling back at him. Moses felt great respect for him and cared for him as though they were brothers. In fact, he thought of Howling Wolf as his brother now, and it pleased him.

One day as they rode far out across the land, Moses asked Howling Wolf the question that had long been bothering him, as more and more that day his thoughts had turned, unbidden, to Sarah. "My brother, I must ask you a question," Moses said, a serious look upon his face.

"Speak, Black Hawk," Howling Wolf replied.

"Can you tell me who Spotted Dog is?" Moses asked. "Though I have not seen him in our village, I have reason to believe he is known there."

"Yes," Howling Wolf answered. "Spotted Dog was one of 'The People.' He was cast out because he brought shame upon our people."

Moses was shocked. Why would Sarah care so deeply for someone like that, he wondered. She must know he is of such poor character. To be cast out by your own people indicated a person of no honor. No decency. How could she give her heart to someone such as this?

All the rest of the day, Moses was troubled by what he had discovered about Spotted Dog. Apparently, Sarah had strong feelings for him, in spite of his unsavory character. He decided he must go talk to her, reason with her, even warn her, if she would listen.

When they returned to the village, Howling Wolf went on his way, and Moses headed for Sarah's. He had decided to speak to her, even though she had made it abundantly clear that he was not to intrude in her life. Well, I care for her, he thought, and that's why I must talk to her. Must try to make her come to her senses.

There was no sign of her at her tepee, so he walked over to his, repeating over and over again in his mind what he would say to her when next he saw her. He had just settled in for the night, when a young boy arrived, telling him that Standing Elk wished to see him. Moses thanked the boy and immediately headed for the chief's tepee, wondering what he wanted.

Upon entering, he was surprised to see none of the other braves there. "You sent for me?"he asked, smiling at the older man.

"Yes, Black Hawk, sit. We will smoke together." Moses could tell that Standing Elk had something on his mind and he wondered what it was that caused him so much concern. They sat there, smoking the pipe—passing it back and forth—and Moses wondered again what was troubling the elderly Indian.

Then Standing Elk spoke. "Many moons ago, a young brave and a maiden fell in love. In their village lived another who wanted the maiden for his own. Lacking honor, he told many lies about the maiden, knowing these stories would be heard by the brave who loved her. Upon hearing them, the young brave felt great anger in his heart and told the maiden he no longer felt love for her. The maiden felt great sorrow, not understanding why he now felt as he did. Many days went by, her sorrow growing, blocking all joy from her heart. She refused the attention of the other brave, her heart growing as cold as the winter winds that blew 'round her lodge. Finally, she left, going far from the village.

Many moons passed, the young brave now old, his hair white, like snow. He knew he would soon die. He had never forgotten the maiden, often wondering where she was. There was great pain in his heart when he thought of her.

One day, while hunting far from the village, he saw an old woman sitting near a wide river. He approached, sitting beside her. "I do not remember this wide river being here," he told her.

She looked at him a long time before answering. "It has been here many moons," she replied, looking into his eyes. "It has grown wide from the tears of one who lost her love."

"It is sad to lose the one you love," he replied. "I, too, have felt the pain. My heart became as the rock that lies there, upon the ground, beside the wide river."

She looked at him then, studying his face, seeing in it the face of the young brave that had long ago broken her heart. At the same time, he realized that the maiden he had lost, many moons before, was the woman sitting beside him now. His anger flew away as he saw the same look of love in her eyes that had been there when they were young.

"We have always been together," he said, pointing toward the rock that lay beside the rushing water of the wide river.

"In our hearts we have," she said, and she knew they would never part again."

Standing Elk finished his story, looking at Moses, wondering if he had understood the meaning behind his words.

"Why are you telling me this?" Moses asked, clearly confused.

"My eyes see the rock that grows inside my friend, Black Hawk, as he goes about our village. He does not smile or laugh. This is not good. I am told Red Bird's tears are many. This, too, is not good. It does not please me to see the pain of my daughter, Red Bird, or my friend, Black Hawk," he said, searching Moses' face as he finished speaking.

Moses cleared his throat, unsure of what to say, of how to explain. Then he spoke. "I love Red Bird...Sarah...but I have heard she loves another."

"I know of no other," Standing Elk replied, sounding concerned.

"I have good reason to believe she cares for him," Moses said, a sadness filling his heart and showing all too clearly in his eyes.

Standing Elk saw his pain and was quiet, many thoughts running through his head, then he spoke. "In the valley two days distance from our village, where the sun rises, there is a cave. It is close to a lake my people call 'Lake of the Burning Grasses.' It was there, as a young man, I had my first vision." He paused, looking intently at the younger man. "It is a sacred place, as you will see. I want you to go there, Black Hawk, to find the answers that will heal your heart and take away the rock that grows within it. Will you go there, my son?"

"Yes, I will go as you ask. I will go and consider all we have spoken of tonight," Moses replied.

"Leave when the sun rises in the sky, Black Hawk. It will guide you to the sacred cave." As they stood there, Moses thought he saw, for just an instant, a twinkle in the old man's eye, but decided it was only his imagination. "May Wakantanka guide you, my friend," Standing Elk said, and with a movement of his hand he dismissed Moses.

Moses returned to his tepee, tethering Midnight beside it, then went inside to pack what he would need for the journey. He had heard his mother speak of the 'vision quest' of the young warriors of her village, long ago, but he had never been on one. The idea of this journey filled him with a sense of adventure and excitement. He would go to the sacred place Standing Elk had spoken of and see if he could find answers there. Would see if he, too, could somehow find a way to heal the pain that filled his own heart, because he, too, had lost *his* love—when he lost Sarah.

As he prepared to leave, at dawn's first light the next morning, he wanted to stop and tell Sarah goodbye, but thought better of it. He was certain she was asleep and would not take kindly to him *intruding*, as she had so bluntly put it that day at the stream. Throwing his saddle over Midnight and strapping on his saddlebags, he glanced again at her tepee, wishing she would walk outside so he would have an excuse to stop and talk to her. But there was no sign of her. He turned away, swinging up onto his horse, disappointment filling him as he slowly headed in the direction of the rising sun. A dog barked as he rode past Howling Wolf's tepee, and from within it he was certain he heard some movement. Otherwise, all was still. Solitude, his only companion.

CHAPTER 16

Sarah rolled upon her side, opening her eyes to the cold darkness of the cave. She rubbed the sleep from her eyes and then stretched, yawning as she did so. She had slept well for the first time since leaving the village, for the first time since seeing Dancing Fawn leaving Moses' tepee. She snorted as she thought of it. "I won't think of him," she vowed. "I won't. I won't." She got up, walked to the entrance of the cave and looked out across the countryside below. A large herd of deer grazed in the meadow far below, and a fish jumped in the center of the lake. All was peaceful and serene and she was glad she had done as Standing Elk had suggested and come here. He had said it was necessary that she gather some of the medicinal plants that only grew in this area, but she suspected that he thought she needed some time alone. Actually, she welcomed the chance to put some distance between herself and Moses and had gladly agreed to go. She was tired of crying herself to sleep every night, tired of feeling the shame of knowing he no longer wanted anything to do with her. 'Be happy,' he had said. How can I be happy? she thought. I love him and I've lost him. She thought again of the morning she had seen Dancing Fawn leaving his dwelling, and tears filled her eyes. She walked back into the cave and pulled a piece of pemmican from her pouch which lay just inside, sniffling as she did so. Then she walked back to the cave's entrance and sat down.

As the sun rose, sending shafts of golden sunlight out across the valley below, the tall prairie grass reflected a marbled shade of muted gold, and Sarah thought of the cave near Hastings. She smiled as it came to mind. She thought of the pleasant times she had spent there, and felt comforted by these thoughts. She remembered the day she had nearly fainted from fright as she realized an Indian was standing on the ledge above it, watching her. Remembered, too, the day the ground had given way, sliding out from beneath where he stood, and the horror she had felt as he yelled out, his body plummeting to the ground far below, amongst the dust and rocks. She shivered as she remembered and rubbed her arms as chills coursed through her at the memory. She had never seen an Indian closeup before and remembered how she had sniffed his hair and chest to see if he stunk, like her father had always said Indians did. "Oh Father, you were *so* wrong," she said, "so *very* wrong." She had thought Gray Eagle so handsome, right from the first moment she saw him standing there, his jet black hair shining in the sun, his skin bronzed by its rays. "I loved him so, Father," she whispered aloud, looking up at the clear blue sky above her. She chewed another bite of the pemmican, thinking how enjoyable a swim would feel, but instead, she remained sitting where she was, lost in a myriad of memories. She remembered the first time he had touched her, how her body had responded. Thought, too, of how he had pulled away, not wanting to bring any dishonor to them or upon his people. Her thoughts turned, suddenly, to Moses, 'I thought I could,' he had begun. "You thought you could love me," she said, and her heart filled with pain. She took a deep breath. "You thought you could love me, and now it will never be... No!" She exclaimed aloud. "I have to forget him! I have to!" She rose and walked back into the cave.

In spite of her intention of wiping him from her mind, her thoughts turned to the day Gray Eagle brought Moses to her cabin after he had been attacked by the cougar. The image of him as he lay there, helpless, completely in her care, brought a feeling of warmth flooding through her. She had been without a man four years now. Four years without a man's' touch, four long years without the fulfillment only a man could give. "Oh Moses," she whispered, then caught herself. "Darn you, Moses Gentry, why can't I stop thinking of you?" She bent to straighten the hides where she slept, her mind refusing to be still. She saw, once again, the look on Moses' face as the handsome bandit, Antonio Gonzales, had pranced his horse before her, that grievous day in Hastings. He had smiled at her as he drew his gun, intending to kill her as he had killed Moses' wife, many years before and she had been too surprised to run, too shocked to even cry out. She had just stood there, knowing she was about to die. She shuddered, remembering. She had not seen the knife as it flashed through the air. The knife that Old John had thrown as he raced down the walkway by Tommy Dawson's store, calling her name, intent on saving her. She remembered the handsome Mexican's look of surprise as the knife found its mark and he fell forward over the neck of his horse—the horse Moses now rode. She had not heard the shots ring out from the Mexican's gun as he fell, or the sound behind her as John Bruce collapsed, his arm outstretched toward her, his life's blood running in an ever-widening circle from within him. She shook her head, seeing it all again, as though it was all happening anew. She remembered Moses saying her name as she knelt down beside John, his voice comforting and soft. She had been stunned to see blood spreading across the side of his shirt, and even more dripping from his hand as he slumped against her then. She thought someone had yelled to go get the doctor and her father, but she had no clear memory of it. No clear memory after she saw the blood seeping through Moses' shirt. "Oh Moses," she said, a tear trickling down her cheek. She shook her head, her eyes pressed tightly shut. "I have to stop thinking of him, I have to!" she exclaimed, knowing in her heart that it would be easier said than done. She ran from the cave, deciding a quick swim might just get her mind off him.

A short while later, she crawled into her bed, snuggling down, trying to get her body to quit trembling. She knew she shouldn't have gone swimming, as cold as it was, but it was too late to change that now. The water and air had both been cold and now she felt chilled clear through. Nestling down further under the hides, her wet clothes in a pile on the floor of the cave, she drew her knees up against her stomach. Her feet felt like two chunks of ice and she rubbed them back and forth, hoping to warm them. She knew she should get up and put on dry clothes and add more wood to the fire, but decided just to lay there until she stopped shaking. She closed her eyes, listening to the night sounds, shivering more and more as time went by. Before long, she noticed that her throat was sore and it had become difficult to swallow. In the morning I should feel better, she thought. If not, I'll head back to the village. Right now, I must get warm!

A coughing spell woke her sometime later and she felt even colder. She reached out, pulling the buffalo robe coat she had made for Moses, over her, hoping it would help to warm her. Another bout of coughing wracked her body as she lay there, aware now that she was, indeed, sick. The thought that she might have smallpox and could die, like so many of her friends had, gripped her heart with fear. Especially as she realized she was now too sick to go for help.

"Dear God," she whispered, her teeth chattering and body shaking, her throat so sore that the words caused her eyes to water. "Please don't let me die here…alone. Please help me. Send someone, God… and please let Moses know that I truly *did* love him…if…" Another wracking cough interrupted her prayers, and as it did, she again closed her eyes, too sick to say more.

CHAPTER 17

Moses rode on, his thoughts jumping from one thing to the other, yet always returning to Sarah. "Lady," he said, speaking aloud, causing Midnight's ears to perk up in response, "how am I ever going to forget you?" He was tormented by his thoughts. How could you love a man like Spotted Dog? A renegade who had brought dishonor upon his people. "And how can I just ride away knowing you love someone like him?" He shook his head, a sad expression upon his face. Worse yet, how can I ever forget you? he thought. Maybe I should have told Standing Elk who it is you care for. Maybe he could have talked some sense into you. He wondered if Standing Elk knew that Spotted Dog had attacked them that night at the creek, obviously not caring that he had also put Sarah's life in jeopardy. How could she think he loved her, when he would do that? Glancing at the sun as it spread out before him, caused him to squint in order to see. He patted his horse's neck, speaking aloud. "It'll do me good to put some distance between Sarah and me. Who needs some fired-up, red-haired gal spouting off at him, anyways? She'll have to do all her yelling at that Spotted Dog fella from now on...and he's welcome to it! I'm gettin' too darned old to have some hot- tempered gal chewing me up one side and down the other!"

He shook his head, his thoughts suddenly going back to the day he had first called her darlin', the day of Nancy Pearly's wedding to Silas Haverty. He had to laugh as he remembered how upset she had been. She had gotten all flustered and started to walk away from him, then saw Tom Dawson heading across the yard toward her and had turned back, her cheeks blazing fire-red. He remembered how he had offered her his arm then, and she had accepted, just to avoid being bored to death by Tommy. He had to laugh at the memory, remembering how her chin always raised when she felt threatened, as it had then. He smiled, the memory making him happy.

The sky began to darken as he rode on, the threat of rain or snow hanging heavily in the air. Moses wished he had a warmer coat, just in case an early snowstorm hit, but his old coat was all he had, and it would have to do. He pulled his hat further down on his head, urging Midnight along.

His thoughts turned back to the day he and Sarah had delivered Melinda Rose's baby. He had come breech and the contractions had gone on all day. Melinda Rose had grown weaker and weaker. They had begun to think that she and the baby would die, though Sarah had tried and tried to turn him. He had seen that Sarah was growing tired and she no longer had much strength left, so he had said something to make her mad. She had quickly gotten all fired-up and called him a 'pompous bag of wind' and shoved harder, and the baby had suddenly turned, slipping from within his mother, into Sarah's waiting arms. He had felt so good, so proud of her, when the little fella burst out, looking like a messy pup, his lungs filling with air as he lay in her arms. He had seen, that day, the strength and fortitude Sarah was capable of, and felt proud to have shared it with her. That was the day he had told her of his wife—of *his* Sarah—and how she had been shot down—years before—by the bandit, Antonio Gonzales, as he rode through town after robbing the bank. How his wife had been crossing the street to go to him and he had looked up just as the shot rang out, killing her and their unborn child. He remembered feeling Sarah's arms go around him after he had told her. He remembered how she had cried and tried to comfort him as they sat there in the dark, on Melinda Roses' porch, the moon shining across the yard.

He pulled up on the reins, dismounting, thinking of how long it had been since he had felt so comforted. He stood there, petting Midnight's neck, then walked back and forth, stretching his legs, his thoughts still assailing him. How long had it been since a woman had held him? How long had it been since he'd lain with one? There had always been plenty of women he could have, just for the asking, but how long had it been since he'd had one? How long since he'd *wanted* one of them? It wasn't just *any* woman he wanted, that was the problem and he knew it. A soft, sweet-smelling body could be easily had, some for a couple of dollars, some for even less. But he had no interest in them, hadn't had for a long time. Hadn't had, since he had realized he loved this woman he called 'darlin'. No, he thought, there's no getting around it. I'm in love with Sarah and I have to tell her so when I get back to Standing Elk's camp. Have to make her believe me. Have to try to make her see that *I'm* the one for her. He took off his hat, raking his hand through his long hair. "Well, Midnight, old fella, this trip might be just what I need to get that gal out of my head...but so far, it's not working," he said, as he mounted and started on his way again.

They traveled on till they came to an outcropping of rock just before dark, then Moses hobbled Midnight and spread his bedroll on the ground, using his saddle for a pillow. He made a fire, keeping it small, so as not to attract any unwelcome company. Gray Eagle's people weren't the only Indians in the territory—only the friendliest—as far as he was concerned, and he didn't want any nasty surprises. He'd had a feeling that he was being followed ever since he'd left Standing Elk's village, and it had grown even stronger, the farther he went. As he prepared for the night, the uneasy feeling continued to bother him. He pulled his old coat tightly around him, rubbing his hands together to warm them. He could see his breath in the air before him and knew it had gotten colder. He made a pot of coffee, taking some pemmican from his pouch, but decided he wasn't really hungry and put it back. When he got to the cave Standing Elk had told him about, *then* he would eat, after he got all settled in and had hunted up a nice tender rabbit or a young buck. He poured himself a cup of the hot coffee, and the smell of it made his stomach rumble. He was used to makin' do with little food, never did fancy his own cooking. As he drank the coffee, he thought again of the night he and Sarah had walked down to the stream near the camp. He had intended to tell her about himself, about his being part Indian. He had even thought about giving her his medallion to wear, as a symbol of the future they would share once they got back to Hastings. Now he wondered if she ever *would* return to Hastings, wondered if she would ever return there *with him*. He shook his head, going over to his bedroll and laid down. Off in the distance, a coyote howled, answered soon by another. He closed his eyes, listening. Rolling over, his thoughts continued. I was just about to tell her how much I loved her when that Spotted Dog fellow attacked, racing out of the dark and straight into us. Nearly split my head open. Reaching up to rub his head, a soft nicker from Midnight caught his attention, and he reached for his gun beneath his saddle, cocking it. He lay still, never moving and scarcely breathing as he listened for any sound that might mean danger. Nothing moved in the darkness and after awhile he sat up, pouring himself another coffee, his gun still within easy reach. Pulling his coat collar high up around his neck, he watched the moon as it lit the ground with its soft white light. Then he lay back down and soon fell asleep.

When he woke, long before sunup, a feeling of immense dread and foreboding filled him. He could not shake the feeling that something was terribly wrong as he quickly packed his pouch and saddlebags, foregoing his usual morning cup of coffee. He had the strangest feeling that he had to hurry, that something was urging him on in a race against time! But what could it be, he wondered, out here, so far from everyone and everything? He saddled Midnight—removing his hobbles—then picked up his bedroll, threw his saddlebags across the horse, and checked his gun.

Only once before had he felt this same feeling! The day he had sat on a hill, watching Sarah Mathews skipping rope with her younger sisters. He had sat there, enjoying the scene before him, listening to their laughter and thinking how pretty Sarah was and how much he wished that he could tell her of his feelings for her. Then, all of a sudden, he had begun to feel such a tremendous feeling of dread that he felt almost nauseous. At first, he had held his stomach, wondering what it was that he had eaten that would tear at his insides like that, but soon other feelings had come. A gut-feeling that something was wrong, and that he had to *hurry*, to stop whatever it was that was about to happen. As his anxiety grew, he began to think of his home. He had no idea *how* or *why* his home had come to mind. The only thing he was certain of was that he had to get home! He felt that it was a matter of life or death! He had raced along, kicking his father's old horse in the sides to make it go faster, his heart pounding frantically. When he reached his home, he was shocked to see his father—in a drunken rage—kicking his mother and hitting her with his fists as she lay curled upon the ground, trying to protect herself. Moses had jumped from the running horse, slamming into his father, sending both of them hurtling to the ground. He had beaten his father that day, beaten him almost to death, as his younger brothers stood nearby. Looks of fear upon their young faces. *Never* thereafter, had his father laid a hand on his mother, though he continued to come home drunk.

Now, for some reason unbeknownst to him, the feeling was back! Moses urged Midnight into a gallop, heading into the rising sun, wondering what it was that he would find at the end of the day's ride. As he raced along, he thought of Sarah, wondering what she was doing, wondering if she was with Spotted Dog. Then, suddenly, he knew— *knew* beyond a shadow of a doubt! It was *Sarah* who needed him! The 'twinkle' he had thought he saw in Standing Elk's eye...that was it! He hadn't seen Sarah around camp for a number of days because she had *left* the camp and gone to the cave where Standing Elk had suggested *he* go! Fear filled his heart as he raced along, fear so strong that it made him feel weak. She had to be all right! She *had to be!* But he knew in his heart he was right. Sarah was in serious trouble, and he had to find her right away!

CHAPTER 18

The sun rose higher and higher in the sky as Moses raced on, intent on finding the cave Standing Elk had told him of, his feeling of dread growing stronger with each beat of Midnight's pounding hooves. Dear God, he thought, please let her know I'm coming. So help me, I'm coming!

When the sun was nearly straight up in the sky, he stopped at a small pond to let Midnight drink. Moses paced back and forth, anxiety filling him as he began to question his feelings. What if he was wrong? What if he was being foolish and taking the chance of running Midnight to death on a foolish whim? He stopped pacing, looking in the direction he was heading, shielding his eyes. The feeling of dread and foreboding filled him, even stronger than it had earlier. He ran to his horse, mounted, and raced off again, his thoughts bleak.

What if I can't find the cave? What if I'm miles from it? What if she's trapped or bleeding? "*No!*" he exclaimed aloud, trying to drive these fears from his mind. Where's my faith? Did my feelings fail me before? he thought. No! They caused me to rush home just in time to save my mother! As God is my witness, I have to believe that they'll guide me to Sarah...I *have to* believe it! Thoughts continued to trouble him as he raced along. Faith is what determines a man's life, isn't it, he thought, when you get right down to it? Faith can move a mountain, my mother used to say. Faith as small as a mustard seed. "I hope you're right, Mother," he said aloud, his words lost upon the wind.

After awhile, he slowed his horse to a walk, watching for the different signs Standing Elk had mentioned that pointed the way to the cave. He knew it would do no one any good—himself include—if he ran Midnight until he dropped. He crooned softly to the big horse, patting his neck. "We have to get to her, Boy," he said. "I *know* Sarah's in trouble! Don't know *how* I know it, just know it in my heart." The horse shook its head up and down, as though it understood. Moses got down, still surveying the countryside, to see if he could get his bearings. He checked the saddle and girth strap, making sure everything was all right. Then he swung back up into the saddle, spurred on by the intensity of his feelings.

Just before dusk, they came to a ridge of rock that ran north and south for about a mile. He rode along, knowing he was on the right track and close to his intended destination. He also knew that he had to locate the cave entrance before dark, otherwise he would have to postpone his search for it until daybreak. His eyes scanned the ridge, feelings of anxiety and dread filling him. They ate at him, making his insides churn. Just when he was beginning to think he would not find her, he saw the lake ahead of him. The lake Standing Elk had spoken of...what was it called...? He tried to remember. "Lake of the Burning Grasses," he said aloud, as it came to mind. Yes, he was certain it was the same lake. It lay in a cove at the base of a precipice. Standing Elk had said there was a path that led up to the cave, not far from it. All he had to do now was find the sign...a drawing of three horses, carved into the side of the rock by one of the 'Ancient Ones' many, many moons ago.

He walked along, leading Midnight, his eyes scanning every inch of the ridge, biting his lip as he searched anxiously for either the path or the petroglyph. He was just about to turn and retrace his steps when he decided to call out, hoping Sarah might be close- by and would hopefully be able to hear him. "Sarah," he called, listening intently for an answer. "Sarah!" To his surprise, Midnight whinnied, lifting his head expectantly, looking off to his left, and a moment later, an answering whinny was heard. Moses rushed to where it came from, being cautious, though, in case it meant trouble. To his great relief, he ran nearly headlong into Glory, who was hobbled behind a large outcropping of rock, near a small stream that fed into the lake. "Glory!" Moses exclaimed, his heart pounding with joy. He knew now that he had been right to trust his feelings. Knew that Sarah had to be nearby! He quickly hobbled Midnight, then began to search for the signs Standing Elk had spoken of. It took him only a few minutes of searching to find them, and the path that was well hidden, only a few feet away. He ran up the path, not taking the time to unsaddle his horse or grab his gear. He had to find Sarah and see if she was all right. His heart beat rapidly—like a drum within his chest—with worry over what he might find.

"Sarah?" he called out, as he reached the entrance to the cave. There was no answer. The cave was pitch-black inside. He picked up a thick branch that lay near the obscure entrance and lit it on fire, then entered the cave. He could see her bed, over near the far wall, but it looked empty. He held the branch up higher, looking around for any sign of her. He saw the pile of wood she had gathered, near the opposite wall of the cave—to be used for both heat and cooking—and walked quickly to it, forcing the burning branch beneath it, setting it afire. It was cold in the cave and he wondered how long she had been gone from it…and to where? He walked over to her bed, calling out to her again. To his horror, as he began to turn away he saw her arm sticking out, ghastly pale against the dark hides. He froze in his tracks, his heart lurching within him at the chilling thought that he was too late, that she was dead. "Sarah!" he shouted and hurried to her, dropping to his knees. "Sarah!" He lifted her arm, horrified to find it ice-cold. "Dear God," he cried. "Let her be alive. *Please* let her be alive!" He pulled back the hides that covered her, terrified at what he might find. She had not moved—even when he lifted her arm—and he paled at the thought that he was already too late. "Please, God," he murmured, again and again, unaware that he was speaking aloud. He pulled the last covering from her, a heavy buffalo robe that felt damp to the touch, staring in horror at the sight before him! Her hair was wet, her body as pale as death, a red rash across her neck, face, and upper body. "Smallpox," he said, his voice filled with dread. "Sarah, Sarah, can you hear me? It's Moses. I'm right here, darlin'. Can you hear me?" To his great relief, she moaned, shifting a small bit where she lay as her body began to shake. He felt her forehead, stunned to realize she was burning up with fever. He covered her slightly then, and dragged her and her bedding closer to the fire so he could see her better. "Need to cool her," he said, getting his thoughts in a semblance of order. Seeing that she still was not moving, he rushed from the cave and down the path to get his saddle and saddlebags off of Midnight, hoping he had something in his saddlebags or deerskin pouch that might help her. He threw his saddle over one shoulder, his pouch over the other, and his bedroll and saddlebags over his arm. Then hurried up the path, not wanting to be away from her any longer than was necessary.

He glanced at her as he entered the cave, seeing that she had not moved. Laying his gear to one side, he pulled a shirt from his saddlebags. It was the same shirt that he had bought with the idea that he would look more "presentable" if she ever came back to Hastings to visit, after she had left to marry Gray Eagle. He tore it into strips, then raced down to the lake to wet all the strips and fill his canteen. Then he rushed back up the path to the cave.

Placing one of the cold wet strips across her forehead, he brushed back her hair with one hand. She stirred slightly, her body trembling, as he lay another cold strip across her skin. She tried to speak, but he could not make out what she was saying. "It's all right, darlin'. I'm here with you. You're gonna' be all right, Sarah. I'm right here," he assured her, hoping she could hear him and in spite of her high fever, would understand.

It was then that he saw the pile of wet clothing that lay in a heap near where her bed had been, on the other side of the cave. Seeing this, he realized what had transpired. "You went for a swim!" he exclaimed. "That's why your clothes are all wet." He shook his head, envisioning what had taken place. She must have gone for a swim, then gotten chilled and undressed as soon as she got back to the cave, he thought. Either the fire went out or she felt too cold...or sick, to get it going again, before she crawled into her bed, hoping to get warm. He replaced the strip of cloth across her forehead with another, realizing she might have died if he had not come to the cave...if he had stayed in the village...if Standing Elk hadn't suggested he come to sort out his thoughts. He shook his head, knowing in his heart that it was only by the grace of God that he was here now, doing what he could to help her. "Oh, darlin'," he said, a cold chill running through him. "What if I hadn't listened to Standing Elk? What if I hadn't had those terrible feelings that something was wrong?" He hung his head, unable to stand the thoughts he was thinking. Replacing the strip of fabric with another cold one, he went over to where his saddlebags lay, going through them to see what he could find to dry her hair.

She began to cough then, a dry hacking cough that worried him. "Sounds like pneumonia," he said, looking in his pouch for some whiskey or some herbs that might be of help. She moaned and rolled onto her side, still shaking. He spread out his bedroll beside the blazing fire and knelt down beside her, removing his coat. He gently wrapped her in it, knowing the heat from his body, still inside it, would warm her. Her bedding was damp, damper still where her hair had laid, and he knew he had to get it dry. He picked her up—-coat and all—lifting her as carefully as he could, then laid her down upon his bedroll. Covering her with his blanket, he began rubbing her hair, to dry it. She coughed again, and her body jerked violently with each expulsion, her forehead hot as fire. He got another strip of dampened material and placed it across her forehead. She moaned aloud as it touched her skin, and he felt sick at heart that he really didn't know what to do to help her.

I'll have to get some food into her tomorrow, he thought. Maybe she'll take some broth. I don't know when she ate last. Don't know how long she's been like this. He tucked his blanket in around her, making sure that even if she rolled, or somehow shoved it aside, it was not too close to the fire to catch afire and burn her. In his saddlebag he had found a flask of whiskey, but there was only enough left in it to get a few swallows. He berated himself for drinking the rest of the bottle that night at his tepee. He always carried that for medicinal purposes. "Darn fool," he said, wishing he could change the events of that night. But that was impossible. He was well-aware that she could die now, and the whiskey he drank that night might have been able to somehow help her, to save her. "I was such a fool," he said. "I'll never forgive myself if she dies." He shook his head, picking up the flask with the trace of whiskey inside it. "We'll have to see if we can get this down you," he said and he walked over to her, lifting up her head, slowly tipping the flask against her lips. She coughed and sputtered as the liquid filled her mouth, but he was relieved to see her swallow, and very little of it ran out the side of her mouth and down her chin. She coughed again, her body still shaking because of the fever. He lay her head back down and walked outside to get some more brush and what branches he could find.

It was a brisk moonlit night, with few stars in the sky. He shivered as the wind hit him, its icy fingers a harbinger of the winter weather that would soon be upon them. He made three trips down to the cove below to gather enough brush and kindling to keep their fire going, and to spread her clothes upon, so they would dry. He knew that it was of the utmost importance that her clothing and bedding dry.

Returning to the cave, he quickly gathered up her wet clothes, spreading them over the pile of brush. Then he spread out the hides she had used for a bed, knowing they, too, were damp. As he picked up the large buffalo robe, he wondered why it was so much larger than she needed, then realized it was probably intended for Spotted Dog. "Damn!" he exclaimed, his heart sinking as he felt his anger grow. "Well, where are you, Spotted Dog, now that she needs you? Is this how you care for your woman?" His anger caused a burning sensation in the pit of his stomach, and a mouthful of vile-tasting liquid filled his mouth. He walked out of the cave and spit into the dark, rubbing his stomach. Then hurried back to her side, to put another damp strip of cloth on her forehead. She was still shaking, and though he wanted to cover her more, he was afraid to do so would make her fever soar even higher. She coughed again, this time a raspy series of coughs that caused him to shake his head with concern.

He knelt down, taking one of her hands in his, a silent prayer upon his lips. It was then he remembered that years ago, when he was young, his brother had gotten a high fever. His mother had put cold wet rags on his forehead, too, but it hadn't helped. Moses remembered the look of fear in her eyes then, as she asked him to carry the little boy down to the pond. Moses thought she had gone crazy, he remembered, asking her if she intended to drown him. She had smiled at his words, explaining that they had to get his fever down or he would die. He wondered at such a thing helping, but said nothing and did as his mother told him. When they reached the pond, she told him to place the boy into her arms. Moses had done as she said, surprised as she walked out into the frigid water with him. The little boy had fought her as he felt the icy cold water cover his body, but she had held on tightly, seeing his glazed eyes, knowing the high fever *had to come down!* Then, just as quickly, he remembered that she had walked back out of the water, handing the boy into the waiting blanket that he had held for her. Moses never could understand why his little brother had not gotten pneumonia from the cold water, but he hadn't. They had rushed him into their cabin, wrapping him warmly. Then their mother had changed out of her own wet clothes and into some dry ones, snuggling the child to her within her arms in front of their fireplace, the heat of both their bodies helping to warm the two of them. Moses smiled at the memory, realizing once again, how deeply his mother had loved and cared for her children.

"Well, darlin', it looks like we're gonna' head for the lake." He took off his gun belt, fastened it closed and looped it over his shoulder. Then he stepped out of his boots, socks, pants and shirt. He hated the cold as much as it was possible to hate it and shivered as the cold air hit his nearly naked body. "I hope this is worth it, darlin'," he said, wondering if *he* would end up sick, too. Then he bent down and gently pulled his coat from around her and wrapped his blanket back around her. She moaned as the cold air circled around them, a series of hacking coughs wracking her body. He picked her up in his arms, blanket and all, and started out of the cave and down the path to the lake below. Nestling her head against his cheek, in the hollow of his neck, he hoped he wasn't making a dreadful mistake. What if her coughing got worse? What if she *didn't* have pneumonia and this gave it to her? His thoughts tormented him as he walked along and he realized how very difficult it must have been for his mother to walk out into that freezing pond that day, so long ago, when his little brother, Lou, had taken sick. Hell, I know how hard it's gonna' be for *me* to walk out into that water, he thought, and knew he would truly give *anything* to not have to do it. "Well, Mother, if you could do it for Lou, I can do it for the woman I love," he said, as he reached the waters' edge. He shifted Sarah around, pulling off the blanket as he did so and laid it upon a large boulder along with his gun belt.

Shivering nearly as bad as she was, he walked to the waters' edge, gritting his teeth. He gasped as he stepped into the lake and had to force himself to go deeper, force himself to ignore the dreadfully cold water, force his legs to move and his arms to keep their grip on Sarah. When the water rose to his knees, he knew it was too cold to go any farther. He bent, hating the cruelty of it, and quickly lowered Sarah into the water. Then he lifted her up and rushed to the shore, hoping he wouldn't drop her as she struggled within his aching arms. His legs and feet felt numb from the cold as he grabbed up the blanket and wrapped it around her. He even covered her head, afraid he had made a horrible mistake, and now she would surely get pneumonia, if she didn't already have it. Be a dog-gone wonder I don't get it myself, he thought, picking up his gun belt and heading as fast as he could up the path to the warmth of the cave's waiting fire. Twice, he almost dropped her as he hurried along, barely able to keep a hold on her because his fingers were so cold. His teeth chattered violently and he felt certain if this didn't cure her, it would surely kill her, and *him* along with her.

"Lord, I hope I didn't make a terrible mistake. I'm afraid it wasn't nearly as cold the day my Mother dipped Lou in the lake to squelch his fever. Please help Sarah get better Lord, and please don't let this give her pneumonia," he prayed aloud as he placed her next to the fire, on his bedroll. He tucked his blanket tightly around her, then pulled on his pants, noticing that his legs and feet looked blue from the cold. Pulling on his shirt, he hurried over to where the large buffalo robe lay, drying. It felt dry to the touch and warm from the fire and he had the strongest urge to wrap it around himself for just a moment, to get some heat back into his own bones. But instead, he put it over Sarah, tucking it in around her. Then he pulled on his socks, boots, and coat, enjoying what little warmth they provided. Sarah still shook and shivered, but not as hard as she had before, and he was certain that was a favorable sign. He hoped so, anyway. He went over to his saddlebags, and got out his coffeepot and coffee. A good hot cup of coffee would hit the spot, he thought, might even chase this horrible chill out of me. He pulled out his old tin cup, noticing that his hands were shaking, and saw that the cup had a new dent in it that he had not noticed before. Shivering, he went to sit beside the fire, spreading his hands above the flames to warm them.

All night long, Moses sat beside Sarah, drinking coffee to stay awake. He kept placing the wet strips of material across her forehead, hoping they would help to cool her. Worry was his constant companion as he sat there: afraid she would go into convulsions from the high fever. He prayed, as he sat there. "Dear Lord, please help Sarah get well. I haven't asked much of You over the years. Never was much of a praying man. But, Lord, my heart was crushed for years by the loss of my wife and child. It laid inside me like that rock Standing Elk spoke of. Laid there as dead as those I loved. Now You've shown me a woman a lot like that first one. A woman that I've grown to love. She may not love me, Lord, but that's not important now. It only matters that she live. Please, God, I'd give *anything* for that. Amen."

Sarah stirred as he spoke and muttered words that he could not understand. He continued to sit there, feeding the fire as the hours went by, keeping the cave as comfortably warm as possible. He left her side only long enough to dampen more of the strips of material and to make himself another pot of coffee. Otherwise, he was there beside her, tending to her every need.

He was relieved when he noticed, just before dawn, that she shook and shivered less and her forehead seemed cooler to the touch. She seemed to be resting easier, too, and he breathed a silent prayer of thanks. The relief he felt did not last, however. He noticed how hot she felt about an hour later and grew more and more worried as her coughing increased. A rattling sound deep in her chest seemed to cause her a lot of difficulty getting air. The red rash he had noticed on her face, arms and upper body seemed fainter though, and he saw there was no further sign of smallpox. A thought came to him as he sat there watching her struggle for breath: Maybe she had something in *her* deerskin pouch that he could give her. Some medicine, he thought, hopefully. He walked over to where her pouch lay and reached inside. To his relief, his fingers touched a bottle and he knew it was whiskey before he even pulled it out. Happiness soared through him as he saw that it was more than half full. He remembered that his wife had poured whiskey down him when he had pneumonia, years before. It had seemed to help him recover. At least, he had felt no pain and had relaxed, no longer struggling as much. "Well, we'll try it," he said, walking over to her. He opened the bottle and lifted her head, tipping the bottle until a goodly amount of the liquid ran into her mouth. She coughed, a long spell of coughing, but he was sure she had gotten most of it.

As morning dawned, he stood leaning against the wall of the cave. He would doze off, in between her raucous coughing spells, then croon words of comfort and encouragement to her while he changed the wet strips of cloth across her forehead. He wondered if God had heard his prayers and would help her to recover. Wondered if she knew he was with her, caring for her. He looked at the buffalo robe he had covered her with and wondered again how she could care for a fellow like Spotted Dog. Wondered if he even knew that she was here and that she was ill. Or if he would even care. Well, he thought, shaking his head sadly, *I* care and *I'm* the one who's with her. That's all that matters now. If she has feelings for Spotted Dog…well, so be it. That's all up to her, one way or the other. I've already made up my mind to go back to Hastings before the snows come. The only reason I stayed here this long was because I still had hopes that things would change between us and she'd decide to go back with me. If not as *mine,* then…well, at least so she wouldn't be alone here, with some renegade Indian mistreating her.

Time and time again, he managed to get a little whiskey into Sarah, noticing as it became light outside that she had again quieted, and slept peacefully. He saw this as his chance to go and hunt up some food, and lit out quickly to see what was about. It wasn't long before he returned with a prairie hen he had shot some distance from the path. He had cleaned it where it fell, in a hurry to get back to the cave and see if she was all right. He had also made a snare on the far side of the lake, in hopes of catching a nice juicy rabbit for the following day's meal, and gathered some cattail roots from the stream that fed into the lake. He had often eaten cattail roots and knew they were not only delicious, but also highly nutritious. They would make a tasty nut-flavored potato substitute. He hoped he would be able to get her to eat some, once she was conscious. Lord knows she's thin as a rail, he thought, as he walked up the path to the cave. The sounds of geese flying high above drew his attention, and he watched them, feeling hope fill him. "She *will* get better," he said aloud. "She *has to!* She just has to." Then he hurried up the path to see to her needs.

CHAPTER 19

Moses entered the cave, glad to be in where it was a bit warmer. He bustled around, getting their meal on to cook. He was ravenous, having eaten very little the past few days, and his stomach growled as he thought of how good the food would taste. He wasn't much of a cook. But right now, he thought, *anything* would taste good—even *his* cooking!

Sarah stirred, mumbling something, and he dropped down beside her, trying to hear what she was saying. A faint, "Moses" came from her lips, and he smiled, hearing it. "Have to get to Moses…need water," she croaked, her eyes opening and looking up at him pleadingly. He could tell that she was not aware that he was there beside her, nor aware of her surroundings or of being ill. Her eyes looked glazed and she moaned as she tried to get up. It was a feeble attempt and only succeeded in baring one of her feet.

He reached down to cover it, talking quietly to her. "Lay still, darlin', I'm right here. I'll get you some water, just lay still." Then he poured some water into his tin cup and took it to her. He held her head up, letting the water trickle slowly into her mouth, careful not to choke her. "You're doing fine, honey. I'm right here, Sarah. Old Moses is taking care of you. Don't you worry."

She coughed and sputtered and some of the water ran down her chin and neck. Then she opened her eyes again, looking up at him, but was too weak to keep them open. He lowered her head and it fell limply to one side as she drifted back to sleep. There were beads of sweat across her forehead and her hair was damp, he noticed, and he was certain the fact that she was now coughing less had to be a good sign. He was sure she'd be coughing a whole lot more, if she had pneumonia. She lay still then, and he went and got the pan he had seen amongst her belongings, and readied the cattails for cooking. He added the last of his flour and some salt to the other pan, pleased that the prairie hen seemed to be coming along just fine. He had eaten one only once before, but couldn't remember if it had been to his liking. It smelled real good, and though there wasn't much to it, it would be enough for now. Tomorrow he would check to see if his snare held a nice-sized rabbit. If not, he'd get them a young buck. He'd seen a lot of deer tracks around the far side of the lake, and was sure it'd be easy pickin's."

Just then Sarah yelled out, startling him. "Gray Eagle! Gray Eagle help me!" she screamed, and began writhing around, unaware that Gray Eagle had long been deceased.

Moses hurried to her side, noticing that she was shaking and felt hot to the touch. "Sarah," he said, leaning close to her. "It's me, Moses. Everything's all right, darlin'."

"There's blood!" she screamed. "Have to stop the blood! Have to get help!" She rolled and tossed frantically, kicking her covers off. "Gray Eagle will *kill you* for this! He'll kill you!" she screamed, and Moses had all he could do to try and calm her.

"Sarah, it's me, Moses. You're all right! There's no blood. You're gonna' be all right. I'm right here with you," he said, wondering what had happened to her after she left with Gray Eagle.

"Got to stop the blood," she cried, over and over again, and she clutched at the blanket that covered her, her knuckles white in the glow of the fire.

"Take it easy, darlin'," he said, trying to get hold of her hands as she groaned and twisted about, becoming more and more agitated.

Suddenly she quieted, a shudder running through her body. Moses watched her, wondering what he should do. Wondering if she would sleep. But to his dismay, she became frantic again and cried out. "Oh, God, look what you've done! You've killed him! Why? Why? Oh, God! You've killed him!" she moaned, and then her head rolled to one side and she was still.

Moses' stomach churned, knowing that she had suffered something terrible. He wondered who had hurt her, and why. Wondered where Gray Eagle had been when she had needed him. He placed another wet strip across her forehead, covering her with his blanket. Then he walked over to stir the pan, and poured himself another cup of coffee. He looked over at her as he drank it, his thoughts solemn. I don't know what happened to you, darlin', but I can guarantee it won't happen again, if I can help it, he thought. He walked to the cave entrance and stood looking out over the land below. He thought of his life in Hastings and the friends he had there: Amos, Rosie, Doc and Judith, and the O'Leary's. He thought about Jonas Hart, the big man who had spent most of his life ridiculed because he was shy. He smiled as he thought back to how shocked everyone had been at Silas and Nancy's wedding, when Jonas had begun to sing. You could have knocked them all over with a feather! He shifted, leaning against the wall. It was funny, how people were. So accepting, as they discovered his voice, rich and pure as heaven itself! He turned, glancing into the cave, glad to see that Sarah rested peacefully. He took a sip of coffee and then resumed his daydreaming. He remembered the day Samuel Justus shot him. He hated to have to tell Sarah about it, but knew it would be best she heard it from him, and not some "well-meaning" friend. It was a miracle he was alive, though he still had a mark on his chest, from the impact. Another flock of geese flew by overhead, their cries sounding eerie in the otherwise silent surroundings. He walked back into the cave, adding the last of his canteen's water to the pan of cattails. Sarah lay fairly still, though she mumbled sometimes. Moses put on his coat and walked down the path to the lake, to refill the canteen. As he filled it, he listened to the evening sounds, then walked through the brush to check on the horses. They were grazing peacefully, so he hastened back up to the cave.

Sarah's cough was now a wracking dry cough that tore from her, worrying him. He hoped the broth from the prairie hen would soothe it, and give her strength. He took a taste of it. Hot, it burned all the way down, but had a good flavor. He poured some of the broth into his empty cup, giving it a few minutes to cool, then walked over to where she lay. He called her name, lifting up her head so she wouldn't choke. She resisted, at first, then took in some of it. She tired quickly, though, and he lay her head back down, letting her rest, and fixed himself something to eat. He hadn't realized how hungry he was and ate rapidly, wondering if he would ever get filled up. Thoughts of Sarah's cabin came to mind as he ate, and he smiled, knowing how he had enjoyed being there after she had left with Gray Eagle. He hoped one day soon that he would return to it, that they *both* would. He was proud of all he had accomplished there: the little herd he had built-up for her, the new addition he had put on the barn, and fences he had fixed. He felt 'at home' there, like he had never felt anywhere else. He had always thought he'd be the kind of man to put down roots, never had liked the idea of just drifting. Well, if Sarah decides she doesn't want to go back, maybe she'll sell it to me, he thought, but in his heart he knew he really wanted her there with him.

As time went by, she continued to cry out, her fever peaking as each evening drew on and he would hurriedly put cool wet pieces of material across her brow. He was pleased to see that her rash had begun to disappear. Well, darlin', that's one thing in our favor, he thought. He brushed her damp hair back off her face, her words stopping him in his tracks each time she cried out. "Sh-h-h, honey, it's all right. It's me, Moses. I'm right here with you, darlin'. You're all right, Sarah," he crooned, trying to comfort her. She was shaking again, her teeth chattering, as the fever began to climb. He pulled off her covers and began to dampen the torn shirt strips in the cold water from his canteen and spread them all over her. He dreaded the thought of putting her through another dunking in the lake. The weather had grown steadily colder the past two days and he was afraid as weak as she was, another dunking would *definitely* give her pneumonia. It was then he remembered the whiskey! He rushed to get the bottle, and lifted her head, holding the bottle to her lips. The amber liquid ran slowly into her mouth. Some of it ran from the corners of her mouth, but he knew she was getting the majority of it. When she resisted, he eased her head back down and capped the bottle, returning it to her pouch. There was very little left.

Instead of quietly resting, however, she cried out, "Gray Eagle, help me. Gray Eagle, where are you?" Then, she began to call for *him*. "Moses, help me, Moses...help!" Every time she cried out for him, his heart wrenched within him. The sun was setting, a bright pallet of red, pink and lilac spreading across the sky to the west. Moses looked out at it, wishing Sarah could enjoy it, too, but he knew it would take more than a beautiful sunset to wipe the bad memories from her mind. The words she uttered were the same words she had screamed at him at that old cabin, he realized, when they were on their way to Standing Elk's camp, and now he knew beyond the shadow of a doubt that something terrible had happened to her, after she left with Gray Eagle. He shook his head at these thoughts. Well, if she wants to tell me, when she recovers, I'll do all I can to make it better, he thought, if it *can* be made better. Then he decided to see if he could get her to take more of the broth.

Later, after he'd managed to get some into her, he hurried down to check the snare he had set earlier. A pint-sized rabbit was caught in it. "Small," he said aloud, "but, big enough for the two of us." Then he went to check on their horses. Both Glory and Midnight whinnied a greeting when they saw him coming, and he petted first one, and then the other. He knew he had ridden Midnight awfully hard on the way to the cave, and was glad to see that he looked none the worse for wear. "Midnight, old boy, you got us here just in time," he said, rubbing the horse's neck. He patted Glory next, assuring her that her mistress would soon be up and about, voicing his own hopes, to comfort *himself* more than the old horse. Then he gathered up an armload of sticks and brush and walked quickly back up to the cave.

Sarah was thrashing about when he entered, yelling out, "I'll kill you, Spotted Dog!" as he knelt down beside her. He shook his head, sadly, knowing she was delirious and wondering just how long she could go on like this. Earlier, she had screamed the very same thing, but he had shrugged off her words, remembering that she had also screamed them at *him*, after he tackled her in the pond by the old cabin. He knew that people made little sense when they ran a high fever, but it seemed strange to him that she would threaten to kill the man she loved. He rose, walking around the cave to stretch his legs, as thoughts assailed him. What if she *had* meant it? What if Spotted Dog *was* the one who had hurt her? Could *he* be the reason she seemed so afraid, a lot of the time? No, he thought, look at that day by the creek. She had whispered his name, when I said that someone must be jealous of our closeness, and then she had refused to tell me who he was. Obviously, she was protecting him. He shook his head, his thoughts upsetting him. Then he walked over to her, wondering if she was warm enough with just his blanket covering her. He bent down and picked up the buffalo robe coat that lay beside her, and as he did, he noticed some small stitches inside of the neck. There, in tiny, even stitches he saw his name, 'M. Gentry,' and his heart swelled with a happiness so strong that tears filled his eyes! He picked up her hand, holding it gently within his own. "Oh, darlin'," he said, "my sweet, sweet darlin'."

Four days later, as he stood by the fire, pouring himself a cup of coffee, Moses heard her call out to him. He knew even before he turned, by the sound of her voice, that she had beaten the illness and come back to him. He smiled, walking quickly to her side. She looked terribly pale and was still too weak to raise herself up. "Moses?" she questioned. "Oh, Moses, I thought I was dreaming when I saw you standing there."

"No, darlin', it's no dream. Old Moses is right here," he answered, kneeling at her side. He kissed her on the forehead, more than a little pleased to find that her skin felt cool. He was even more pleased when she snuggled her head into the hollow of his neck and kissed his cheek. He held her close, a feeling of contentment filling him.

"How did you get here? How did you find me?" she asked, a confused look upon her face.

"A wise old Indian sent me here," he replied, "to find an answer to what troubled me."

"Standing Elk," she said, yawning. "What was troubling you?"

"You rest now, darlin', I'll tell you all about it when you wake up." She smiled at him and was soon fast asleep.

Sarah slept all that day and half the next, waking to the smell of coffee boiling and venison cooking. Her stomach rumbled with hunger. She glanced around, surprised to see that Moses was nowhere to be seen. Very slowly she rolled onto her side, pushing the blanket back, surprised to see she wore nothing beneath it, but her smile. She sat there a few minutes, trying to get her bearings. She tried to stand, but found she was too weak, so she pulled the buffalo robe coat around her, and leaned her back against the wall of the cave. Wherever he was, she had no doubt he would be back soon. Her stomach growled at the aromas filling the cave. She realized that he had taken care of her, bathing and feeding her, and tending her every need. She also realized that he had seen every inch of her! She felt embarrassed because of it, but knew that without his care, she would have died.

"Well!" Moses exclaimed, as he came into the cave. In one hand he carried a cup of berries, in the other, a bouquet of flowers. She smiled up at him, grateful for all he'd done. "Glad to see you're awake," he said, smiling at her.

"Can't stand," she replied, "but, at least, I'm sitting."

"Got any idea of how long you've been sick?" he asked, sitting down beside her.

"No," she answered, taking the cup of berries from him. "M-m-m, these are good!"

"I found you ten days ago," he said, a look of sadness in his eyes.

"Ten days!" she exclaimed, unable to believe she had been ill that long. "No wonder I feel so weak!"

"You scared me to death," he said, taking her hand in his. "I thought you had smallpox. Thought I was gonna' lose you. It was...*bad"* He cleared his throat. "I love you, Sarah. I know there's a whole lot of things we need to talk about, but I don't *ever* want to lose you, darlin'."

She smiled at him, at the look of hope that filled his eyes, and answered softly, "I love you, too, Moses." He put his arm around her, holding her close, silently thanking God for giving her back to him and giving them another chance.

CHAPTER 20

Idyllic days followed, as Moses continued to care for Sarah, her health steadily improving. They reasoned that she had only had a rash, and not smallpox, and a cold bordering on pneumonia. Moses didn't doubt the reason she had become so ill, what with the long trip back to Hastings, then back to the Sioux village, then all the long hours she had spent caring for those who were sick. Nearly half the tribe had succumbed to the disease. It was a wonder she hadn't gotten it, as tired and rundown as she had become. Now it looked as if she was on the road to recovery, and they were both relieved.

He brought water up to her, heating it over the fire, so she could wash herself, discretely turning his back when she disrobed. It was hard for him to be close to her, his need for her was so great. Holding her was both pure joy, and pure torture! He longed to make love to her, his desire nearly overwhelming him whenever she looked at him with her beguiling smile. Knowing she loved him, too, made it all the harder to ignore the needs of his body, but he vowed to do so, regardless of how badly he ached to be with her.

As she gained her strength back, they grew closer. They ate together, walked together and laughed together as the days turned cooler and the weather began to change. The only thing they didn't do was to have the talk they both knew they had to have, sooner or later. That, and make love. Sarah wondered why he held her close, obviously enjoying her kisses, then made some excuse and walked away. She was certain of his love for her, yet every time they started to get close, he distanced himself.

One night, as he held her in his arms, she felt the awakening of desire within her that she had thought long dead. She heard him groan as she sighed, pressing her body against him, and yet, once again he began to move away. "Don't," she pleaded, unable to help herself. "Moses, make love to me," she whispered, her voice trembling. She felt him shudder in response, then he got up from where they sat, and walked to the other side of the fire. She turned away from him then, laying down upon her bed, her back to him. She knew now that nothing had really changed between them. Pulling the blanket up around her, she began to cry.

Moses heard her and felt torn between his desire for her and his sense of right and wrong. "Sarah," he said, his voice a mere whisper, "I'm sorry…I…I *can't*"

"I *know!*" she exclaimed. "You've made that *very clear!*" her pain at his rejection turning to anger. "You told me *once!* I don't need to hear it again!"

He looked at her, totally taken aback by her words and how angry she was. "I told you *what?"* he shouted. *"When?"* His voice had risen to the same level as hers. "Darn fool woman," he said. "I try to do right by you and you don't appreciate it, at all! Do you know how hard it is to walk away from you? Do you have *any* idea how bad I want you? Want to make love to you?"

"Sure you do, Gentry," she growled. "I know *exactly* how much you want to make love to me! You explained *perfectly* the *first* time!"

"What?" he exclaimed, completely dumbfounded by her words. *"When?* What are you talking about?"

"The night at the old cabin, after you tackled me," she hissed, "you said you 'couldn't,' that night, too." She jumped up and began to rush toward the cave's entrance, wanting to get as far away from him as possible, but he caught her by the arm, his fingers pressing into her tender flesh.

"Let me go!" she shrieked, her eyes blazing with anger.

"No!" he hollered, getting the feeling that she might try to slap him. She was a fiery wench when angry, and he wouldn't put anything past her!

"I asked you to lie beside me and hold me," she said. "What was your answer, Gentry? Go ahead, tell me your answer *that* night, too!"

Moses looked at her, his dark eyes flashing, furious that she hadn't understood, then or now. "I said I couldn't!" he replied, fuming. "I said I couldn't, you little fool, because I love you! Because I want things right between us...*decent!* What's wrong with that?"

She stared at him, her eyes widening in surprise at his words. She looked dumbstruck, and stood there, the anger going out of her instantly. "But, I thought..." her eyes began to fill with tears, "I thought..." She began to stammer and cry at the same time. "You want things *decent* between us? But, I thought..."

"Sarah, I don't know what you thought when I wouldn't hold you, but I know what *I* thought. I thought you were the most beautiful woman in the world, the most beautiful woman I had ever seen. You were naked when I carried you into the cabin, and more desirable than I ever dreamed a woman could be..." he paused, a smile crossing his features as he remembered his first glimpse of her body. She watched him, her heart filling with happiness as he spoke. "I wanted to take you, right then and there. To claim you for my very own. Wanted you tonight, *too—still* want you—but I'm not that kind of man." He reached out slowly, opening his arms to her. "I've had some misconceptions about that night, too, Sarah. About that night at the old cabin." He felt her stiffen and saw her raise her chin defiantly. "We've got to talk about that, Sarah. Gotta get it all behind us, once and for all," he said, keeping his voice level. "That night at the cabin, you said some..." She pushed away from him before he could say more. He saw the blaze of red that suddenly colored her cheeks and it made him all the more determined to get to the truth of the matter. "You screamed that Gray Eagle would kill me for...for what I'd done. I never hurt you, Sarah. Don't you know that? I never will. You believe that, don't you?" She nodded, slowly. He continued. "The words you said that night...you said again, the other night, when your fever was high. You were out of your head," he paused, trying to get some order to his thoughts, "you said..."

"Go ahead," she ordered, turning to face him, anger filling her voice again. "Tell me the *real* reason you wouldn't be with me! Go ahead!" she hissed.

Moses stared at her, totally confused by this outburst. "Why don't *you* tell me," he shouted. "You seem to have all the answers, Lady!" He regretted his words as soon as he said them, but it did no good trying to explain his feelings to her. Obviously something else lay behind her tears and anger.

"You *know* the truth," she said. "I don't have to spell it out for you."

He shook his head. "Apparently you DO!" he roared.

"The *real* reason you won't sleep with me is because you know about..." she paused, too upset to help herself, "you know...about... Spotted Dog! *He's* the *real* problem between us," she said, and she started to cry.

Moses felt as though the wind had been knocked out of him. As if his heart had a hole in it the size of a cannonball. He could have accepted *any* answer...*any* answer, but that one. So that's it, he thought, she really *does* love Spotted Dog. Loves me, too, but as a *friend*, nothing more.

Before he could say anything, Sarah stood and ran from the cave, nearly falling in her rush to get away from him. Moses ran after her, for no other reason than to catch her before she hurt herself, though his heart felt crushed. He found her out by Glory, her face buried in the old horse's neck, as she sobbed. "Sarah," he said, going over to her. She wiped her eyes on her sleeve, looking up at him. "We can still be friends, can't we?" he asked. "I understand now, darlin'," he flinched as he called her the name that came so naturally, the name his heart had given her, long before he even knew he loved her. "You know I love you, Sarah, but I guess we just weren't meant to be. It's all right," he assured her. "I wish you all the happiness in the world. I always have. I always will. But, can't we stay friends...in spite of Spotted Dog?" She felt her heart break into a million pieces at his words and dare not answer for fear of sobbing once again and letting him know how much she loved him. Moses placed a hand on her shoulder, his touch gentle. "He's a lucky man, Sarah...a real lucky man."

Sarah's face registered total confusion. "*Who's* a lucky man?" she asked.

"*Who's* a lucky man?" he repeated, becoming confused, himself. "Spotted Dog. Because you love him."

Sarah gaped at him in shocked surprise. "I don't love Spotted Dog!" she exclaimed. "I *hate* him!"

Moses stared at her, totally bewildered. "But, you said..." his thoughts were racing, "you said..." he stammered, not finishing his line of thought.

"Moses Gentry, I love *you* I *hate* Spotted Dog!" she stated, emphatically.

Moses stood there, not daring to believe her, his heart hammering in his chest with renewed hope. "But, you said...the night that he attacked us near the camp, you wouldn't tell me who he was. I knew then that you were protecting him."

"Oh, Moses, I wasn't protecting *him* I was protecting you!"

He reached out, at the same time she moved into his arms. He held her close, kissing her over and over, his heart soaring with the tremendous happiness he now felt. His mood turned serious, however, when he released her. "Sarah, tell me why you hate Spotted Dog. What did he do to make you hate him?"

"I thought you knew," she said, her voice a mere whisper.

"Tell me," he ordered, his voice low, but insistent.

He felt her shudder, her face becoming a mask of sadness as she began to speak. "When Gray Eagle left with the men to hunt buffalo that fall, I was five months pregnant." She looked down at the ground, shaking her head at the memory. "I went to the creek to get water for the journey. I was alone." She shuddered as she remembered. "He was there, waiting for me." Her words a mere whisper as she continued, Moses leaned in closer to hear. "He raped me, again and again, and beat me. Then left me there, bleeding, beside the creek. Everywhere there was blood. Just everywhere." Her voice had become a monotone. "I lost our baby. A little boy." She felt Moses stiffen as she spoke, then felt his arms encircle her. "As he rode away, he yelled threats, saying he was going to kill Gray Eagle." She shuddered. "Gray Eagle never returned from the hunt."

She started to cry then, the pent-up tears she had held inside so very long.

Moses held her, unable to ease the pain of the woman he loved. He stroked her hair as she cried, holding her tightly, feeling overwhelmed by all she had suffered. When at last, she quieted, he spoke, his voice shaking with emotion. "Darlin', I'm so sorry. I'm *so very sorry*. He'll pay for what he did to you, I give you my word. Oh, Sarah, *I promise you he'll pay!*"

Later that night, after they had eaten and talked of happier things, Sarah rested in his arms beside the fire. "Moses," she said, "we've had so many misunderstandings between us, I can't believe it. I thought you didn't want me because I'd been raped by an Indian. It doesn't make a difference, does it? I know it would, to a lot of white men. Most of them would turn away. Are you *sure* it won't ever make a difference to you? Are you *absolutely* sure?"

He laughed at her words, looking her straight in the eyes. "Absolutely no difference. No difference, *ever*, darlin', and in the morning I'll tell you why, all right?"

"All right," she said, snuggling down next to him, feeling happier than she had in years.

CHAPTER 21

A shout woke them the next morning at dawn. "Hello!" called a booming voice from down near the lake, surprising them.

Moses got up, pulling on his shirt and tucking it into his pants, then picked up his gun. He walked cautiously to the entrance of the cave. Far below, a burly fellow with a snow-white beard and hair stood looking up at him.

"Hello," he called again, and Sarah woke, asking Moses who it was.

"Looks like we're getting a visit from old Saint Nick, darlin'. You best get up," he replied.

"I'll put on some coffee,"she said, rolling out from under the warm covers. Moses shouted a greeting to the old man, who laughed heartily, in response.

"Mind if I sit a wee bit, and warm meself by yer fire?" the man asked.

"Are you alone?" Moses asked, scanning the area below for others and seeing none.

"Aye, tha' I am, lad," he replied. "Jist me, and me auld mule."

"Come on up, then," Moses said and watched the old fellow start up the path to the cave.

"Did you ask his name?" Sarah questioned.

"No, darlin', but I'm sure he'll tell us, soon enough. Looks pretty harmless," Moses replied.

"Well, how do," the man said, entering and stopping a moment to let his eyes adjust to the darker interior of the cave. "Grand, it 'tis, t' find some friends t' sit a spell wi'," he added, walking over nearer to the fire. "Saw yer horses doon below and decided t' pay ye a visit."

"Make yourself comfortable," Moses said, gesturing toward the fire. "My name's Moses...Moses Gentry, and this is Sarah."

"'Tis pleased I am t' meet ye. Du na' see many folks way oot here." He shook Moses' hand, then sat down in front of the fire, groaning, as he did so. "Name's Angus...Angus Charles MacGregor. Angus, after me father; Charles, after bonnie Prince Charlie. Originally from Dunfermline, Scotland, near Kirkcaldy. Last few years, from whaure'er I hung me hat."

"What brings you to these parts?" Moses asked, as Sarah handed him a coffee. Angus was busy removing his deerskin pouch, tobacco bag, knife sheath, and pipe bag, all beautifully decorated with beads, quills, and fringe, along with his red wool capote—with wide black stripe—that he was all bundled-up in. He laid his things beside him—within easy reach—along with his flintlock rifle, then reached up to take the cup of coffee Sarah held out to him.

"Thank ye, kindly, lass. Nuthin' like a good hot cup o' coffee to git the day started right."

Sarah smiled, noticing that his thick, white mustache blended into his bushy, white beard, and truly *did* make him look like Father Christmas.

"Been huntin' in them hills yonder," Angus said, pointing toward the south, where only a faint outline of higher land could be seen. "Did some prospectin', too, a wee bit, here and thaur."

"Any luck?" Moses asked, as Sarah started to cook them all some breakfast.

"Now and then, laddie, now and then. Took me a nasty fall a few months back. Laid me up awhile. Bones stiffen up on me e'er since," he replied, rubbing his knee. "Thinkin' 'tis aboot time I git me some pritty lassie t' keep me company this winter. Gittin' too auld t' take many more winters up here, jist me and the auld mule." Sarah smiled, and Moses laughed, outright.

"Seriously," Angus said, after taking another swig of his coffee, "I'm headin' fer a town a far distance from here, a town called Hastin's. Got a friend thaur that I've been meanin' t' look up fer many a year. Gitting too auld t' put it off much longer. Hope he's still thaur."

"Hastings!" both Moses and Sarah exclaimed, in unison, looking at the old Scot in total amazement.

"Seems ye've heard tell o'it," Angus said, looking at them curiously.

"Heard of it? We're *from* it!" they replied.

"I'm sheriff there," Moses stated, "and Sarah lived there most of her life, until a few years ago, when she married and moved away."

"Well, I'll be!" Angus remarked. "I was told I'd be wise t' come this way today, and lo and behold, I run right int' folks from the verra place I be headin'!" Angus slapped his knee and let out a loud 'Woowie.'

"Who told you to come this way?" Sarah asked, sitting down at the far side of the fire.

"Why, me 'Sixth Sense,' lassie—all good Scots got the "gift," dinna ye ken?"

"Who is it you're going to see in Hastings, Mr.MacGregor, if you don't mind me asking?"

"An auld friend o' mine, lassie. But du na' call me "Mr." if ye please; me friends call me 'Mac.'"

"Mac it is, then," Sarah replied, anxious for him to go on.

"I could tell ye right oot who it be, lass, but, instead I'll tell ye a tale, if ye du na' mind."

Sarah noticed how Angus MacGregor's large blue eyes twinkled when he talked, and suddenly she knew who he reminded her of; Old John, John Bruce. "Go on with your story, then, Mac, please," she said, anxious for him to begin. Moses poured them all a second cup of coffee and Angus began his tale.

"Many, many year ago, I come t' America, from me beloved homeland, o' Scotland. Come t' git work and make me fortune. On the boat o'er t' this grit rich land was anither Scot. A young lad me ain age. A fine lad, from an auld family. In fact, kin, he was, t' the King o' Scotland, Robert the Bruce. Ha'e ye' heard tell o' Robert the Bruce, lassie?" Sarah shook her head, affirming that she had, indeed, her interest more than a little peaked.

"Well," Angus continued, after taking another sip of his coffee, "the lad and I become the best o' friends." He smiled, his eyes twinkling. "Upon landin' we parted company; him goin' his way, and me, mine. Being a bright lad, ye see, he had a job waitin' fer him at a university, though he would, indeed, be their youngest professor. Being so bright, tha' he'd graduated years earlier than the rest o' his classmates. Woowie!" He exclaimed, laughing heartily. "'Boot forty-some year ago, thaur I was, livin' in an Indian village and jist settin' doon t' a delicious bowl o' venison stew, when I hears this sound far off…a gun shot, I was sure. 'Twas the worst winter I'd e'er seen! Even round them parts! So cold, tha' the wee children were kept inside, so as they wouldna' freeze. Woowie! Tha' snow was as high as a horse's back in some places! Anyways, thaur I be, all ready t' take a big bite o' tha' delicious stew, and off in the distance I hear wha' sounds like a shot. Now, mind ye,' no Indian was fool enough t' go oot in tha' weather, so I put doon me bowl…me stomach grumblin' sumpthin' fierce, and oot I go all bundled-up like a papoose! I listen, first one way, then t'other, then I listen again. Then I hear anither shot. Woowie! I'm wonderin' wha' kind o' fool would be oot in tha' kind o' weather." He paused, pulling an old, dark-brown pipe from his pipe bag, and getting out his beaded tobacco pouch; shifting around to get more comfortable. Then he laid them aside.

When he was settled, once again, Sarah pleaded, "Please go on.

"Well, whaur was I? Let's see…Oh!…Thaur I was, settin' me bowl doon and traipsin' oot in tha' freezin' weather t' find the fool tha' was oot thaur." His blue eyes seemed to dance as he spoke and Sarah felt as though Old John was in their presence. Both she and Moses were certain he was talking about John. Breakfast was done cooking then, however, and Sarah excused herself, dishing it up while it was hot. They ate quickly, anxious to hear more of the surprising story.

When Angus finished eating, he took up the old burnished pipe, lit it, and puffed merrily. The cave filled quickly with the smell of tobacco. Moses excused himself and walked down by the lake to tend to their horses. Before he left, he told the old Scot not to say another word until he returned. Happy memories filled Sarah's mind, and she smiled as she sipped her cup of coffee.

Soon, they were all settled again and Angus resumed his story where he'd left off. "A good distance from me dwellin', was whaur I found the fella doin' the shootin'," he said, "dressed all in store-bought clothes and near' froze t' death. His horse was stuck whaur it stood, too tired t' push through the deep snow tha' was still afallin'." He took a pull on his pipe, then continued. "Well, says I, 'twill be all right, lad, I'll git ye t' me camp. Ye jist lean on me 'till we can git t' me horse.' All covered up, he was, ye see, and 'tween the clothes he was bundled-up in and the heavy snow afallen, I had me nary an idea who I be helpin'." He laughed heartily and slapped his knee, his jolliness adding to the story.

"Go on, go on," Sarah pleaded, drinking the last of her coffee.

"Whaur was I? Oh...well, I figured tha' fella would be froze t' death, time I got him and his horse back t' me camp. Tha' horse was plumb-tuckered oot, I'll tell ye, and so was he. Fell doon on me bed soon's I took me arm from 'round him. Woowie! Near dead, sure as I be a MacGregor! Figured I'd rest up a bit, then git them fancy clothes off o' him and see if he'd fit in some o' me long-johns, 'till he thawed a wee bit, or died. Seemed pritty dumed possible he'd ne'er make the night; coughin' and shakin' wi' cold like he was." He paused, and they could see he was thinking back to that day. "Now, whaur was I? Let me see...so I gits meself unbundled and takes a wee dram o' John Barley Corn. T' warm me bones, ye understand, na' being a drinkin' fella. And I warm up me venison stew. Git it boilin', fillin' the place wi' smells tha'd please the saints. Then, jist as I'm aboot to spoon me up a big spoonful, I hear from me bed these words: 'Why, Angus MacGregor, ye auld sidewinder'. Made me jump near oot o' me skin!" He laughed heartily, his beard shaking as he did so, and Moses and Sarah couldn't help laughing right along with him. "Why, I jumped up, near' spillin' me bowl o' stew, and I sees tha' fella sittin' up in me ain bed, laughin' at me! I grabbed me gun, saying 'Who's thaur?' Thinking maybe he's some kind o' ghost er spirit come t' haunt me! Well, he busts oot laughin' even harder—'tween coughs—and raises up on the side o' me bed. I pointed me gun straight at him, thinkin' no ghost nor spirit I e'er heard tell o' was fool enough t' get near froze t' death in a snowstorm! Then, he says, 'Well, are ye goin' t' shoot me, Mac, or are ye gonna share a bowl o' tha' good smellin' food wi' me'? Woowie! When I hear him say me name, right oot, I near t' dropped dead meself! I jist stood thaur, like I was frozen, too, an' he starts pullin' off his hat 'n coat, and all I could do was stand thaur awonderin' how he knew me name. Then he takes off his scarf and I can see tha' it ain't a young lad. Nor a ghost! Fer there ain't no ghost wi' them devil's eyes and tha' grin t' match!" He paused, nodding slowly, then drew on his pipe, his eyes full of merriment. "Whaur was I?" he said, "Oh, I looked tha' fella straight in the eye, and sure enough, thaur was me friend. Near, dinna recognize him, 'cept fer them devil-eyes. His hair was white as snow and his face was bearded, na' like last I saw him. I kept staring at him, na' believin' me ain eyes, then I hauled off and hit him—smack in the jaw—and knocked his tooth plumb oot! T' git back at him, ye see, fer near' searin' the life oot o' me. Then I helped him up and hugged him, and we had us a good laugh. 'Twas, aye, a good one, tha'! And a delicious bowl o' me venison stew, soon after!" He chuckled, then excused himself to take a walk down by the lake, while Sarah and Moses looked at each other in disbelief.

"John," Sarah said, softly, her eyes filling with tears.

"I'm sure it is," Moses replied, shaking his head in wonder. Sarah walked to Moses, hugging him close, her heart filled with joy at the miracle she knew they had received in the person of Angus Charles MacGregor.

"Do you ever feel that things happen for a reason, Moses?" she asked. "Like things were all planned-out—long before—by the Lord, and you are but a small part of it?"

He smiled down at her, asking, "You mean you think the Good Lord sent that old man to us for some *special* reason?"

"Yes!" she replied, excitedly. "Like a *miracle*, Moses, like a real out and out miracle!"

Moses laughed, "I wouldn't go that far, darlin'. Sounds like you've been listenin' to one great story-teller, that's all."

"But he's talking about John, Moses. We both know he is! How do you explain *that?*"

Moses saw the joy on her face, the radiance of her smile, and was glad to see how happy she was. "I'd like to hear what else he has to tell us, darlin', before I decide if he's a miracle, or not," he replied, bending slightly to kiss her on the forehead.

CHAPTER 22

The next morning found the three beginning their journey back to the Sioux Village. Sarah and Moses had talked, long into the night, as their surprising guest slept soundly, snoring loudly and oft' times, talking in his sleep. Sarah believed more than ever that he was a 'miracle', sent by God, while Moses still had his doubts.

Long after Sarah had fallen asleep, Moses had lain awake, remembering the last of the old-timer's story. 'Well, whaur was I?' he had said, 'Oh, aboot me friend. His company sure helped t' pass the time through tha' long, hard winter! The snow continued blowin' and howlin' 'round our small shelter, but, inside was all the warmth an' happiness of a Christmas morn'! Took a long time fer his feet t' mend. I told ye they'd been near froze-off...I reckon?' Angus had said. 'Well,' he had continued, 'thanks t' me dear mither's special concoction and the many long hours each day whaur we had only t' rest and pass the time, 'tweren't long afore me friend's feet begun gittin' some color back into 'em and stopped itchin' and burnin'. Soon, saints be praised, the skin lost its raw look and begun t' heal. Course we had us a heap o' games t' play, afore tha' day come. He taught me card games, the likes o' which ye'd ne'er hear tell o' today.' Angus had smiled at the memory, sitting by the fire like a jolly old Saint Nick, Moses remembered, and just for a moment, Moses wondered if he *was,* indeed, a miracle. Or, if the miracle lay in their surroundings. Standing Elk had told both Sarah, and him, that their journey would bring them to a sacred place, where

'The People' were given special blessings and gifts. His exact words were, 'Journey there, Black Hawk, and you will find answers to all that troubles you.' Moses smiled, as he lay near Sarah, who slept peacefully. "Now our "miracle" has *me* startin' to believe," he whispered aloud, listening to the old man snoring and talking in his sleep, where he lay, farther on into the cave. Moses smiled. Some miracle, he thought, a miracle who talks, even in his sleep. He rolled over, smiling at this new turn of events, feeling a sense of contentment fill him. It took him only a few moments to drift off to sleep.

In the morning, they woke refreshed and ready to head back to Standing Elk's village. As they traveled that day, Sarah felt disappointed. Angus—or Mac—as he preferred to be called, had never finished his story or confirmed the name of the man. When she had nearly blurted it out, he had shushed her quickly saying that no story was good, if'n the folks tellin' it told the most important things right at the beginning. She knew it was about old John: the gap in his mouth, where he had lost a tooth—though she had heard he lost it in a saloon fight. The many different card games he knew, how many of them had *she* learned from him? Yes, she *knew* the story was about John Bruce, there was no doubt in her mind.

Moses, on the other hand, had many doubts. Not so much about the identity of Angus' friend, but doubts about Angus, himself. He looked harmless, and had a truly jolly nature that tended to cheer his listeners, but Moses just had an odd feeling about the old Scot that he couldn't seem to shake.

They rode all day, stopping only to water the horses, down a morsel of food, and tend to their needs. Sarah was anxious to return to the village and see how her friends were faring, praying that there were no more sick with the pox. Moses was anxious to get back also, first, to thank Standing Elk for his wise counsel and the happiness the journey had brought him, and second, to settle the score with Spotted Dog, as he had vowed to do! Angus, on the other hand, was happy for their companionship along the trail and liked nothing better than to have someone to talk to. He also liked the idea of riding with folks who knew the direction to Hastings, for Moses had told him that he planned to go back to Hastings soon. Angus wondered if Sarah would go back with Moses, or if she would stay with her dead husband's people, the

Lakota Sioux. He had heard of Chief Standing Elk and knew he was revered among the Indians for his innate wisdom. Angus had never met an Indian he didn't like, and had many friends among them. In fact, he had lived among the different tribes and enjoyed their ways and respect for all things. Oh, there were some blood-thirsty ones, but he had found that was true in all folks, whites, included. In fact, he had seen more down-right contrariness and deceitfulness among whites than any other folks, and it saddened him. Yes sir, when it came to chicanery, the whites seemed destined to win, hands down! That was one of the reasons he had decided to go off by himself and live peacefully amongst the Indians, tending to his own business: trapping and prospecting.

Now things were changing, for the Indians and for him, too. That fall he had taken awhile back had laid him up good, and common sense told him it was near time for him to settle in with some sweet gal—if indeed, one stole his heart—and put down roots in a town where he could enjoy the rest of his days. That was when he got to thinking about his old friend, and decided to go check out Hastings. There was another reason, too, that he wanted to find his friend: the reason being a promise he'd given that cold, long ago winter, after he had found his friend near froze to death. Now the time had come, and saints be praised, he thought, God had led him directly to these folks from Hastings, and Angus Charles MacGregor was not one to question God's leading!

That evening they reined in under an overhang, tying their horses and the mule to some bushes nearby. Moses made a small fire, as the weather was quickly getting colder and colder, and all three knew it could snow, any day now. Sarah busied herself, gathering brush and sticks and soon had a pot of coffee boiling and the stew reheating. As they settled in around the fire, the aroma of the fresh coffee and stew filled the air, and soon had their stomachs growling. It was then, that Angus began, once again, to reminisce. Sarah sat enthralled, as the story of Mac's friend continued to unfold.

"Well now, whaur was I ?" Angus said, as he so often did. "Oh!

I was telling ye aboot me friend's feet...well, aboot spring, he got t' hobblin' around and being an ornery cuss, he made up his mind tha' he was goin' wi' me on me trap-line. Now, I told him it'd be too much walkin', him being off his feet so long, but he was determined, and nuthin' I said would change his mind! So, we set oot. At first, he got 'boot half-way, waitin' thaur fer me t' return. But he was stubborn—he was—an' kept pushin' hisself further and further, and in a month or so, thaur he was—makin' the rounds wi' me an' keepin' me company. Woowie! And could tha' man talk!"

Sarah and Moses looked at each other, trying their best not to bust out laughing. If *anyone* could talk, it was Angus Charles MacGregor, himself!

Shifting closer to the fire and setting his plate aside, Angus continued, "Seems me friend had come near t' freezing, tha' winter, due t' his ain plumb stubbornness! Ye see, lassie," he winked at her, a big smile breaking out all over his face, "me friend had fallen head o'er heels in love wi' a wee lass near his family home in Scotland, and afore he left Scotland, he promised he'd send fer her as soon as he saved up enough money. Well, the lass, being young, had no real understandin' o' me friend's ways, fer though he was pure o' heart, he was also of a mind t' fergit things. Ye see, he'd set his mind t' somethin', and soon fergit all other things. Let me explain; me friend promised t' send fer the lass, and tha' was all well and good. She accepted his proposal the night afore he left, and agreed t' wait fer him. The trouble was, me friend got t' saving tha' money, workin' all day at tha' professor-job, and even got hisself a night job on the docks, so's t' save up the money faster. I du na' ken how he did it—workin' day an' night—and sleepin' verra little. Told me he worked and worked, havin' nae life, at all. Nae friends, nae ladies—on the side—beggin' yer pardon, lass. Like some men du. All he did was work an' save his money. Set hisself a goal, and was determined t' reach it, as soon as was humanly possible! And save it, he did! In jist five year! The trouble come when he wrote his lassie, back in Scotland, tellin' her he could now provide fer her the style o' life he'd set his mind t' fer them. Woowie!" Angus exclaimed, slapping his knee and roaring with laughter until his eyes grew wet. Sarah and Moses couldn't help laughing along with him, in spite of themselves. When, at last, he quieted, he continued. "Me friend had done *exactly* what' he had set his mind t', but ne'er once had he written the wee lass, tellin' her he'd arrived safely in America! Lo and behold, three year after he left—thinkin' he'd fallen sick er died at sea—she'd married anither! When his letter arrived, she had the sorry task o' returnin' his ticket money and tellin' him tha' she was wed—near on three year—and had a wee bairn, and anither on the way!" Angus stopped to catch his breath, his eyes twinkling with merriment, and Sarah and Moses had to laugh, in spite of themselves. When they all quieted, Angus excused himself and strode off, while Moses checked the horses, and Sarah cleaned up.

Before long, the two men returned, Angus whistling a merry tune. He pulled out his pipe, tamped it, then lit it, and settled back down beside the fire. Sarah asked if he'd like another cup of coffee, then asked him to please go on with his story. "Did your friend ever find another to love?" she asked, hoping with all her heart that he had.

"Aye, lass, tha' he did," Angus replied, "and a prettier woman ye've ne'er seen. I think she loved him 'boot as much as he did her; na' tha' I was payin' all tha' much attention, ye see, cause jist aboot tha' same time, I found a lovely lass o' me ain!" His blue eyes danced with joy as he pulled on his pipe, and they could see that he was remembering back by the look in his eyes. Then he continued. "Thaur we were, livin' among the Indians, all settled in, and goin' aboot our business; me and my gal, and me friend and his. But, alas, 'twas na't' be." He pulled on his pipe, again, and for the first time, Sarah and Moses could not help notice a sadness in his eyes. "T'was near on t' winter again and me friend had jist learned his lass was wi' child. Oh! They were so happy, them two! He was laughin' and so pleased, the day he come t' tell me thaur'd be a wee bairn, come summer. He was slappin' me on the shoulder and hootin' and hollarin'. I ne'er seen a man so happy, no siree!" He stopped talking, rubbing the knee that he seemed to favor, and looked long into the fire as he continued to smoke his pipe.

Sarah reached over, squeezing Moses' hand, a smile upon her lips. Moses wondered what she was thinking, but he said nothing, because Angus seemed to be deep in thought—his breathing quiet, and eyes shut. But soon he opened his eyes and cleared his throat, took another pull on his pipe, and began to speak.

"Ne'er knew wha' happened t' her. She said she was goin't' see the chief 'boot somethin', her father was the chief, ye see. Me friend come t' me at first light the next day. He'd been oot all night, searchin' fer her, along wi' some o' the tribe. We ne'er found a trace o' her."

Sarah felt Moses stiffen, as he remembered back to the sad life *his* mother had endured. He began to say something, but looked intently at

Sarah, a few seconds, and then remained silent.

"Moses, what is it?" she asked, knowing something was bothering him.

"Nothin', darlin'," he replied, looking at Angus, who sat quietly, smoking his pipe.

"What happened to your friend, after that?" Sarah asked, a plaintive tone in her voice.

Angus glanced at her before answering, "I've made ye sad, lassie, and fer tha' I apologize."

"It's all right," Sarah replied. "It's just that I'm certain your friend *was* also *my* friend, and I'd have wished better for him than that."

Angus searched her face in the shadows of the firelight before speaking. "Ye say ye suspect me friend *was* yer friend," he said, his voice quiet. "Tha' bein' the case...I guess I'd best tell ye his name," he hesitated, and they could tell he was gathering his thoughts. "Tha' changes things," he said, "if indeed, yer right. Me promise, I mean." He looked long at Sarah. "I'll be heartfelt sorry, lassie, t' na' be keepin' me promise, if 'tis me friend. His name was Johnny ... Johnny Bruce."

"Old John," Sarah said, and tears began to fill her eyes. Moses, too, felt sad, not for himself, but for the obvious sadness Sarah and the old Scot felt. He shook his head, then got up, gathering up their cups to refill them. Sarah looked at Moses, wiping the tears from her cheeks.

Angus rose, walking a short distance away, then stood there, looking out into the darkness. Sarah had seen the tears come to his eyes when he realized his old friend was dead. She rose and walked over to him, laying her hand on his arm. "I'm sorry, Mac. I didn't mean to hurt you."

He turned to look at her. "'Tis na' yer fault, lass, na' at all." He patted her hand, then wiped his eyes. "Friendship... *true* friendship has more value, lassie, than a ton o' gold. Been many, many a year since I last saw Johnny, but...well...he was me *friend*. A rare thing, t' *truly* be a man's friend. Especially t' a man like Johnny Bruce." He shook his head, looking down at the ground. "Can ye be tellin' me how he died, lassie?"

Sarah took his arm and walked with him, back to the fires' warmth, sitting down beside him. "He died saving my life," she said, softly, tears once again glistening in her eyes and trickling down her cheeks.

"Then he's in the *best* o' company, lass, wi' God and His saints!

Praise be!" Angus exclaimed, his voice filled with renewed happiness. "And a *fine* time he's havin', nae doobt!"

Moses smiled, and surprisingly, so did Sarah, as Angus tapped his pipe on his boot, a smile once again upon his face. "About time we turned in," Moses said, glad for a change in the tone of things.

"Aye, lad, tha' it tis," Angus replied. "I'm plumb-tuckered. Think I'll go say g'night t' me auld mule, afore I turn in. G'night t' ye both."

"Good night," Sarah replied.

"Good night, Mac," Moses said, wondering if it was, indeed, a 'miracle' that brought the old Scot their way.

CHAPTER 23

A light dusting of snow covered the ground when they woke the next morning. "We'll be making the village just in time," Moses said, wrapping himself in the warm buffalo robe coat that Sarah had made for him. He stuffed his old coat into his saddlebag, enjoying the warmer wrap.

"I hope so," Sarah replied, shivering as she crawled from her bed of hides into the chill of the morning.

"Good mornin'," Angus greeted them cheerfully.

"Good Morning," they both answered, in unison.

"I've decided t' go on t' Hastin's and pay me respects t' Johnny," he said. "He *is* buried thaur, aye?"

"Yes, he is," Sarah replied. "When are you going?"

"I'll be waitin' fer yer lad, here, t' decide tha', if he du na' mind me accompanyin' him, tha' is."

"Moses?" Sarah looked at him with a questioning look upon her face. "Are you going back to Hastings?"

Moses had wanted to tell her himself. Wanted to see if she would go back with him. More importantly, he had planned to ask her to go as his *wife*. Now, she knew he planned to go, and he had not had a chance to ask her. He looked at her, wishing Angus had not mentioned it.

"Seems I opened me mouth at the wrong time, laddie," Angus said, watching the facial expressions of the couple. "I'll jist be takin' me a short walk—go stretch me legs a wee bit—so's ye can talk a bit by yerselves." With that, he turned and walked away toward where his mule was tied.

Moses took Sarah's hand. "Come with me, darlin', let's walk a ways" he said. "There's some things I've been meaning to tell you, and it looks like it better be now."

Sarah felt crestfallen. Moses had planned to leave her and return to Hastings and he had not even thought to tell her. Worse yet, he had *obviously* spoken to Angus about it. A total stranger, mind you. She braced herself as she followed him, her chin raising defiantly. I lived alone before him, she thought, and I can do it again. But, deep in her heart, she knew she could *not* live alone without him—not happily, anyways. Moses had become her morning sunshine, her evening star, and everything in-between! She watched him walk in front of her, wondering how she would ever live, or laugh, or even smile, if he left her.

A fair distance from their camp, he stopped walking and turned to her. "Sarah, I'm sorry you heard of my plans from Mac. I wanted to tell you, myself. There's a *couple* of things I've been meaning to tell you, in fact."

She searched his face, seeing the tension in his eyes and his worried look. He was leaving without her, she could tell, and her heart felt torn and crushed, clear through to her soul. "Moses, I understand," she said, *not* understanding, but not wanting to hear any more. She couldn't bear the thought of hearing him say goodbye!

"Sarah," he said, taking both her hands in his. "Remember the question you asked me the night before Angus showed up? Remember what I answered?"

She thought back to that night, and suddenly knew! So that was it! She thought, and after all we've been through, after all we've shared! He's realized that he *can't* accept me, because of what Spotted Dog did to me. She tried to pull her hands away, but he held them tightly, watching her and reading her thoughts in the sorrow that filled her eyes. "It's all right," she whispered, looking down at the ground. "I understand." She pulled her hands from his, trying not to cry.

Moses reached into his shirt and pulled out the medallion he wore around his neck. The medallion his mother had given to him.

Sarah watched, her heart filled with dread at the thought that he was leaving. Moses removed the medallion, holding it carefully in the palm of his hand. Sarah looked at it, then up at Moses. "I guess now's as good a time as any to tell you about this," he said, his voice filled with emotion. "I'm not gonna tell you the whole story now, cause it would take too long, and all you really need to know is about this." He grew silent, looking at the medallion he held. Sarah could tell he was choked up with emotion. She glanced at it, trying to get a better look. Then Moses began to speak. "You asked me if it would ever matter... what Spotted Dog did to you," he began, and Sarah hung her head, not daring to look at him. "I told you it didn't, do you remember?" She shook her head, unable to say anything. "Well, it *doesn't* matter, Sarah, and never will. It wouldn't matter, *regardless*, darlin', because I love you." His voice was firm as he continued, "But, there's *this*," he said, holding the medallion up for her to see. He cleared his throat nervously, "You see, darlin', my mother gave this to me when I was just a small boy. She gave it to me so I would never forget who I am." Sarah stared at him, surprised by his words. "You see...my mother was an Indian. A beautiful woman who taught me not only the ways of my white father, but also the ways of her people." Sarah's mouth dropped open in stunned surprise. "You loved Gray Eagle, Sarah, and he was a half-breed. Do you think you could find it in your heart to love another one?" Sarah was shocked! She had never had the slightest idea that Moses was part Indian. She stood there, too stunned to say anything, trying to make sense of all he was saying. "If you think you could love me, Sarah, knowing the truth, I'd be so dog-gone happy."

"Oh, Moses..." she said, but he cut her off.

"I know it comes as a shock, honey, to find out something like this about a person you thought you knew, but, I love you, Sarah. I have for a long time. If you can find it in your heart to love me... well...I want you to be my wife. I don't have much to offer...but if you think you could spend the rest of your life with me, darlin,' I want you to have this medallion as a token of my love for you. If you decide otherwise..." Before he could finish his sentence, Sarah reached out and took the medallion, carefully placing it around her neck. Moses grinned happily and picked her up in his arms, whirling her around. His shout of joy reverberated far and near upon the air, making Angus Charles MacGregor smile as he heard it, and there beside his old mule, he danced a little jig!

CHAPTER 24

The smiles on the young couple's faces told Angus all he needed to know. Seemed like they couldn't stop smiling! A glowing radiance seemed to fill the very air around them.

Angus followed behind them, on his mule, feeling like a benevolent Genie. Moses and Sarah rode, side by side, sometimes holding hands, sometimes sharing a kiss, or happy laughter. At one point, Angus was certain he heard Moses singing a little tune, slightly off-key, but Sarah didn't seem to mind. Far be it fer me t' complain, he thought, smiling.

Along toward noon, with the sun high in the sky, they came to a small, clear pond. Along the bank the tracks of deer, bear, raccoon and some small critters showed in the dirt. "Let's stop a bit, lad, wha' du ye say?" Angus asked, riding up alongside of Moses.

"All right," Moses replied, smiling happily.

"I'll be takin' me a wee rest," Angus stated, surprising the couple.

"I'll fix us something to eat," Sarah said, quickly dismounting.

Moses looked at her, beaming as if she had blessed him, and in his heart he felt like she had, indeed, because she had accepted his proposal and agreed to become his wife. "I love you so much, darlin'," he said, taking her into his arms and holding her tightly. His breath was warm against her cheek as they stood there, her heart pounding, in unison, with his.

"I love you, too, Moses Gentry," she replied, touching his arm.

"There's something else we need to talk about," he said. "Can we talk as you rustle up something to eat?"

"Don't know why not," she answered, then noticed how serious he had become. She bit her lip, nervously, looking over at him. "It can't be all that bad, can it?"

He hesitated a moment, before answering. "I...ah...I want to go back to Hastings," he said, at last. "I want us to grow old among our friends, there: Amos and Amanda, Rosie, Lilly and Jonas. They're your friends, too, Sarah. Are you set on staying here...with Gray Eagle's people?"

She thought before answering, taking her time, choosing the right words. "My time with Gray Eagle's people was wonderful, Moses. They were good to me; kind and caring. I love many of them as though they are my actual family." He watched her closely as she spoke. "I never thought things would end the way they did, you know? First, with Gray Eagle dying, and then our baby. Standing Elk is like a father to me. I love him, Moses, like my own father." She paused, looking off into the distance. "He exiled Spotted Dog from 'The People'—from the *whole tribe*—for what he did to me, when word of it reached him." She paused, shaking her head sadly before continuing. "He had his wife, Wind Runner, care for me and tend to my...my wounds." Her eyes filled with tears as she spoke. "I became a *daughter* to them." She reached up, then, laying her hand against Moses' cheek. "When you go, Moses, there's no question that I'll go with you. But I do have a few concerns about going back, about being shunned" She shushed him as he began to speak. "My...*our* friends will stand by me, I know that, but what about the others? It's the others I'm worried about," she paused, adding, "but, if *you* can face them, I guess I can, too."

He beamed at her, her words a healing balm to his worried heart. "We'll face them together, darlin'," he replied.

"When do you plan to leave?" she asked, stirring their food.

"As soon as possible. Best we get back before the snows come. How long will it take you to get ready? To say your goodbyes, and all?"

"A day or two," she answered. "All right?"

"Yup," he replied. "I've got a couple of things I have to do, too. That'll be fine." She saw the pensive look that came into his eyes.

"What do you have to do?" she asked, a strange feeling coming over her, suddenly.

"Nothing for you to worry your pretty head about, darlin', just a few goodbyes of my own to tend to, that's all," he said.

"Oh," she replied, and she thought of his friend, Howling Wolf, while Moses' thoughts turned to Spotted Dog: the man who had caused Sarah so much pain. He'll never hurt you again, Moses thought, you, or *anyone else!* This is *one* goodbye I'm looking forward to!

CHAPTER 25

They reached Standing Elk's village just before dark, happy to see the Indian friends that hurried out to greet them. The children were surprised to see heavily bearded Angus MacGregor and his small, sway-back mule, and followed him to Standing Elk's tepee. They giggled and pointed at the mule and, to Sarah's surprise, Angus spoke to them in their own language, complete with Scottish burr!

Dogs ran to and fro around their feet and curious braves approached. The Indian women staying back, due to shyness. Chief Standing Elk walked toward them, raising his hand in greeting, obviously happy to see them. "My children," he said. "I welcome your return." His eyes seemed to dance with merriment as he studied their happy faces. "You are well?" he asked, looking at Sarah.

"Yes," she replied, wondering why he would ask that.

"Then Wakantanka has smiled on *both* of you," he replied, smiling at her and at Moses.

"How did you know I'd been ill?" Sarah asked.

"Standing Elk see many things written in sky."

Sarah took Moses' hand in hers, smiling at the elderly Indian, wondering how he could have known. "We're going to be married," Sarah said, her joy more than evident.

The chief smiled back at her. "So it was written. When do you leave for your people?"

Sarah was taken aback by his question and at a total loss for words.

"Soon," Moses answered, "a matter of days...before the snows come."

"My heart feels great joy for you, Black Hawk. The sacred cave of our ancestors bring many answers and much happiness to all who go there."

"Thank you for sending me there," Moses said, gratitude filling him.

"It was written in the stars, Black Hawk, that you should go there." He looked past Moses to where Angus stood, saying, "Now we must smoke the pipe with your new friend."

"Oh!" Sarah replied. "Chief Standing Elk, this is Angus Charles MacGregor. Angus, this is Chief Standing Elk of the Lakota Sioux."

Standing Elk and Angus exchanged greetings, then the men went into the chief's tepee to smoke and talk. Sarah walked over to her own dwelling, waving at friends as she passed. It made her sad to know that soon she would be leaving, though she also felt excited at the thought of returning to Hastings. She smiled, as she thought of Lilly and Jonas, and wondered how they were. And wouldn't Rosie be surprised to see her? she thought. She thought, too, of her father, and wished he was still alive. Wished she could see him just once more. Could tell him of the good life she had had with Gray Eagle's people. She saw Laughing Water running with a group of other little ones, over by Little Moon's tepee, and decided to go over and tell her friend her news. She glanced, once more, back at Standing Elk's tepee, knowing how hard it would be to say goodbye to him and his wife, Wind Runner. They had shown her as much love as any parents could show to their own child, and she knew they would always have a place in her heart. She smiled, remembering the care Wind Runner had lavished on her when she had gotten so ill after Spotted Dog attacked her. Yes, she thought, it was going to be just as hard—and painful—to leave them, as it had been to leave her father. She shook her head, continuing to head for Little Moon's. She knew she had to look ahead to the future. The future she would share with Moses. Thinking this, she began to smile. It was funny how a person's life could change, she thought, funny how it always seemed to lead in a direction you never expected it to, and yet, somehow, it seemed as if it worked out according to a plan. Well, she thought, I got the life of excitement and adventure I always wanted, when I married Gray Eagle. And knowing Moses, I expect there'll be plenty more to follow. She smiled at these thoughts, ready to face whatever lay ahead.

CHAPTER 26

Sarah fell asleep as soon as she lay down, tired from the journey and glad to be back in her own comfortable surroundings. Moses and Angus retired to Moses' tepee, settling in for a good night's rest. They talked of their upcoming journey back to Hastings and other things of less importance. Before long, Howling Wolf joined them, happy to be in the company of his friend, Black Hawk, once again. They talked: Moses telling of his plans to return to Hastings and to marry Sarah.

Howling Wolf enjoyed seeing Moses' happiness, though he knew how much he would miss the friendship they had shared.

"I am glad Wakantanka give you fine wife, Black Hawk. Red Bird good wife to Gray Eagle. Bring him much happiness. Red Bird teach 'The People.' Teach good. Now many talk white man's talk as good as Howling Wolf!" They laughed with him, enjoying each others company.

"Howling Wolf," Moses said, his tone suddenly serious, "before we leave, I must find Spotted Dog and settle things with him." There was a stillness in the air as Howling Wolf looked at his friend, and then at the old Scot, Angus MacGregor, before replying.

"When Black Hawk go to sacred cave, I follow," he said, "and watch for Spotted Dog. He not like white man. Not like Red Bird...or Black Hawk. I follow; watch he not attack Black Hawk on journey."

"I know," Moses replied, "but, that wasn't necessary."

"Was *most* necessary, my Brother," Howling Wolf replied. "Spotted Dog angry when Gray Eagle return to village with wife: *white* wife!

Spotted Dog *hate* white people, start much trouble. Attack many white lodges. Bring small, white child to camp with sickness, then many of our people die."

Moses listened to Howling Wolf, more certain than ever that Spotted Dog had to be stopped. "Do you know where his camp is? I have to settle things with him," Moses replied.

Howling Wolf looked at the friend he called 'Brother,' knowing it would do no good to try to change his mind. "Camp not far from place Black Hawk and Howling Wolf see mato—bear. Five, six braves ride with him. Spotted Dog ride black horse with white feet and white face."

Moses thanked him, each man lost in his own thoughts, momentarily, until Angus spoke: "Per'aps, 'twould be better t' jist git on our way, lad? Ye're aboot t' start a new life wi' yer lovely lassie. Aboot t' return t' yer people in Hastin's. Wouldna' it be best t'jist git on our way and fergit aboot this...encounter? Are ye sure 'tis really necessary?"

"More necessary than you know," Moses replied. "I'll leave at dawn."

"Well, if yer mind's made up," Angus replied, hearing the finality in Moses' voice, knowing it would be useless to try to change it. "The saints be wi' ye, then. The saints be wi' ye, lad."

"Thank you," Moses said, looking into the blue eyes of Angus MacGregor a moment, adding, "I'm counting on you to see that Sarah gets back to Hastings, Mac, if...if I can't."

"Aye, lad, aye. Tha' I will. Tha' I will. Ye dinna' have t' ask."

"Howling Wolf, you've been a good friend to me. I'm grateful to you for following me and covering my back when I went to the sacred cave. When I get back from my..."visit" with Spotted Dog, I plan to leave right away for Hastings. Want to get there before the snow flies, if possible. Anyway, I'd like you to be there when I marry Sarah. It's called being a 'best man'. I'll explain more when I return, if you're willing?"

"You and Red Bird will marry in white man's village?"

"Yes," Moses replied.

"Your people not like Indians, Black Hawk. They not..."

"Hang my people!" Moses exclaimed. "You're my best friend! I think of you as my brother, Howling Wolf, and I'd be honored to have you by my side!"

"Howling Wolf do it! Howling Wolf be Black Hawk's best man!"

They all laughed, amid hand shakes and heartfelt slaps on the back, then wished each other good night. Howling Wolf had to smile as he walked back to his tepee, pleased to be so honored by his white brother. A pack of wolves serenaded the moon in the distance as he walked, and he felt a wealth of happiness and contentment. It was only when his thoughts turned to Spotted Dog and the intended confrontation between him and Black Hawk that he felt uneasy.

CHAPTER 27

Sarah woke at dawn the following morning, feeling well rested. She was surprised how soundly she had slept. Dressing quickly, she walked down to the creek to wash. Few were up and about, and she felt somewhat disappointed, because she wanted to tell everyone the wonderful news...that she and Black Hawk were going to be married! She felt like dancing and singing with joy, she was so happy. "Sarah Elizabeth Gentry," she said aloud, trying out what her name would be when they were wed. "Sarah Gentry. Mrs. Moses Gentry." She laughed at herself, so happy that they had finally mended all their misunderstandings.

As she passed Moses' tepee, she wanted nothing more than to rush inside and wake him with a hug and a kiss. But thought she had better not, because Angus was also bunking there and might think it highly improper...or, at best, not entirely fitting.

She stooped to pick a small yellow flower that poked its head up from beside the path to the creek, seeking any warmth from the sunrise that it could get. The morning air was brisk, a chill in the air that trumpeted the arrival—very soon—of winter. Glancing around at her surroundings, she breathed in the pristine beauty, unable to suppress a prayer of thanks for the unsullied grandeur that she saw. "In years to come, Wakantanka, will the people who come here have reverence for this beautiful, bountiful land? Will they, too, give thanks for it and respect it, treating it with the dignity it deserves? The dignity I've seen only *one* people show it. Oh, Lord, remember when I was much younger and used to wonder if Indians went to church, or if they even prayed? I was so very ignorant of their ways, then." She sat down on a rock outcropping, her prayer continuing: "I've enjoyed my time with Gray Eagle's people so much. Enjoyed their quiet, peaceful ways, their simple joys, and strong beliefs. I've marveled, so often, at these beliefs. Beliefs that have been handed down from generation to generation. These are good people, Wakantanka...really *good* people, and I ask you to always watch over them and protect them. There is talk of white men coming in great number, taking over the land, and bringing death and destruction in their wake. I fear for my friends—Standing Elk and Wind Runner, Little Moon and Howling Wolf, and all the others. Take care of them, please." She glanced out across the land, her gaze following the easy gliding spirals of a pair of Eagles in flight. She smiled contentedly, then got up and began to walk along toward the creek.

Suddenly, she stopped, turning back to look toward Moses' tepee. The mule belonging to Angus stood peacefully beside the dwelling, its ears twitching, its gray-brown hide coarse. "Well, I wonder where Moses' horse is?" she said. She looked about, hoping to see it with the other horses of the tribe, but it was nowhere to be seen. He must be out hunting, she thought, or out for an early morning ride with Howling Wolf. Satisfied with this conjecture, she smiled and turned, resuming her walk to the creek.

At the creek, she saw Wind Runner, washing in the frigid water. "Good Morning," Sarah said, kneeling beside her. "You're up early."

"Good Morning. Yes, I have many things to do today. I am glad to see you, Red Bird. I have heard you are to marry," she said, smiling.

"Yes, Moses...Black Hawk has asked me to be his wife," Sarah replied, beaming with joy.

"I am happy for you. You will return to your people?"

"Yes, in a day or two, we leave," Sarah replied, and Wind Runner reached over, patting her arm. "I will miss you, Red Bird."

"I will miss you, too, Wind Runner, and all 'The People.' But we will come back to visit, I'm sure."

Just then, Howling Wolf's sister, Dancing Fawn, arrived and quickly knelt down beside the two women. "I wish you and Black Hawk much happiness," she said. "I have heard you are to marry."

"Yes," Sarah replied, a triumphant gleam in her eyes, her chin lifting.

"I am glad. When Howling Wolf sent me to care for Black Hawk, he call your name, then nearly knock me down when he open eyes and see *me*, and not Red Bird."

"Then you didn't...you weren't..." Sarah felt her face flush with embarrassment and could not say more.

Dancing Fawn looked at Sarah, her gaze steady. "Black Hawk love Red Bird, not Dancing Fawn. Dancing Fawn try help Black Hawk when too much firewater make sick."

Sarah reached out, gently squeezing the young woman's hand. "Thank you, Dancing Fawn. You are truly a good friend, and I am sorry I thought otherwise."

Dancing Fawn smiled at Sarah, then, and Sarah felt happy, knowing she had misjudged the young woman, and had no reason to be angry with her, *or* with Moses.

CHAPTER 28

Far from Standing Elk's village, Moses came upon the camp of Spotted Dog and his band of renegade followers. He tied Midnight some distance from the camp and covered the space on foot. One lookout stood on an outcropping of rock, guarding the others. Moses crawled closer, his gun drawn, eyes alert for any sign of trouble. He knew he would suffer a painful death, if his presence was discovered. The guard yawned and turned to gaze off into the distance, his back to Moses. Moses slid his knife from its deerskin sheath and grasped the point, then threw it, as his Mother had taught him. The blade hit its mark, lodging up to the hilt in the Indian's back. The Indian turned, his mouth open in surprise, but no sound issued forth from him as he crumpled upon the ground in a heap. His blood ran red among the rocks and his dark eyes stared vacantly. Moses crawled over to where he lay, retrieving his knife.

A horse whinnied from the far edge of Spotted Dog's camp, tossing its chestnut-colored head and stomping one foot, before beginning to graze, once more. There were six tepees at the far side of the camp, each painted with its own symbol. The one Moses guessed to be Spotted Dog's, had a large buffalo and three horses painted upon it. The others had less adornment.

Moses inched back the way he had come, running quietly to where Midnight stood waiting. He untied the reins and swung up onto the horse, knowing that he had as good a chance of being killed as he had of killing the man who had so savagely raped and beaten Sarah, causing her to lose her baby, that day, long ago. Thinking of what Spotted Dog had done, fanned a fire within Moses that spurred him on. Hatred filled him, hatred so vile that he felt as if *nothing*—short of Spotted Dog's death—could alleviate it! He dug his heels into Midnight's sides, and they raced forward, Midnight's hooves pounding the earth. As he flew down the hill into the camp, Moses let out a blood-curdling scream, his gun drawn and ready! A brave ran from one of the tepees, yelling, surprise showing upon his face. Moses shot him between the eyes, then turned his horse, starting back in the opposite direction! Three more braves rushed from their tepees, all hell breaking loose, as they drew back on their bows, shooting a trio of arrows in Moses' direction! Moses fired rapidly, seeing one brave drop where he stood and another grab his head, blood spurting from between his fingers as he fell! The third brave screamed in agony, clutching his gut, then crumpled to the ground as blood began to run from his wound! Moses pulled up on his reins, leery now. He yelled out to Spotted Dog, first in English, then in his native tongue. All was still.

Midnight pawed the ground, nervously, his nostrils flared and breathing ragged! Moses jumped from the horse and hit the ground hard, rolling over and over. Then he got to his feet and ran from one tepee to another. There was no sign of life. He bent low, crouching, alert for any sign of movement, or attack. There was an eerie silence. He reloaded, his heart hammering in his chest, as he listened intently and tried to catch his breath. Only silence prevailed.

He was halfway back to his horse when he heard the sound of pounding hooves, as two riders came into sight, clearing the top of a rise. One horse was the black, with white feet and face, that Howling Wolf had told him Spotted Dog rode. The riders were both brandishing bow and arrows, and one, a lance. Their faces were covered with angry red and black splashes of paint. Moses ran for cover, hearing their angry cries, knowing he could not reach the safety of the rocks before they would be upon him. He felt a gust of wind as an arrow passed a mere breath away from his cheek, and the lance pierced the ground not a foot in front of him. He drew his gun and threw himself to the ground, rolling to face his attackers, firing as he fell. The brave to his right yelled out in anguish as one shot tore into his chest, and a second made a dark hole in his face, just below his eye socket! He screamed and fell backwards off his horse, his body hitting the ground with a thud!

The second Indian hurled himself from his horse, and Moses knew it had to be Spotted Dog! The hatred alone that burned in his eyes left no doubt! He threw his knife, its blade slicing through Moses' shirt, pinning his sleeve to the ground! Then he threw himself upon Moses, his eyes wild with hate! *"You die!"* he screamed, grasping the handle of the knife and wrenching it free. Moses' gun had been knocked from his other hand as Spotted Dog landed on him, and he grasped the Indian's wrist, struggling to keep himself from being stabbed! Spotted Dog realized he had the advantage, at that moment, and straddled Moses, his heart filled with unbridled hatred!

"Now you *die!*" he screamed. "Spotted Dog kill Gray Eagle! Now you die! White woman *not* refuse Spotted Dog *again!*"

Moses could not believe what he was hearing. He gathered every last ounce of strength and pushed with his feet, causing Spotted Dog to lose his balance, and his hold on the knife! Moses thrust himself away from the Indian, who continued to seethe with hatred and scream out more insults and threats toward Sarah, adding what he'd do to her after Moses was no longer alive and able to protect her! Moses jumped to his feet, bent low, circling his enemy. Spotted Dog quickly retrieved his knife. Eyes filled with hate, *both* circled, knives drawn! They lunged forward often, the knives not hitting their targets. Then Moses' knife was knocked from his grasp! He was tiring, his breath coming in labored spurts, while Spotted Dog seemed to have energy to spare. Then, Moses saw his chance! Spotted Dog lunged at him, and he caught Spotted Dog's leg with his, tripping the Indian, causing him to fall. Moses knew he had only *one* chance now! He was getting too tired to keep going and the younger man was rapidly gaining all advantage! As Spotted Dog fell, Moses threw himself toward where his knife lay, grabbed it, and turned, instantly lashing out! The blade caught Spotted Dog along the front of his throat, blood gushing from the pencil-thin line that severed his windpipe. He fell back, a look of astonishment upon his face. Moses lay beside the Indian's inert body, hearing his final gurgling rattle. His heart thundered in his chest and his breath was ragged from all the exertion. He lay there—listening to the silence that followed—filling the air with an unnatural quiet, after all the screaming and yelling.

Then he rose, standing still, his legs trembling slightly, realizing there was a niggling pain in his left arm, just above the elbow. He glanced at his shirt and saw the bloody area and the small slit where Spotted Dog's knife had pierced the hide. "Looks like he got me," he said, pulling off the shirt to see how bad it was. There was a small cut, one that barely broke the skin. Greatly relieved, he pulled his shirt back on and bent to pick up his knife, wiping the blade on his pant-leg. Then he bent to pick up his gun and saw the knife that Spotted Dog had carried. He picked it up, looking it over closely, certain it was the one Sarah had given to Gray Eagle—the one that had originally belonged to Old John. He had no doubt now that Spotted Dog had killed Gray Eagle as he had claimed. He walked slowly to where Midnight stood waiting, looking back at the dead warriors, shaking his head at the sight, then led Midnight over to where the Indian ponies stood. He picked up their leads, then mounted his horse, thankful to be alive. A slight smile crossed his face as he realized he had won the fight, and now Spotted Dog and his followers could no longer cause pain or suffering to anyone ever again. With one last look back at the scene of battle, he turned his horse, and began the long ride back to Standing Elk's village. The long ride…back to Sarah.

CHAPTER 29

The sky was filled with a gray haze, dark clouds—heavy and ominous looking—hung in the distance as Sarah, Angus, and Moses began their journey back to Hastings. Moses rode ahead, Midnight's black coat standing out sharply against the snow that had begun to fall. Sarah felt chilled clear through, and dreaded the long trip. She closed her eyes, trusting Glory to follow Midnight's lead. Pulling her heavy buffalo robe up higher, so not only her neck, but also her chin and nose were warmly covered, she urged Glory on. Only her eyes peeked out from the soft, warm folds of the robe, as the icy blasts of wind and snow swirled 'round, causing her to blink as it touched her lashes.

Angus MacGregor had wrapped his red, woolen capote around him and looked for all the world like a red-cheeked Saint Nicholas. His mule trailed behind Glory, never quite catching up, yet never losing sight of her. Sarah had more than once, worried that he would become separated from them as the snowfall became more and more dense. What if he lost his way, she thought, but so far he had not, and she made it a practice to turn and see that he was following, as they journeyed on.

It had begun snowing the night before they left Standing Elk's village and had not let up since. Sarah had expected *some* early snowfall, but *nothing* like this! Not the ever-deepening, unrelenting fury they found themselves in! If this kept up, they would have to seek shelter at the old, abandoned cabin again, *if* Angus could make it that far! She noticed that Moses kept looking back, also, to make sure that all was well with the old Scot! If *he*'s worried, she thought, then I *know* I have good reason to worry! Moses would smile at her, before turning back to watch the trail, his face reddened by the wind and cold. His hat was covered in white, as were his shoulders and back, and she hoped the buffalo robe coat she had made for him was ample enough to stave off some of the icy chill. She smiled at him, then realized that he couldn't tell she was smiling because only her eyes showed above her wrap.

The snow continued to fall, and was nearly ankle-deep. She wiggled her toes in her fur-lined moccasins, glad that they came all the way up to her knees. The sun was hidden, almost totally, behind the heavy, gray clouds now, and Sarah knew they would be doing any eating as they rode, not stopping until nightfall. Her thoughts drifted back to those they had left: Chief Standing Elk, a man she had grown to love as a father, his wisdom; strengthening, his quiet countenance; endearing. She thought, too, of his wife, Wind Runner. A tall, slim woman, who often reminded Sarah of Rosie because she was so cheerful. Wind Runner had the ability to look on the bright side of things, and her quiet, cheerful attitude always changed the mood of those around her, as did Rosie's. Of course, Rosie isn't all that quiet, Sarah thought, and had to smile at the thought. Funny though, here are two women, similar in attitudes and personalities, yet so unalike in their lifestyles, all because one is an Indian, one white. It seems strange, Sarah thought, that I find so very many similarities in the two of them.

Then there's Little Moon, my friend since my very first day in the village. While others had whispered, giggled, or poked at me—touching my hair—surprised by its color. Curious about it. She had stood back shyly, a smile upon her face that seemed to speak to me and to welcome me. Soon after, we became friends, as she taught me the ways of her people, and I told her of the loved ones and friends in Hastings that I had left behind. Little Moon had been quick to learn. I remember how we used to sit, talking quietly, late into the night, sharing information and advice. At first we grew in knowledge—often with great difficulty— as we learned to converse through signs and an awful lot of pointing! Sarah smiled as she remembered, but then she remembered the other reason their friendship had grown—when Spotted Dog attacked me, it was Little Moon and Running Deer who stayed with me while I healed, and sang to me: songs of healing and hope. I'll always be grateful to them—and to Wind Runner—for their care at that horrible time, Sarah thought. She felt a great sadness well up inside, and sniffled loudly, her eyes filling with tears.

Moses turned, looking questioningly at her, though she was certain he had not heard her. "Is everything all right, darlin'?" he asked, pulling back and waiting, as Glory came abreast of his horse. He sensed, by the look he saw in her eyes, the sadness she was feeling. It had been hard on her to leave those she had grown so close to. It was obvious that she would miss them after living with them so long. Sarah shook her head, unable to answer, for fear she would begin to cry. "It'll be all right," he said, reaching out and touching the end of her nose with his fingertip. "We can always come back and visit."

She sniffled again, smiling at him, appreciating his concern. "Are you warm enough?" she asked, her voice somewhat muffled by her wrap.

"I've been warmer," he replied, smiling. His devilish grin brightened her day. "Don't know what I would have done without this buffalo robe coat, though," he said, pulling it closed around his neck. "Thank you, again, for it."

"You're welcome," she replied, smiling.

"Are we here, yet, laddie?" Angus MacGregor's voice boomed as he came to a halt beside Moses.

"Well, we're *here,* " Moses answered, "but, we're not *ther* ...yet." Moses laughed at his own play on words. Angus looked at him, then Sarah, a merry "ho, ho, ho!," bursting forth from the old Scot.

"True, 'tis not Hastin's," Angus said, looking around at the snow-covered landscape that stretched endlessly in all directions. "Dinna' think it 'twas." His blue eyes twinkled and Sarah could not help laughing at the two men. "Goin't' stop a bit," Angus said, "take a short walk o'er yonder hill. Guess ye can think o' somethin' t' du whilest I'm gone, aye?" Moses grinned at the old man, in answer. "A wee bit o' "spoonin'," per'aps?" Angus suggested, smiling. Then he winked and ambled off, his slightly bowed legs moving stiffly, after the long ride. His mule hung its head, intent on staying alongside Moses' horse as though it knew that the horse's body would block some of the gusts of wind.

Moses reached out, putting his arm around Sarah, as she in turn snuggled closer to him, burying her face in the folds of his coat at the hollow of his neck. Glory stomped her foot, then stood quietly, her body also sheltered from the wind's fury by Midnight's larger body. "I love you," Moses whispered into Sarah's hair as he wrapped his arms around her, pulling her tightly against him.

"And I, you," she said, enjoying the extra warmth his closeness afforded her. "Do you think the snow will ever let up?" she asked, looking up into his eyes.

"Sooner or later, darlin'," he replied, adding, "here comes Angus." He winked at Sarah, pulling her wrap back up around her neck, then turned to Angus. "Ready to go, Mac?"

"Aye, lad, tha' I am," Angus answered.

They rode till just before dark, then made camp in an arroyo that ran up to and under a rock overhang, where they were sheltered on three sides. Glad for the protection from the falling snow and unceasing wind, they soon had gathered enough sticks and brush to start a roaring fire that provided much welcomed warmth. As they sat before it, warming their hands over the flames, a coyote yipped off in the distance, and was quickly answered by others. Sarah shivered and slid closer to Moses, while Angus rearranged his capote and other paraphernalia, somewhat, settling in closer to the fire. Sarah took pemmican from her pouch and passed it to the two men.

"Thank ye, kindly, lass," Angus said, smiling at her. "Canna' seem t' keep me auld bones warm, anymore...least not in weather like this. When I think tha' I used t' track fer days in it, and weather a hundred times worse—na' tha' long ago—I have t' admit I'm gittin' auld."

"How old are you, Angus, if you don't mind me asking?" Sarah questioned.

"Many a winter, lass. Many a winter. Time seems t' sneak up on a fella when he least expects it. One day ye're a lad, all full o' hopes an' dreams an' ambition. Ye're workin' hard, er dodgin' it, best ye can," he winked at her, smiling. "Then ye stop fer jist a minute and look o'er yer shoulder at a shadow, and when ye turn back, yer an auld man, seein' yer hopes and, especially yer ambition, all gone. Yer dreams all dreamt."

Sarah smiled at him, saddened by what he said. "Will you stay in Hastings, Mac?"

"Aye, per'aps," he replied. "Na' too auld t' enjoy the warmth and comfort of an obligin' lass. Per'aps one will catch me fancy in yer fine town o' Hastin's."

"He should meet Rosie," Moses volunteered, his eyes twinkling with pure devilment. Sarah shook her head, laughing.

"And who might this Rosie be?" Angus asked, noticeably perking up with immediate interest.

Moses let out a hardy "Aha!"

"Moses!" Sarah admonished. "Rosie is my step-mother, and a dear friend of mine," Sarah replied, noticing the same look of devilment in Angus MacGregor's eyes, as in Moses'. "My father died a few years back," she continued, "and...well...I guess she's just about the nicest woman you could hope to meet. She's Irish, and the best cook!"

"Well, well, looks like I jist might be likin' yer town, after all...and maybe a certain Irish lass, too." Sarah poked Moses, who had slapped his knee, grinning.

After the fire had chased some of the chill from their bones, and they had eaten, night settled in around them, hiding the snow under its velvet-black coat. The wind abating, Sarah snuggled into Moses' arms, her head against his, his breath warm against her cheek. Angus tapped out his pipe, coughed, then curled as close as he could to the fire and slept. Every now and then, he shivered.

CHAPTER 30

At first light, they were already up, had eaten, and were ready to ride. The day promised to be near perfect, though a bit chilly. A bright burst of sunlight stretched out from the east and both the snow and the wind had ended.

Moses lifted Sarah up onto Glory, kissing her soundly, once she was seated. Then he swung up onto Midnight, asking if she and Angus were ready to begin. Angus was moving a bit slower than usual, both Sarah and Moses noticed, stopping often to get his breath after coughing bouts.

"Are you all right?" Moses called out, concerned.

"Aye, fit as a fiddle, lad, fit as a fiddle—lead on, lead on," Angus answered, getting on his mule and pulling his red, woolen capote more securely around him. Its fabric dotted, here and there, with holes and threadbare areas they could easily see through.

A couple days later, when the sun was once again straight up in the sky, they arrived at the abandoned cabin. It looked more dilapidated than when they had stopped on their previous trip, and both Sarah and Moses felt uneasy when remembering the events of that stay. Moses knew that Sarah would be uncomfortable there, but he was more concerned with the terrible coughing spells that Angus was suffering. The old-timer's face grew furiously red with each coughing spell, and he often placed his hand upon his chest when they were most severe.

Sarah tried to get him to eat something, but he pushed the food aside and bent nearly double as one more bout of coughing occurred.

"Nae, thank ye, lass, jist a mug o'coffee, if ye please," he managed to say before another round of coughing began. He shuffled over to a bed in the far corner, brushing off the dust, dirt, and droppings of the rodents and other critters that had inhabited the cabin, after the human occupants had moved on. Removing his pouch and other paraphernalia, he spread out his blanket and laid down, covering himself with his capote.

Sarah had put on a pot of coffee as soon as she managed to get a fire going in the old fireplace, using wood she found nearby, and part of an old, wooden chair that had been broken for just that purpose, it seemed. Moses unsaddled Midnight and turned both horses and the mule into the barely adequate corral. At least they could get under the lean-to, he thought, and have a bit of shelter if the weather turned bad again. He looked out toward the pond, not happy about stopping so early in the day, but knew Angus was needful of a good rest and some hot victuals. The old Scot's health was Moses' first concern. *I don't like the sound of his cough. I hope he has enough strength to make the rest of the journey. Once we get to Hastings, we can get him some medicine from Doc. If he can make it to Hastings*, he thought.

"Moses?" Sarah called out, walking toward him, her hair shining in the afternoon rays of the sun, her wrap pulled closely around her.

"What is it, darlin'?" he asked, reaching out, his arm encircling her waist. She lifted her face to him, feeling the need in him grow as he began kissing her—at first tenderly, and then with mounting passion—his lips moving against hers, then across her cheek and down her neck. Fire flamed within her as his tongue made a wet trail along the side of her neck, causing her to moan in response.

"Oh, Moses!" Sarah exclaimed, her arms tightening around him, pulling him closer against her.

He groaned and gripped her upper arms, holding her slightly away from himself. His heart pounded in his chest like a drum, his breath coming in short, sharp gasps. "Oh, darlin'," he whispered, a look of pain upon his face as he struggled to gain control of himself. Sarah stood still, knowing even the slightest move would topple their resolve to wait any longer. Their desire for each other threatened to overwhelm them. It had been a long time since either had made love, and they both knew it would take very little to make them forget propriety and give in to the fire that threatened to engulf them.

Moses opened his eyes, a slow smile covering his face. "Oh, lady," he said. "I'll sure be glad to see our wedding night arrive!" Sarah smiled up at him, in total agreement. "Did you come out here purposely to seduce me, darlin'?"

She blushed. "No, I came out to talk to you about Mac. I'm worried about him, Moses, his breathing seems to be getting worse. Do you have any medicine? Any whiskey?"

"No, I don't, I... wait a minute! There might be a little whiskey left in the flask in my pouch! I'll check." He walked over to his saddle and pouch, hung on the corral fence, and reached into the pouch. He felt the flask and pulled it out. "There's a little in here," he said, shaking it.

"Good!" Sarah exclaimed, and she took the flask from him, leaning up onto her toes to kiss his cheek. "I love you, Gentry. It'll be a wedding night worth waiting for!" She smiled flirtatiously and turned, walking away from him, her hips swaying in a manner *most* unbecoming to a proper lady!

Moses watched her, the heat rising in him like a flag of surrender. "Oh, darlin'," he intoned softly, "you don't know just how close we came to having our wedding night!" Then he lifted his saddle and other gear off the corral fence and started toward the cabin, enjoying the welcoming smell of boiling coffee.

CHAPTER 31

The next morning the sky was once again clear and the air was still. Sarah cooked their breakfast from the meager selection of rations that remained and enjoyed the cup of coffee she had with Moses. She glanced toward the far corner where Angus lay, coughing and talking loudly as he slept. She wondered what his life had been like when he was younger, and if he had ever been married. More importantly, she wondered if he could make the rest of the trip to Hastings. He wheezed when he breathed now, and she knew how quickly a person could die from pneumonia.

"Angus sounds bad," she said to Moses, nodding toward the bed where Angus lay, "but I do think the whiskey we got him to take helped him sleep."

"Seems like it," Moses replied, "unless he was just plain tuckered-out from traveling."

Sarah poured them a second cup of coffee, the chipped and cracked cups reminding her of the cups at her cabin. Remnants of life, she thought. "I wonder who lived here? How many folks lived here over the years? And why they left?"

"Probably froze out," Moses replied, as he sat on the side of the bed that had been his the previous night. "Looks like they burned the table legs to keep warm. See the top of it over there near the fireplace?" Sarah glanced over at it, wondering if a woman had been in this very room: a woman with a young daughter, perhaps. "What are you thinking?" Moses asked, noticing the faraway look in her eyes.

"I found children's clothing…a little girl's dress…and a piece of quilt," she explained. Her words drifted off as she imagined the plight of that woman and child, and the fear she must have felt for her child.

"Don't think about it," Moses suggested. "Whoever they were, they're long gone. This cabin has been empty for years, by the looks of it."

"I hope they survived," Sarah said, sighing.

"Let's see if we can get some food into Angus," Moses said, rising and walking to the far end of the room. "Angus. Angus! MAC!" he called out, and the old Scot groaned and stretched, beset by a siege of coughing. He sat up on the edge of the bed, one hand on his chest, the other over his mouth. Moses stepped back, not liking the sound of his coughing. It was plain to see that he was having trouble breathing.

At last, he caught his breath and attempted to stand, succeeding on the second try. "Mornin' is it, laddie?" he asked, his voice hoarse, as he rubbed the sleep from his eyes.

"Are you up to traveling, Mac?" Moses asked, placing a hand on the old man's shoulder.

"Aye," he answered, "but, if I'm t' git t' Hastin's, 'tis best we go soon."

"There's a doctor in Hastings, he'll be able to give you something for that cough."

"'Tis na' the cough tha's botherin' me, lad. 'Tis the fire in me chest, an' the shortness o' breath."

Sarah walked over to Angus, feeling his forehead. "Far as I can tell, you've got no fever," she said, a relieved look on her face.

"Then, 'tis best we go," he said, picking up his capote and wrapping it around him.

"Why don't you take my buffalo robe coat," Moses offered. "It'll be a lot warmer than your capote, and I have another coat in my saddlebags that I can wear."

"Thank ye, kindly," Angus replied, "but I been trappin' an' travelin' fer many a year, and this auld coat al'ays done a fair job o' keepin' me warm."

"Well, if you change your mind, you just let me know."

"Indeed I will," Angus answered, between more wracking coughs, and shuffled over to pour himself a cup of coffee. He swallowed it down quickly, keeping one hand on his chest.

"Don't you want something to eat?" Sarah asked, as he struggled to clear his throat after another coughing spell. He shook his head in answer, wiping his mouth on his sleeve, then walked outside.

"Moses..." Sarah began, but Moses shook his head. "We'd better go, darlin', while he *can*!" They quickly gathered up their belongings and closed the door, glad for the night's shelter, but more anxious than ever to get to Hastings.

CHAPTER 32

When they woke Angus, two days later, he could not get up without help. Dawn had come breathing its moist, chilly breath upon the earth and its inhabitants, and the old Scot was seriously ill. Moses was amazed he had gotten as far as he did, and knew a less hearty man would have succumbed long before this. They had cut across country due to him being so sick, hoping to reach Sarah's cabin quicker, but it looked now like he still might not be able to make it. Moses knew they would be at the cabin by late afternoon, but even *that* might not be soon enough.

"Oh, Moses, what'll we do?" Sarah asked, wringing her hands and looking pleadingly at him.

"Well, we can't stay here, that's for certain," he replied. "He needs to be inside, in a warm bed. Guess we'll just go on now as best we can."

"He needs a doctor...and some medicine," Sarah said, picking up their things, handing Moses the last piece of pemmican from her pouch. "Not much of a breakfast," she said, reaching up to touch his face.

"You take it," he said.

"No. You'll need to keep up your strength, Moses. Angus will be heavy, love." He smiled at her, pleased to hear her call him "love." It was a first, and he reached out to her, wrapping her in a quick embrace. All too soon it was over, however, and they bustled about, getting ready to travel. They secured Angus' gun, pouch, and personal things onto his mule and tied a lengthy lead to its halter to be sure it would follow. Then Moses helped Angus to his feet, almost totally supporting him: a not too easy task, while Sarah held Midnight's reins to keep the large horse still. Struggling, Moses helped the seriously ill man up onto the horse's back. Then mounted behind him, and pulled him back into a sitting position against his chest, wrapping his arms around him for support. Angus tried to speak, but got to coughing again, instead; dry, hacking coughs that threatened to unseat *both* men. Sarah held the reins, looking anxiously up at them, wondering if they could *possibly* get very far, and even if they did, if Angus would still be alive?

"I've got him, darlin'. Let's ride," Moses said, as he took the reins from her. Sarah swung up onto Glory and their journey began. Moses seriously doubted that Angus would survive the rest of the trip. The only positive aspect being, that his body heat against the old man's back would warm him a bit.

By noon they enjoyed the first decent temperature they had had on the whole trip. Sarah shed her heavy outer garment and Moses pulled off his hat, careful not to lose his hold on Angus, or his balance. Angus' head drooped forward, his shoulders slumped. His arms hung limply at his sides. His breathing was ragged and loud: a disturbing thing to listen to. Moses felt his head and realized it was a good deal warmer than it had been that morning. "He's got a fever," he said, as Sarah rode up beside him.

"Better loosen that old blanket he's got around him," she said, gingerly tugging at it.

"Don't pull too hard, darlin', or it'll be *all* holes, instead of *mostly* holes."

She smiled at his comment as he helped her loosen it, somewhat, from around the old Scot. Angus groaned, coughed a series of deeply wracking coughs, then slumped forward. Moses quickly tightened his grip around him, his arms already beginning to ache from the effort. "We need to keep going, Sarah. Can you do it?" he asked, a worried look upon his face.

"Yes," she replied, looking anxiously at Angus. "We'd better hurry." Her stomach growled loudly as they set off again, and she hoped Moses hadn't heard it. She longed for a hearty dish of venison stew, a glass of milk, and a large piece of Rosie's special chocolate cake. She was so hungry she could almost taste the things she envisioned, and her stomach rumbled again. She moaned, shaking her head.

"Are you all right?" Moses asked, his own stomach growling as he spoke.

"Just my stomach crying for a bowl of venison stew," she replied, and Moses groaned in response, hurrying Midnight along. They were following a different route than they had ridden before. The terrain was strewn with boulders, at first, then became dense forest, and extremely difficult to traverse under the circumstances, though ultimately a much shorter route.

At dusk, they crossed the meadow near Sarah's cabin. When Sarah realized where she was, she spurred Glory on at a faster pace, hurrying on ahead of the two men. All of a sudden she had no qualms about going home! Her friends would not turn away because of the choices she had made, and her enemies—though she didn't think she had any—were welcome to their opinions. Soon she spied her cabin sitting in its pristine setting of scrub oak, maple, cottonwood and box elder. The barn looked freshly painted and all the fences were standing straight, none in disrepair. Sarah looked back at Moses, her smile saying it all. He was pleased to see her so happy, but had his hands full. His arms had long before felt pricks and tingles as they began to fall asleep, and he wondered how he would manage to get Angus off of Midnight. It would be hard. He hoped he wouldn't let the old fellow take a tumble.

Sarah dismounted at the cabin door and as she did, a young man opened it, surprise showing on his face. "Miz Justus?" he questioned, gaping at her, "is that you?"

"Yes, it is," she answered, wondering why in the world he had been in the cabin. "Would you help him, please?" she said, pointing back at Moses.

"Sure enough! Hello, Sheriff, didn't see you there," he said, hurrying to his side..

"Can you lift him down? He ain't light."

"Oh, sure," the young man replied, reaching up for Angus and supporting him while Moses dismounted and walked around, flexing his stiff arms and legs.

Sarah went on into the cabin, at once pleased to feel the warmth inside. The smell of boiling coffee made her stomach growl as she hurried to the bed and threw back the covers. Everything looked so comfortable and inviting. She smiled a contented smile and ran to open the door for the men. Moses and the young man lay Angus down on the bed. His white hair was disheveled and though his cheeks burned fire-red, his face—

what they could see of it, beyond his beard—was extremely pale. Moses quickly removed the old Scot's boots and pulled off his socks. They were stained black with dirt and grime, and reeked! Moses held them up with one hand, holding his nose with the other, and walked over to the door, tossing them outside. "Don't think those will *ever* wash clean," he said, wrinkling his nose and grinning. Sarah could hardly suppress a giggle, seeing his expression. He winked at her, and went back to his work.

First, he unwrapped Angus from his tattered capote, and considered throwing it into the fire. But that wasn't up to him, he decided, and he laid it aside. Sarah had read his thoughts and agreed. "Better not," she said. "It seems special to him."

Moses groaned. "Almost as "scented" as his socks," he commented, and they both couldn't help grinning. "I'm gonna shuck off most of his duds. You want to turn your back, darlin'? I sure could use a good, fresh cup of hot coffee."

"You've got it," she replied, going to the cupboard for two cups. "Where's the boy? And *who* is he?"

"Why, that's Michael. Michael O'Leary. I thought you'd recognize him."

"Oh, my! He's so grown-up. I thought he was an O'Leary—the red hair, you know—but...I can't believe how he's grown. He's tall as a man now."

"He's a good young man, one of the best," Moses replied. "He kept the place going since we left. Took care of the cattle and all. Stayed right on here, hope you don't mind?"

"I don't mind at all. In fact, I'm grateful—to *both* of you. Thank you, Moses."

"You're welcome, darlin', but like I told you a long time ago, there's no need to thank me." He covered Angus with a blanket as his buckskin leggings came off, one leg at a time. "Got a cold, wet rag? Our friend is burning up. Hope Michael gets back soon with the doctor. I sent *him* to get him. Too tired to go, myself."

Sarah hurried to find a towel, dipped it in the bucket of water by the door, then took it over to Moses. "Have I told you how much I love you, Moses Gentry? And what a wonderful man I think you are?"

"I'm listenin'," he said, and he looked at her with that old devilish look in his eyes that she remembered so well.

CHAPTER 33

Later that evening, after they had eaten and continuously tended to Angus' needs, Moses and Sarah sat side by side in front of the fireplace in the pair of old rockers. Moses sat still, his long legs stretched out toward the fire's warmth, his eyes closed. Sarah rocked gently, her head leaning back against her old feather pillow, the only noise to be heard, the rasping and rattling of the old Scot every time he took a breath.

Sarah had just begun to doze—her hunger satisfied and the warmth of the cabin lulling her to sleep—when the sound of an arriving buggy was heard, causing her to stir. "Moses," she said, but he was already rushing to open the door.

"Hello, Doc. Come on in." A second figure hurried inside after the doctor, so bundled-up that they could not tell who it was. Sarah stood, relieved to see the doctor. Hopeful that he would be able to help Angus.

Doc Valentine hurriedly removed his coat, then rushed over to the bed. "Let's see what we have here," he said, adding, "hello, Sarah, welcome home!"

"Hello, Doc. Thank you." Then she squealed in surprise and delight as the second person removed her coat, scarf and mittens, and there stood a red-cheeked, smiling Rosie! "Oh, Rosie!' Sarah said, rushing over to hug the older woman, tears filling both their eyes.

"Oh, dear, dear child, I've been missin' ya' so," Rosie said, wiping the tears from Sarah's face, and then from her own. "I was at Doc's when Michael arrived—visitin' with Judith—and I just had to come along with him."

"I'm so glad you did, Rosie," Sarah said, turning to watch as the doctor examined Angus. "I've missed you, too, more than I can tell you."

Moses turned his attention from Doc and Angus, to his two favorite women, happy to see their joyful reunion. Rosie looked at him, a smile upon her face. "Well, sheriff, I've, got a hug for you, too," she said, and walked over to him, enfolding him in her arms. "It's happy I am to see ya', Moses. Thank you for bringing our girl back."

Moses hugged her to him, smelling the faint scent of lavender as he kissed her on the forehead. Her unruly, nearly white locks tickling his cheek as he did so. "I don't intend to let her get away *this* time, Rosie. I've asked her to be my wife."

"Oh, dear! Oh, my! I'll have to tell Amanda and start baking and..." Rosie began.

"Now, wait a minute," Moses said, enjoying her response, "we haven't set a date, yet..."

Doc Valentine interrupted just then, "Moses, can you give me a hand, here? Help me lift him and turn him so I can get his shirt off. He's burning up with fever. You ladies might want to avert your eyes. We'll have to completely undress him and...do you suppose we can mange to get a lot of wet towels? We're going to have to cover him with them, to cool him. His fever's way too high."

"Sure can, Doc, and the O'Leary boy's out in the barn, he can help, too."

"I'll call him," Sarah said, going to the door. Michael came on the run, when he heard her call.

"Sounds like pneumonia," Rosie commented, looking anxiously at Sarah. "Don't like the sound of it. Sounds just like your dear father had." For just a moment there was a sadness in her eyes, and then they brightened, as she asked: "So, who is the old gent? A fine looking fella, ain't he?"

"Looks like old Saint Nick," Sarah replied.

"That he does," Rosie agreed, laughing softly. "He's not an Indian, by the looks of him, and I doubt he's Saint Nick, so why don't I pour us a cup of coffee, Sarah? And while the men tend to him, you can tell me all about him."

The women sat at the kitchen table, talking, as the coffee began to reheat, ignoring the men as they huffed and puffed, helping the doc to turn Angus. He wasn't a tall man, but short and stocky, and at the moment, "dead weight." They rolled him and pulled him and struggled to do what the doctor asked, hoping it would all be worth it and he wouldn't die.

"His name is Angus Charles MacGregor," Sarah told Rosie, and proceeded to tell her the story of the old Scot and his surprising connection to John Bruce. Just as she finished, Doc, Moses, and Michael finished doing what was necessary for Angus. The doctor bid them goodbye, in a hurry to get back to town to see to a patient who had been laid up at his office for a few days, after having an unexpected encounter with a bear and her cubs. Michael also excused himself, saying he was going back to town with the doc, but would be out the next day to tend to the chores, as usual.

Sarah poured Moses a cup of coffee, rubbing his shoulder as she handed it to him. Then he pulled the large rocker over by the bed, so he could keep an eye on their patient, while the ladies talked quietly at the kitchen table.

They had all been surprised, earlier, when Angus called out, his words making little sense to them: "Johnny! Johnny! We done it, lad! We done it!" His words had been a bit garbled, his accent making it all the harder to understand him. They had *all* laughed, even earlier, when he shouted out, "Move yer arse, Johnny! Saints be praised, lad, move yer arse!" A bout of coughing, worse than any he had suffered earlier, interrupted his words, but not before Rosie and Sarah had covered their mouths with their hands and twittered with laughter.

"He thinks he's talking to John," Sarah explained. "They were more like brothers, than just friends." Rosie shook her head sadly, looking over at the older man who was now thrashing about in the bed. "How is he?" Sarah asked, looking questioningly at Moses.

"Let's just say he's a hearty old fella, or he wouldn't have made it this far," Moses replied, his words interrupted by another series of coughs, and more thrashing about by Angus.

"She canna' be far, Johnny! We'll find her, lad, we'll find her!" shouted Angus, as he rolled and tossed, his voice filled with so much anguish that it left no doubt that he and John Bruce had shared a most trying and terrible ordeal.

"I brought a pan of good venison stew and some of my special chocolate cake," Rosie said. "Would you like some?"

"We already ate, but, I never could resist your cooking, Rosie," Moses replied. "I wouldn't mind having a small dish of stew, and maybe a small piece of cake, too."

Sarah smiled at him, wondering what he would look like, if he ate Rosie's good cooking everyday. "None for me, thanks," she said, enjoying watching Rosie bustle right over to the stove, heating up the stew for Moses, humming contentedly as she worked. Though her hair had turned more white than red, and sometimes there was a sadness in her eyes, Sarah could tell that she was more than a little happy to have someone to look after, again, as she always had been.

"Rosie, could you bring me a large bowl of water?" Moses asked, noticing that Angus was getting more feverish.

"Indeed I can," Rosie stated, hurrying around to do his bidding. "Why don't you go eat, sheriff? I can put rags on Saint Nick's head. Best you eat it while it's hot."

Moses quickly agreed, winking and grinning devilishly at Sarah, who guessed what he was thinking, and shook her head at him. Moses, the matchmaker, she thought, and she couldn't help smiling. She had thought many things of him over the years, but *never* that he would be that! The man constantly surprised her! She looked at Rosie, who busied herself at the bedside of the old Scot. She wrung out a rag in cold water, placing it on the old man's head, crooning: "There ya' go, darlin'. You just lay still an' stop your frettin'. Rosie's here, an' will take good care of ya'." She had to smile as Rosie brushed back their patient's shock of white hair, patting it back as carefully and as tenderly as if it was a baby she was tending. She smiled at Moses, thinking *maybe* he *was* right!

When Moses finished eating, he walked over to stand behind Sarah, wrapping his arms around her. "They make a good pair, don't you think?" he whispered.

She poked him gently with her elbow. "Sh-h-h," she ordered, then added, "but, you might just be right, Mr. Gentry."

"Oh! So it's "Mr." Gentry, is it now, *Miz* Justus?"

"Only until we say our vows," she answered, placing her hands over his.

"And how soon do you think you could be ready to say those vows?" he asked, teasingly. He kissed her on the back of her neck, watching so Rosie wouldn't notice and be embarrassed.

"I'll leave that up to you, Mr. Gentry."

"I *hoped* you'd say that! In fact, I *counted* on it!" he whispered excitedly. " It'll be two weeks from now, on the ninth of November," he said, smiling happily.

"November nine it is," Sarah said, happiness filling her whole being. And she turned, throwing her arms around him, kissing him a resounding smack on the lips! They were both too busy to catch sight of the radiant smile on Rosie's face, as she turned *her* attention *back* to Angus MacGregor!

CHAPTER 34

Three days later, as she tended Angus MacGregor, Rosie let out a squeal, exclaiming, "Why, of all the…" and blushing furiously, she scurried away from the bedside of the old Scot.

Angus raised his head, looking puzzled. Seeing Sarah and Moses, he looked even more confused. "Whaur am I?" he asked, wiping his eyes and pulling up on the blanket that covered him, his hair standing out from his head all wild and unruly.

"You're at Sarah's cabin, Mac," Moses replied. "You've been awful sick."

"Whaur is she, lad? Saints be praised, tell me whaur she is?"

Thinking Angus was still suffering a bit of the delirium that had plagued him during the fever, Moses went to stand beside the bed, to reassure the older man. "I'm sorry, I don't know who it is you're asking about."

Angus looked at him, a troubled look upon his face. "Aye, laddie, then 'twas only a dream." He shook his head sadly. "'Twas the angel, I'm askin' aboot. Dinna' ye see her, lad? I was so sure she was here. Could almost feel the material o' the dress she was wearin'."

"No, sorry," Moses replied. "Haven't seen any "angels" around here, Mac."

Angus lay back, closing his eyes. "Oh, laddie, I wish ye coulda seen her. Eyes as green as an emerald sea. Hair the color o' the sun shining on the snow in me beloved Scotland." He sighed, looking plaintively at Moses. "I was so sure she was here, lad. So sure she had held me hand and tried t' comfort me. A beautiful angel, wi' a smile only God could make."

Sarah shook her head, having walked over to the bedside, also. She felt so sorry for the old man. Then, suddenly, she gasped, realizing who he meant! "Angus, you don't mean the "angel" who's sitting in my rocker, over by the fireplace, do you?" And she nodded toward Rosie.

Both Moses and Angus looked toward the rocker, where Rosie sat, smiling demurely.

"Saints be praised! Saints be praised!" Angus shouted, then promptly had a coughing fit.

"Saints be praised," Moses whispered, and he looked at Sarah, a huge grin upon his face!

CHAPTER 35

No one was surprised, a few days later, when it was decided that Angus MacGregor would be the convalescing houseguest of Rosie O'Day, Mitchell, Justus. After all, she explained, it made no good sense for a man who had been so ill to be such a far distance from the doctor—in case he had a relapse, you see—when she had a large, empty house all to herself, and was only a few doors down the street from the doctor!

Angus was recovering at remarkable speed, under the tender care of his green-eyed "angel." And his angel had taken to giggling a lot, and singing Irish ditties as soon as she woke in the early morning.

The younger couple had caught Angus holding Rosie's hand, on more than one occasion, and couldn't believe their eyes when they walked in from the barn one fine morning and caught Angus kissing her cheek! Rosie had blushed crimson and giggled like a schoolgirl, then hurried to get their breakfast dished up.

Soon after, while the two women were at the pond just beyond the cabin, washing out a few garments, Angus called Moses aside. There was a worried tone to his voice. "Laddie, du ye think a man me age has much chance wi' an angel like Rosie?"

"Well, what do you mean?" Moses asked, thoroughly enjoying himself.

"Ye know, laddie. A *chance!* A *chance!*"

Moses put his hand up to his chin as though deeply studying the question. "Exactly what do you have in mind, Mac?" he asked, at last.

"Oh, fer Heaven's sake, man! Ye canna' tell? 'Tis *smitten*, I am!'" Angus replied, his total frustration with Moses clearly showing.

"Well, Mac, it's just that…well…how would a lady like Rosie feel when you decided to move on…have you thought of that, my friend?"

Angus glowered at Moses, as though he had just struck him. "Laddie, if ye be thinkin' so little o' me, then I'll be steppin' outside wi' ye, as soon as I'm able!"

Moses couldn't help himself and laughed aloud before replying. "Angus MacGregor, I can't think of a finer man for Rosie! I've never seen her so happy! But truly, Mac, what would she feel when you took up your trapping and prospecting again, and left her?" He realized it was no longer a subject to make light of, and didn't want to offend the older man, whether seriously, or in jest.

Angus looked at him, long and hard, as though to be certain Moses was sincere. Then, he spoke. "Laddie, 'tis a fine life I've had. I've traveled far and wide, wi' verra few cares and nae ties t' bind me." He paused, looking across the room, while choosing his words, then continued, "I've sowed a few oats, and had a fine time o' it. Even left a lassie weepin' a time er two. I've seen men smitten and thought them fools…t' give up their freedom fer the shackles o' matreemony. Even me friend, Johnny Bruce…I give him a hard time when he begun t' see his Indian lass. Told him his heart would get broke, as sure as all git-out, when some handsome, young buck come strollin' by." There was silence, then he continued: "I was *wrong*, laddie! *Dead wrong!* As God is me witness, I've lived t' regret those words I said t' him. Ye see, Johnny Bruce wasna' like jist any man…*nae!*…when he lost tha' first gal; the one in Scotland…well, it tore him up somethin' fierce. Fierce enough, lad, tha' he left everything! *Everything!* Du ye understand? And got hisself lost an' near froze t' death cause o' the grief he was feelin'! *Nae!*," he shook his head, sadly, "he wasna' like any other man when it come t' the women-folk he loved! Ye see, when Johnny fell in love tha' second time, 'twas the *same* thing all o'er again. He loved tha' lass, more than most men are capable o' lovin', and she, him. They were inseparable, always laughing an' enjoyin' each other's company. Needin' no one else and nuthin' else, t' see 'em through the day er night." He paused again, hanging his head, and when he looked up, there were tears in his eyes. "Johnny was makin' her a special gift. Finished it the day afore she disappeared. He'd jist been told she was carryin' a wee bairn—a baby—*his* baby, and he wanted t' make somethin' special fer her t' show his love fer her and the wee bairn. She cried when he give it t' her. Cried, na' only wi' happiness, but wi' sadness, too, 'cause she had nuthin' as precious, t' give him in return. He told her the wee babe was her gift; the *finest* gift she could e'er have given him, and I seen him place his hands on her stomach and vow tha' as long as he lived, *no one* had e'er, or could e'er, give him as wonderful a gift!" He shook his head as a tear or two traced a path down his cheeks. "Oh, laddie, the verra next day she rose early, and in spite o' the deep snow and terrible winds, she left the camp. A friend o' hers told Johnny, later, tha' she had gone t' a special place, known only t' those Indians. 'To a cave, some distance from the camp,' she said, 'whaur beautiful golden rocks lay thick upon the ground.' She wanted t' give him a gift as fine, ye see, as the one he had given her. She dinna' feel the babe was her gift t' him, because they had made the babe *t'gither*, from the love they shared." Angus sniffled loudly, and wiped his eyes. Then he continued, his voice filled with anguish: "We found tha' cave, the next spring, but thaur was nary a sign o' her. Fer two months, er more, after she disappeared, Johnny searched and searched fer her, comin' in e'ery night long past dark. I'd know, wi' oot askin', by the look on his face, tha' he had na' found her. He quit eatin' an' sleepin', jist sat starin' oot into the dark, rockin' to and fro." Angus sniffled loudly, looking directly at Moses. Moses had a lump in his own throat, at the realization of the sadness John Bruce had suffered. "Tha's how I feel, laddie, as God is me witness. I knew it, at first sight o' Rosie. I'm *smitten*, jist like Johnny was. I canna' think o' leavin' the lass, canna' think o' being away from her. I want t' *marry* her, laddie, and make me home wi' her fer the rest o' me life. No more trappin' er prospectin'. Me days o' tha' are o'er. 'Tis time t' share me life and riches wi' the love o' me life, me sweet angel...Rosie." He paused, looking plaintively at Moses. "So du ye think I have a chance? Tell me straight oot, lad, fer 'tis smitten, I am."

"If it's smitten ya' are," Rosie said, from the opened door, *"why* are ya' tellin' *him*, Angus MacGregor, and not me?"

Angus stared at her as she stood there, her hands on her hips, and an irate look on her face.

"Ye heard?" he said, his voice quiet. He looked at Moses, a pleading look upon his face, as though asking for help.

"Well?" Rosie said, approaching the foot of the bed. "Are ya' goin' to ask me your question, or not?" She stood there, looking formidable, Moses thought, and he was glad it wasn't him she was talking to.

Sarah entered the cabin, at that moment, suddenly aware of the anxious looks on the faces of *both* Moses *and* Angus. "What is it? What's going on?"

Rosie spoke first, standing where she was, her back to Sarah, her eyes on Angus. "This fine, old man has asked the *sheriff* if I will marry him," she said, and Sarah's mouth dropped open in surprise.

Moses looked at Sarah, shrugging his shoulders, looking almost as guilty as Angus. "Oh! And *will* you...ah...*marry* him?" Sarah asked.

"Not a chance!" Rosie replied, totally surprising everyone. Then she continued, "I've had me two fine husbands, child, both of 'em good men. But, neither one was afraid to ask me to wed!"

Angus gulped, and stirred upon the bed, sitting up, a grimace beginning to cross his face. "'Tis na' tha' I'm afeared t' ask ye, lass," he said. "'Tis afeared, I am, tha' ye'll turn me doon."

"Well, we'll never know, then, will we?" Rosie replied, and began to turn away.

"So...will ye have me, then, lassie, t' have and t' hold, in sickness and in health, fer richer, and all tha'? I'm asking ye, Rosie, me angel."

Rosie took two more steps, then turned back slowly, and both Moses and Sarah realized they were holding their breath! *"Indeed I will*, Mr. MacGregor. I thought ya'd never ask!" and with that, Rosie hurried to his side, and found herself wrapped tightly within the burly arms of the old Scot.

CHAPTER 36

The following morning, Rosie and Angus left for town in Sarah's old buggy, his old mule tied on behind, and Rosie fussing over him as though he was at death's door. Sarah and Moses stood in the doorway, enjoying the peace and quiet, glad to be alone, at last.

As they turned and went inside, Sarah noticed that Moses seemed troubled by something. He seemed distant, somehow, and paced back and forth before the fireplace as she washed off the table and gathered up the dirty dishes.

"Moses, is something wrong?"

"No," he replied, lowering himself into her father's larger rocker. But he sat there, staring pensively into the fire, and she knew something was bothering him.

"Not getting second thoughts, are you?" she said, walking over behind him and running her hands across his shoulders.

He was silent a long time before he finally spoke. "Sarah, there's something I have to tell you. I've just been trying to find the right time, and...well, I guess now's as good as any."

"What is it?" she asked, feeling a sense of uneasiness.

He reached up, taking her hand, and drew her around in front of him and onto his lap. She couldn't help but see the tension in his face, and wondered what was bothering him. "What is it?" she repeated. He ran his fingers over hers as though studying each of them, then raised her hand to his lips and kissed it.

"I don't want you to hear this from someone else," he said. "Best I tell you myself. It's about your father." She sat very still, not speaking, her heart racing in her chest. "I took your letter to your father, as you asked, darlin'. Told him you loved him. Told him you were gone...with Gray Eagle. Told him he was a good man and really loved you." Sarah watched the expression on his face, not saying anything. "He took it hard." Moses reached up, brushing an unruly wisp of hair from her cheek, then he continued. "He took it harder...*a lot harder* than we figured he would, I'm afraid." He paused, choosing his words, "I noticed that things didn't look right at the house, his house, about a week later. Realized I hadn't seen him or Rosie out and around town since I had told them. I got to wondering if they'd taken ill, or something. So we went over to pay 'em a visit...me, and Amos Culpepper." He tightened his arm around her waist, then sat quietly, looking at the bow on the blouse she wore.

"Go on," she said, when he had been silent too long.

He looked at her, sadness filling his eyes. Then he continued: "Rosie answered the door...not like now, all happy and bubbly, but looking like the worst tragedy in the world had occurred. Her hair was hanging down and her cheeks were tear-streaked. She looked like her heart was broken."

"*Why*? Where was my father? Tell me what happened!"

Moses ran a hand across his eyes. "Your father was...under the weather."

"Sick?" she questioned, jumping off his lap to stand closer to the fireplace, her back to him, her arms crossed over her breasts. Moses got up and went over to her, attempting to put his arms around her, once more. She shrugged him away, angrily. "Go on!" she demanded. "Is there more?"

"Yes," he said, his voice subdued. "He had been drinking ever since... that first day, and was out of his head from it."

"Go on!" she demanded.

"He didn't even recognize Amos or me, at first. He told Rosie to go get him more to drink and...well...he hit her."

"Oh, no! Oh, poor Father! And poor Rosie!" She was trembling now and had begun to cry.

Moses reached out slowly and she let him pull her into his arms.

"Sh-h, darlin', don't cry, don't cry." She sniffled a couple more times, then quieted.

"Is there more?" she asked, and he nodded, solemnly. "Tell me."

"Amos talked Rosie into going next door to stay with Amanda, while we tried to reason with Samuel. He was furious, and as belligerent as a drunken man can get. He began raving about all Indians being heathens and...other things...and I lost my temper. I'm sorry I did, but...well, I did. I told him that my mother was an Indian, and...for the time being, that quieted him down. But, soon, he had a lot of other things to say. Amos went to put on a pot of coffee to help sober him up, and I left. I felt like hitting him, Sarah, that's *why* I left! I *had to* get out of there, and away from the things he was saying about my mother and her people. *My* people!" Moses had tightened his arms around her as he talked, not realizing it, as his anger built, once more, at the memory of Samuel's words. She listened to the thud of his heart and felt his quickened breathing against her cheek, but said nothing, waiting for him to go on. Soon he did. "When I came back inside, Amos and I walked into the parlor where we'd left Samuel...and...before we had a seconds warning, he...shot me."

"*What!* My father wouldn't shoot you! *What are you saying?*" she cried, backing away from him.

"It's true, honey," he said, speaking quietly. "I thought I was a goner. Knocked me down. A perfect shot to the heart. Amos dropped the coffee he was carrying and ran to my side, fearing the worst. Your father was suddenly sober, saying over and over how sorry he was, that he didn't mean to do it."

"How can that be? How could he shoot you? *You,* of all people! And how could it be a perfect shot to the heart, if you're still here? Still *alive?* I don't understand," she cried.

"We didn't either, darlin'. Still don't, really. Amos tore open my shirt, looking to see how bad it was. I guess 'Somebody up there' was keeping His eye on me that day. The bullet hit directly in the center of my sheriff's badge and deflected away, putting a terrific dent in it. The gun was small, and really old. Maybe that explains it, too. I don't know."

Sarah stared at him without moving, one hand against her mouth. "It's *my* fault," she said. "It's *all* my fault."

"No, darlin', it's not your fault *Listen to me*...Samuel had good reason to hate Indians. But, not *all* Indians. He told us his reasons. Told us how he'd seen a family slaughtered by Indians, and...well...he had reason, believe me. Good reason."

"But, I almost got you *killed,* Moses!" she exclaimed. "It's all my fault. I was so selfish," she cried, her body trembling, shocked by the horrible possibilities. "And look how I hurt Father! Even my letter didn't ease his pain!"

Moses cleared his throat. "He never saw the letter, Sarah, he..."

"You never gave it to him?" she cried out.

"He burned it, darlin', without opening it."

"Oh, no!" she cried. "Oh, poor Father. He never knew how much I loved him, or..."

"He *did* know, Sarah, later. I went to see him, after...and we talked. Not just one night, but often. We *both* missed you, you see. I told him everything I remembered from your letter. He even planned to invite *both* of you to the house, if he heard you had come back and were at the cabin."

Sarah wiped her eyes on the back of her hand, a slight smile upon her face. "Do you think he forgave me, Moses? *Really?*"

"Yes, I do. He loved you, darlin', same as always, once he realized how wrong he had been to hate all Indians."

She looked up into his eyes, moving into his arms. "Can you forgive me?"

"Nothing to forgive you for. I love you, too, same as always."

CHAPTER 37

The time flew by quickly, before their wedding day. Moses got back into his usual routine as sheriff, relieving Amos Culpepper from his round-the-clock duties. Except for word of a stagecoach robbery near Black Dog Lake, all had gone smoothly. Jonas Hart had reported missing two head of cattle from his south pasture while Moses had been gone, and two ranch hands had gotten into a fight at the Lucky Lady Saloon and spent a night in jail, sobering up. Other than that, all was peaceful. Except for Melinda Rose filing a complaint that someone had made off with a nickel's worth of candy from her husband's store, that is. Other than that, all seemed peaceful.

Sarah, on the other hand, was running around in a dither, between fittings at Rosie's and tending to the planning of the wedding. She wanted her wedding dress to be the absolute best! One that fit her lifestyle, spoke volumes about her, and looked beautiful! She knew exactly the dress she wanted, and hoped she and Rosie could get it sewn and ready in time. She also went to see her friend, Lilly Hart. She enjoyed her comradery and all the news of things that had happened while she was away. She told Lilly of her life with Gray Eagle's people, the surprise encounter with John Bruce's long time friend—Angus MacGregor—and the troubles they had gone through on the journey back to Hastings, afraid that Angus would die before they could get there. She spent the whole day with Lilly and enjoyed herself, immensely.

However, everywhere else she went, she found herself the main topic of conversation. Lilly might not have changed toward her, as she knew she wouldn't, but Melinda Rose had been positively "catty" when she went into Dawson's General Store. As usual, the Dawson children were everywhere underfoot, chasing each other around the counters and squealing at the top of their lungs. Tommy had rushed up to say hello as soon as Sarah entered the store, but soon retreated into the back as Melinda Rose hurried forward, a youngster hanging onto her skirt, and another younger one in her arms.

"Heard you're marrying the sheriff?" she said, her first words to Sarah.

"Yes," Sarah replied, smiling happily.

"That'll be two half-breed husbands you'll have had," she remarked. Sarah stepped around her, ignoring her nasty words. "Don't plan to have any half-breed children, do you? Folk's may not take too kindly to that in Hastings."

"If I do, or if I don't, is none of your business. It seems you've forgotten, Melinda Rose, that if it hadn't been for Moses and me, you and Danny might not be here." Melinda Rose's mouth dropped open in surprise, and just as quickly she shut it. "Excuse me," Sarah said, and walked past her, glanced over toward Tommy, dodged two Dawson children, and left the store. Melinda Rose's comments had cost them a regular customer, and Sarah was certain she wasn't the only one who had had to endure such senseless and vicious barbs!

She crossed the street, list in hand, and never looked back, heading for the other general store in Hastings: the Mercantile. She had only been in it once before, when it first opened, and was surprised to see the nice variety of goods it now offered.

"May I help you?" a man asked as she stood there, looking around. He was a nice looking fellow about her own age, taller than Moses, of bigger build, with a friendly smile and brown eyes.

"I...I'd like to look around," she stammered.

"Certainly. I'm Cal, Cal Dunnevey. If you need any help, Miss, just call out."

Sarah nodded, realizing she was somewhat mesmerized by him, by his wonderful smile. Or, was it his manners, she thought, or the tone of his voice? Rather soft and...she turned away, scanning the counters and shelves for the items on her list, ignoring the slight blush she felt upon her cheeks. Here she was, an old woman of thirty-five—and about to be married—and she was gawking at some total stranger like a silly schoolgirl! She gathered up most of the items on her list, glancing over at him as he bent forward at a desk in the back, studying some figures in a ledger, a shock of brown hair falling forward across his forehead as he worked. He wore a white shirt and dark pants and she found herself thinking how handsome he looked, sort of rugged, yet refined.

She picked up a bolt of blue cloth, and to her complete embarrassment, dropped two or three of the smaller items she had been carrying. "Oh!" she exclaimed.

Cal Dunnevey hurried to her side and quickly bent down and picked up the items, then straightened, his eyes smiling kindly into hers. "No harm done, Miss. Here, let me take those for you," he said, taking the bolt of cloth from Sarah, who stood there feeling dumbstruck!

"I'm sorry, I'm not usually so...clumsy," she stammered.

He smiled at her, his brown eyes seeming to caress her as she stood there, his smile warm and gentle. "Can I get anything else for you?" he asked.

"Um...no," Sarah said, wondering why she couldn't concentrate. "Yes, yes you can," she said, changing her mind, certain her cheeks were on fire. "I'd like some...some chewing tobacco, for my...my "intended." We're getting married soon."

He went and got the tobacco, then added up her purchases, including the chewing tobacco for Moses, who did not happen to chew. Then wrapped her purchases and handed them to her.

Sarah paid her bill and thanked the man for his help.

"Glad to be of help," he replied. "Please come back."

"I will," she answered, gathering her parcels into her arms and leaving the store. She hummed as she crossed the street, feeling happier, somehow, though she could not explain why.

Cal Dunnevey watched the woman leave his store, glad for the first time, that he had moved to Hastings. He smiled as he looked at her beautiful auburn hair, silky as the finest fabric his store had to offer. And her eyes, he thought, like emerald pools. Their sparkling depth would be easy for a man to get lost in. Especially a man way out here in Hastings.

A man far from home and too long alone. He thought of how her dress had clung to her body, not indecently, but enough to start a hunger in a man who had spent too many nights without a woman's company.

"Well, I have to find out who that pretty lady is, that's for sure, and who her "intended" is, if there really is one," he said aloud. He had seen only one other woman who caught his fancy since he moved to Hastings, the year before. A schoolmarm by the name of Ophelia Denter, or Denton, something like that. And yes, she was pretty, but lacked the spark he detected in the beauty with the auburn hair and the tobacco-chewing "intended."

Yes, sir! Things were looking up in Hastings, he thought, and if he played his cards right, his nights of loneliness might soon be ending! He smiled, walking to the door to watch her cross the street, her auburn tresses shining like the rays of the sun.

CHAPTER 38

Sarah hurried across the street, wondering why she had acted so foolishly. How could she explain her purchase of chewing tobacco to Moses? Of course, she didn't have to explain it. He wasn't her husband, after all. Yet, why had she felt it necessary to buy it? But she knew the answer to that: To let that man, what was his name?—Cal, Cal Dunnevey—to let him know she was betrothed. To make certain he knew she was unavailable. She giggled as she walked toward Rosie's. It must have been his voice, she thought, or…maybe the way he looked, bent over his books, his shoulders so wide…not like Tommy's. Why he could have been a drover for the Crowley Ranch, with his build. That would be a job more suited to him, it seemed. But, a clerk at the Mercantile? Hardly! He was too powerfully built for that.

She tripped, nearly falling, not watching where she was going. It isn't like me to be so flustered over a chance encounter with a man. Gray Eagle never made me act so ridiculous, she thought, nor had Moses, if the truth be known. She walked slowly on, lost in her thoughts. Moses had aggravated her something fierce, with his devilish grin and rogue's smile, when she first met him. She smiled at the thought, thinking back to the day of Nancy's wedding. Moses had kept looking at her, teasing her as only he could, until she had gotten positively furious! But, Moses hadn't been at all like Cal Dunnevey. Dunnevey, for some reason she did not understand, was a force to be reckoned with! "Oh, well," she said aloud, "I'll just stay clear of him. That'll settle it!"

"Settle what, darlin'?" Moses asked, as he heard her words. He had nearly been run into by her as he came out of his office, though she was obviously unaware of it. He had fallen into step beside her, waiting for her to realize he was there, but she seemed lost in thought. He had tipped his hat to Mrs.O'Leary, who smiled and said, "Good morning, Sarah, Sheriff Gentry." But, Sarah had been too preoccupied with her own thoughts to even acknowledge the greeting. Must be the wedding, he supposed, all the plans and things to tend to. But then, she had spoken: 'I'll just stay clear of him. That'll settle it' and Moses had noticed how she jumped when he asked, "settle what, darlin'?"

"Oh! I didn't see you there." She stopped walking, looking up at him, obviously upset.

"I know," he replied. "I've been walking along with you ever since you crossed the street. What is it that you need to settle, darlin'?" She stared at him, her eyes widening, in what he took to be alarm. "Are you all right, Sarah? Did someone give you cause to be upset?"

"Of...of course not! Why Moses Gentry, where would you get such an idea? I'm just preoccupied, that's all. I have a *million* things to take care of...to...to *settle,* before our big day arrives, that's all!"

Moses saw how her cheeks flushed, reddening more, it seemed, with every word of her explanation. He didn't know why, but he did know that something—or someone—had upset her. Even to the point of making her keep the problem from him. Well, he meant to find out the reason—and settle it—himself! He wasn't deaf. He had clearly heard her say, 'I'll just stay clear of him.' If someone had been able to make her this upset, well, he meant to find out why! He leaned down, pressing a quick kiss on her forehead. "I've got work to do, darlin', best I let you get on with your shoppin'."

"Yes, I...I bought a few things at the...the Mercantile, but I still have a couple things on my list," she said, looking meek and apologetic, he thought. He turned and started across the street.

Sarah watched him go, noticing his easy stride and slim build. His dark hair, mixed with just a smattering of gray, against the collar of his coat. I love you, Moses Gentry, she thought. I do so love you.

Then, without intending to, she glanced back across the street at the Mercantile, to where Cal Dunnevey stood in the doorway, still watching her.

Moses crossed the street, heading toward the Mercantile. If Sarah had just come from there, obviously someone in it had upset her. As he neared it, he saw the owner, Cal Dunnevey, standing in the doorway. He was looking in the direction Sarah had gone, smiling a smile that spoke volumes! Moses stopped, turning his head to see the object of Cal's attention, although there was no need to confirm it. He already knew. Dunnevey was smiling at Sarah!

CHAPTER 39

Sarah stayed in town, at Rosie's, all the while her wedding dress was being made and Moses spent his nights at the jail, in his old bed. Nancy Pearly's father was lodged in the jail the first night, and complained loudly and harshly about the wrongs he had suffered in life. In particular, the injustice he was suffering now, by being locked up.

"So I fight a bit. Don't see that other fella being locked up. Weren't my fault!" he railed. Moses finally ordered him to shut up, and was mighty obliged when he did, though he grumbled to himself for a long while after that.

Moses lay on his cot, trying to find a comfortable position on its hard surface. He had spent the majority of nights, the past five years, staying out at Sarah's cabin, in a bed, while she was gone. There was a big difference between this cot and that bed! He turned and tossed—fairly comfortable, at last—trying to get to sleep. That was not to be, however, as his thoughts kept drifting back to the day Sarah had first shopped at the Mercantile and met Cal Dunnevey.

Moses had gone over to the Mercantile after, trying to find out just what had transpired to make her so upset. As he crossed the street, he saw Dunnevey standing in the doorway, smiling a smile that could only be construed as *trouble,* to a fellow less sure of his woman!

Moses lay on his bed, his eyes closed, remembering…"'Lo, sheriff, what can I do for you?" Dunnevey had called out, looking away from Sarah, and at the approaching lawman.

"Hello, Cal," Moses replied. "How's things going?"

"Pretty slow. Boring as can be, in fact, up 'till a minute ago," Dunnevey had answered, "when the most beautiful gal in the whole world walked into the store! You wouldn't happen to know her name, would you, sheriff? The gorgeous, red-haired filly over there, in the light green dress?"

Moses had smiled at him, choosing his words carefully. "Yup, I know her. Name's Sarah, Sarah Justus...soon to be Gentry." Dunnevey had stepped back, a look of total surprise upon his face. "Gentry? As in Mrs. *Moses* Gentry?"

"Yup," Moses had replied, rather enjoying himself.

"Well, I'll be! I had no idea, Moses. I hope you'll accept my sincere apology for...well, you know. It isn't often that a beauty like that comes in here. Where'd you meet her, if you don't mind me asking?"

"She and her father lived in a cabin west of town. A few years back, she married a fellow and moved away. To make a long story short, we were friends then. When her husband died, she came back to Hastings to get medicine for his people. I saw her safely back with the medicine and, well, here we are."

Dunnevey had reached out to shake Moses' hand, saying, "Well, congratulations then, Moses. Good thing I didn't see her first. Wouldn't have let a fine lady like that get away!"

"I know what you mean," Moses had replied, then walked over and picked up a box of bullets. "Guess I'll take these, Cal."

"You said she came back to get medicine for her husband's people. What people would that be, if I'm not being too nosey?" Cal asked.

"The Sioux," Moses had replied.

"Well, I'll be!" Cal exclaimed. "I knew, just by lookin', that she was a feisty gal!"

"You've got that right," Moses had answered, laughing. Then he asked the question that lay heavily on his mind. "You don't happen to know what upset her when she came to your store, do you?"

"Didn't realize she was upset...guess she was a little jumpy, now that you mention it, but, well...no offense, Moses, but maybe it was my charm that got to her, do you suppose?"

Moses had looked at the man who had been his friend ever since his move to Hastings the year before, when he bought the Mercantile.

He could tell he was joking, and hoped it was not the actual truth. "I suppose that could be it," he had replied.

Dunnevey had laughed then, and winked at Moses. "There had to be some reason your intended would buy chewing tobacco for you, when she knows you don't chew," he had stated, getting the last laugh.

Moses rolled over, shoving his pillow over to the other side of the cot, trying to fluff it up a little. "Darn!" he exclaimed, wondering why he couldn't get to sleep. He lay there, thinking again of the 'Dunnevey incident'. That evening, he had gone to Rosie's and visited with Rosie and Angus for awhile, then asked Sarah to join him for a walk. The night air was cold and crisp, he remembered, but it was their only chance for some privacy. As they walked along, Moses had brought up the subject, asking Sarah why she had seemed so preoccupied and upset when she left the Mercantile. She had looked sheepish, at first, then squared her shoulders and answered. She told him, then, of Melinda Rose's comments about their up-coming marriage, commenting about two "half-breed" husbands, meaning himself and Gray Eagle. She also told him her comments about the possibility of them having any "half-breed" children. Moses was glad she had walked out of Dawson's Store. It made him furious to think of Melinda Rose's insensitive and cruel remarks. No wonder she had been upset! Moses had waited to see if she would say anything else, and to his surprise, she did!

"The owner of the Mercantile upset me, too, Moses, but for the life of me, I can't rightly say why," she said. "He was polite, and helpful, but I had the feeling he was...don't laugh," she said, "smitten with me. He kept watching me and smiling the *nicest* smile, but I...well, I got so... so embarrassed, my face felt positively afire! I finally told him I needed to buy some chewing tobacco for my...intended! Isn't that silly? That was all I could think of at the time, to let him know I was spoken for." Timidly, she had taken the pouch of chewing tobacco from her pocket. "You couldn't take it back, could you, Moses? Tell him you quit the nasty habit, and I forgot?" He had to laugh, then, glad that *he*—and *not* Dunnevey—had seen her first!

The next day he had returned the chewing tobacco, telling Dunnevey that is was, *indeed*, his charm, that had made her buy it. Dunnevey then promised—man to man—to keep the full effect of his charm under wraps from then on, whenever the sheriff's beautiful lady graced his humble shop.

Moses wondered, as sleep continued to elude him, if someone like Cal Dunnevey might not make a better husband for Sarah. Cal was a prominent businessman, excelling in all facets of the Mercantile trade. He wasn't rich, but he had a steady income: one that grew as his business grew. Plus, he's a nice dresser, putting my buckskins to shame, Moses thought. And he's schooled, and well-read, you could tell that, just from talking to him. And, as he himself readily admitted, he does have a great deal of charm. In fact, I can't see why some pretty gal hasn't already set her brand on him. He rolled over onto his stomach, all tangled in the blanket now, and kicked it to straighten it somewhat, stretching out his legs. Plus, he happens to be more Sarah's age—about thirty-five, not pushin' forty-five—like I am. He groaned, as he thought of how age had saddled him with the usual old man's aches and pains. "Well, I had better start thinking young, again," he said aloud. "By this time next week, I'll have me a pretty, young wife to satisfy." And with that thought in mind, he finally drifted off to sleep.

CHAPTER 40

With only a short time left before the wedding, Sarah returned to her cabin, cleaning it thoroughly, from top to bottom. She enjoyed the peace and quiet. Her only visitor was Michael O'Leary, who dropped by daily, to do the chores and oversee the property. He was an extremely conscientious young man, and a hard worker, and Sarah was happy to see all the progress he had made in the management of her place. Thanks to Moses and him, it was no longer a small spread, but a much larger and very prosperous undertaking. Moses had acquired two hundred acres on the west side of her original property, while she was gone, and easily tripled the size of her herd! Even the chickens had grown from half a dozen, to thirty or more, and every day on his way back to town, Michael sold eggs. Not only at the homes in town, but to both Dawson's Store *and* to the Mercantile.

Moses had insisted Michael supply his mother, Kathleen O'Leary, with all the eggs, cream, and milk she needed to keep her household running well, and that any and all egg money was to be given to her to spend as she saw fit. Though Mr. O'Leary had left no stone unturned in his effort to support his large family, when he had died—unexpectedly, two years earlier—they were, again, suddenly back to eking out a meager existence and barely getting by. When Moses had discovered their situation, and the hardships they were experiencing, he immediately set about hiring Michael to mend the fences and manage the operation, making certain he could provide more and more security for his family. Before long, as the herd grew, he had seen to it that they had a cow and some chickens of their own. He let Michael work off the cost of the animals—an extremely small amount—so he would not feel like they were a charity case.

Sarah smiled, thinking what a kind-hearted and caring man Moses was. She felt so lucky that she would soon become his wife. Sarah Gentry, she thought, Mrs. Moses Gentry! There was nothing she wanted more! She sat down in her rocker before the fire, her sewing on her lap. She was mending the tear in Moses' old shirt. She shivered as she realized it was not a tear, but the slit where Spotted Dog's knife had stabbed into the shirt, when they had fought. She was glad Spotted Dog was dead. Glad that she could sleep easy from now on, never seeing the vicious hatred in his eyes as she had, so many, many nights after he had raped her, killing the child inside her. Ever since Moses had told her he was dead, she had felt relieved! He had also told her that Spotted Dog had made claim to having killed Gray Eagle. She didn't know *how* he had died, only that he *had* died, and Spotted Dog had been in possession of John Bruce's Bowie knife. The same knife she had given to Gray Eagle, after John was killed while protecting her.

She quit sewing, folding her hands in her lap, her thoughts turning to her mother. "Can you hear me, Mother?" she said, into the silence of the room. "I'm going to be married Sunday, over at Reverend Higgin's little church. To a good man, who loves me with all his heart, just as I love him. I wish you could be here to share my happiness, you and Father." She paused a few moments, then added: "I'm sorry, Father, for all the pain I caused you. I love you *both* so very much."

As she finished, there was a knock on the door, and Moses called out, "Sarah, open the door, my hands are full!"

She got up and hurried to the door, overjoyed at his surprise visit. His arms were full of packages, both large and small! "Moses!" she exclaimed, taking some of them from him and brushing the snow off. It had begun snowing earlier that afternoon, large fluffy flakes that melted almost as quickly as they landed. Now, she saw that more had fallen, and she brushed off not only the packages, but Moses' coat and hat.

"What have you got here?" she asked, surprised.

"Wedding presents," he said, grinning at her. "Go on, open them. Rosie said you didn't have to wait." In the largest, which Sarah opened first, was a beautiful quilt in a variety of rich colors.

Sarah cried out, upon seeing it! "That'll keep us warm," Moses said, enjoying seeing the pleasure she felt. Next, she opened a small box. In it lay a soft, muslin gown, its bodice decorated with tiny, pink satin rosebuds. Every tiny stitch, hand-sewn by Rosie. "Rosie said you needed a proper gown for our wedding night," Moses explained, smiling his rogue's smile, as Sarah's face reddened. She held the lovely gown against her cheek, feeling the softness of the fabric, tears filling her eyes.

"She did *all this* for me?" she said, not believing the great kindness Rosie had bestowed.

"Well, I do believe *part* of those things are for *my* enjoyment, too," Moses drawled. Sarah laughed and threw her arms around him, kissing him soundly upon the lips.

A third box contained a healthy supply of medicinal herbs and a bottle of whiskey. "Don't know if this is for medicinal purposes, or for celebrating our wedding night," Moses questioned, holding up the bottle.

Sarah giggled. "You won't be needing that bottle on our wedding night, Mr. Gentry, unless it *is* for medicinal purposes!"

Moses let out a hearty laugh and pulled her onto his lap in her father's rocking chair. "Now, I've got a little somethin' for my "bride-to-be," he said, and he handed her a small box, wrapped in white paper. Sarah took it, her eyes dancing with joy, and quickly began to unwrap it! Inside was a silver bracelet, with tiny turquoise stones all around it. Each stone sat in the center of a small silver setting shaped like flowers. Sarah squealed with delight and let him fasten it around her wrist. "This was my mother's, darlin'. She gave it to me just before I left home. I vowed I would keep it always, to remember her by. No one else has worn it, or even seen it, 'till now. I want you to have it. Maybe someday, you can give it to our daughter, or son." She nestled against him, kissing his cheek, and then his lips. Moses held her, very aware of the effect she was having on him. He was glad that she would be his wife in only two days, and then he would never have to hold her at arm's length again. He enjoyed one more kiss, then pushed her gently off his lap and away from him. "I have to go, darlin'...unless you want an *early* wedding night!"

"Well..." she drawled, teasingly.

He stood up, swatting her on the backside, then started for the door. "I'll see you, tomorrow, darlin', and *forever*, the day after that!" he said, closing the door behind him.

Sarah blew him a kiss, then picked up the beautiful quilt and began to twirl around and around with it in her arms, singing a tune her old friend, Cassandra Winthrop, had taught her, many years before.

CHAPTER 41

The next morning Sarah left for Rosie's. The snow was still falling, its lovely pristine whiteness blanketing the ground to nearly a foot. Sarah pulled on her Indian moccasins and favorite dress, braiding her hair in a single, thick braid down the center of her back. Pulling on an old hat to keep the snow off her head, she walked out to the barn where Michael had Glory all fed, saddled, and ready to go. In just a moment, she was on her way!

She planned to spend the rest of the day and that night at Rosie's, going to Lilly's early the next morning. Lilly had agreed, readily, to be her Matron of Honor, and was almost as excited as Rosie about the wedding! Only one thing worried Sarah. She had asked Moses if he had chosen a "best man," even going so far as to suggest Amos, or Jonas, or Doc. But, to her dismay, he told her that he had already taken care of it, and not to worry! But, it *did* worry her, because he refused to tell her whom he had chosen. Everything else had gone along smoothly, so although she could imagine how embarrassed he would be if no best man showed up, she knew he could always ask someone else. After all, Amos, Jonas, and Doc would be there. Finally, she decided she was being foolish to worry, knowing Rosie was worrying enough for all of them! Poor Rosie! She was rushing around—in a dither—cooking, cleaning, praying, and worrying, far more than *anyone* else! Even more than I am, Sarah thought.

Angus was much better now, and often puttered around in Rosie's way, asking what he could do to help. He still called her his "angel," and seemed unable to be near her without patting her hand or arm. It was so obvious he was smitten, that even if he had denied it—which he didn't—only a blind fool could have missed it.

Rosie told Sarah he had proposed three or four times, and remarked that, 'of course they would get Sarah and Moses' wedding over with first,' but as soon as the hustle and bustle from *that* was over, he meant to claim his sweet angel, in front of Reverend Higgins, the goodly folks of Hastings, and *all* the saints! Rosie had giggled, saying she had told him to hush, then sent him into the parlor or off for a walk about town.

In a matter of days, he had introduced himself to nearly all the residents of Hastings, and counted the majority of them his friends. It seemed they could not help liking the old Scot, with his tall tales and jovial manner. He often bought a bag of penny candy for treating the children he encountered on his walks, and soon had a regular entourage surrounding him, everywhere he went.

They would listen, enraptured, all vying for his attention, as he told them of his many adventures as a trapper and prospector. Many a young lad decided to follow in his footsteps, as he told them his tales, embellishing them "just a wee bit" in the telling!

Sarah also knew that many times, he dodged his young followers and went to stand at John Bruce's grave. She had seen him there, more than once, talking to his deceased friend as though death had not separated them. One day in particular, she had passed him at the cemetery gate while going to visit her father's grave, and found, not only a handful of colorful leaves adorning John's grave, but two or three candies! When she told Moses about it, he had laughed, making a comment about Angus being a bit strange. She thought him sentimental and sweet.

CHAPTER 42

November Ninth came at last. The snow had stopped falling at dawn, and lay like diamonds upon the ground, making everything white and sparkling.

Sarah felt like a young girl, full of hope and pure delight at what lay ahead. She walked downstairs—tiptoeing quietly—so as not to wake anyone, but found Angus at the table, in an old shirt and pants of her father's, sipping a steaming cup of coffee. His eyes twinkled merrily as he spotted her, and he quickly got out another cup, and poured her a coffee.

"G'mornin', lass. 'Tis a fine day fer a weddin'," he said. Sarah nodded in agreement. "I been wantin' t' talk t' ye, lassie," he said, as she sat down at the table across from him. "Seems like now's the only time we might have, fer when me angel wakes, ye know how busy 'twill be." Sarah asked what he wanted to talk to her about. "Well, lass, seems t' me, ye've a fine lad, soon t' be yer husband, and a lovely step-mum who loves ye like ye was her verra ain. But…well, I du na' want t' offend ye…" he paused, reaching over to take her hand, "ye see, lass, 'tis most honored I'd be t' walk ye t' yer groom. T' represent yer father, if 'twould please ye. Rosie says he was a fine man, who loved ye dearly, and I dinna' think it fittin' ye make tha' walk alone." He waited for her to comment, hoping he had not upset her.

Sarah started to smile, then squeezed his hand. "Angus, I would be honored to have you walk me down the aisle," she said. "I can't think of anything I'd like better." She leaned over and kissed his cheek, touched by his thoughtfulness, and couldn't help noticing the look of pure joy upon his face.

By noon they were all at the church. Moses paced back and forth on the steps, looking anxiously down the road. Lilly was dressed in a high-necked, light cream-colored dress, and kept fussing with Sarah's hair. Sarah wore it pulled back off her face with long, wispy curls hanging nearly to her waist in back. The lovely tortoiseshell comb Moses had given her, long before, to one side. Her dress had been handmade by Rosie to Sarah's own specifications, and she knew Moses would greatly appreciate the gesture. It was a soft buckskin with wrist-length sleeves and long matching fringe all around the hem and on the sleeve seams from under her arms to her wrists. Across the bodice was beadwork in turquoise, closely resembling the design of the turquoise bracelet Moses had recently given her. Beads formed the shape of a hawk on the side of one of her moccasins, and the shape of a red bird, on the other, to commemorate their Indian names. She knew Moses would not miss the symbolism. And lastly, she wore the turquoise bracelet he had given her.

She smiled at Lilly, who had her hands full, trying to assure Rosie that all was well. You would have thought it was her *very own* wedding, to see her!

Reverend Higgins had Mrs. Carson, proprietor of the boarding-house, begin to play the piano, while the townsfolk shuffled into the church. Ophelia Denton came in with Johnathon Clark, followed by Doc and his missus, who shook hands all around and then took a seat near the middle of the church. Mrs. O'Leary came in with all six O'Leary children. Each looked freshly scrubbed and in their "Sunday-best." They sat quietly, beside Jonas and Eli, and smiled often. Kevin Landford and Jay Bullard rode over from the ranch, their hair smoothed down and shy smiles on their faces, and Jasmine LaRue and Ruby Deegs arrived, dressed in the fanciest dresses anyone had ever seen! Jasmine's was rose-colored satin with yards and yards of lace, and Ruby's had thin, vertical stripes with a high, ruffled collar and tight bodice.

Lilly peeked out of the ladies dressing room—actually Reverend Higgin's office—looked around, then quickly pulled her head back inside and shut the door.

"Who's all here? Did you see Moses?" Sarah asked, fanning her face, which was getting quite red from all the excitement.

"Moses is still out on the steps," Lilly answered.

"Waiting for his best man," Sarah remarked. "I knew it! I knew he'd..."

"Now don't you go worrying, child," Rosie cut in. She had straightened everything in the room, more than once, sighing as she did so. "Moses knows what he's doing," she added, giggling as if she knew some great secret.

"Rosie..." Sarah began, but Rosie interrupted her, again. "I have to go take my seat. Now don't you worry, love, everything will be just fine." She hurried over to Sarah, giving her a kiss on the cheek, her eyes filling with tears. "If I'd had a daughter of my very own, lovey, I'd have wanted her to be *exactly* like you!" She squeezed Sarah's hand and dried her eyes, saying, "I'm proud to be your step-mom," and sniffled back more tears as she quickly left the room.

Sarah paced back and forth, her heart racing, anxious to get underway. "Who else is out there?" she asked Lilly, who peeked out, trying to see. "It's late. We should have started by now."

"Well, let's see. There's Amanda and Amos Culpepper. They just came in. You should see them, Sarah, they look so cute. She's holding his hand like they're newlyweds. Isn't that nice? Oh, and Tommy and Melinda Rose and their bunch are here."

"I hope they don't make a racket," Sarah said, shaking her head.

"Well, just about everyone from town is out there. Shall I peek out again?"

"Oh, do! Please." Sarah replied.

Lilly opened the door, just a crack, then let out a gasp, shutting it with a bang!

"What's wrong? What is it?" Sarah asked, clutching her stomach as she saw the look of shocked surprise on Lilly's face. "What is it, Lilly, *tell me!*" she ordered.

Lilly leaned against the door, looking at Sarah, her eyes wide with astonishment. "I...ah, Moses' best man has arrived, that's all," Lilly said, blocking the door so Sarah could not see out.

"Heaven's sake, it's about time," Sarah replied, relieved that he had finally arrived, but not able to understand Lilly's strange reaction.

Just then, the wedding music began to play, and Angus MacGregor knocked softly on the door. "Ready, lass?" he asked, as she opened the door and stepped out, taking his arm. She was surprised by the total silence in the church. There wasn't a *sound* from the well-wishers, not a whisper, cough, or sniffle! Only the music, sweet and clear. She squeezed the old Scot's arm as they walked around the corner from the vestibule, and then she stopped! Her mouth dropping open in surprise! In the last pew sat Chief Standing Elk, his wife, Wind Runner, Little Moon, and four braves that she recognized at once! Each looking dreadfully uncomfortable being there. When they saw her, however, they all smiled happily. Sarah met their smiles with one of her own, then looked toward the front of the church. To her surprise, Howling Wolf stood there, dressed in leggings and fine buckskin shirt. A bear claw necklace hung at his neck, atop his dentalium shell breastplate, and a cluster of Eagle feathers graced his long black hair. He stood tall and proud beside Moses as his best man!

Moses was also dressed in buckskins and was smiling at her like he had pulled off the very best surprise of all, which he had! She smiled at him, shaking her head, then glanced at the many townsfolk who all stood watching her. Some smiled, some looked as though they expected to be scalped at any moment. For once, even the Dawson children were totally quiet!

"Shall we go, lass?" Angus whispered to her, and they began to walk down the aisle. Sarah was so happy and nervous, she was afraid she might faint, but kept her eyes on Moses' face, concentrating on his beaming smile. Howling Wolf smiled, too, looking handsome in his native attire. She was delighted that she had chosen to wear the finely decorated buckskin dress Rosie had helped her sew, knowing it would mean *so much*, not only to Moses, but also to Standing Elk and his people.

As they reached the front, Angus kissed her lightly on the cheek, his fluffy white beard tickling her chin and neck. Then he did a little jig, a happy grin upon his face. Rosie's face blushed scarlet at his antics, and she waved him into the pew beside her, flustered by the soft laughter that could be heard throughout the small church.

Moses took Sarah's hand and Reverend Higgins began to speak, but to everyone's surprise, Sarah interrupted him. "Wait, please, wait one minute, Reverend Higgins," she said, reaching beneath the neck of her dress to bring forth the medallion Moses had given her as a token of their engagement. "Moses, as we stand here to be married," she said, "I think it's only fitting that *you* wear the medallion that you gave me as a symbol of your love for me. I give it back to you now as a symbol of the love I, too, feel for you." She reached up, slipping the long leather strip over his head. The medallion his mother had given him when he was young, now hung at his neck: a symbol of love, as it had *always* been! "Please continue," she said to the reverend, noticing the moistness in Moses' eyes, and she had all she could do not to bust out crying, she was so filled with love for him.

CHAPTER 43

Reverend Higgins spoke their vows clearly, and Sarah and Moses repeated after him, both their voices choked with emotion. When he asked if anyone knew any reason why they should not wed, Cal Dunnevey cleared his throat loudly, and Moses squeezed Sarah's hand, winking at her. She blushed crimson, recognizing Dunnevey's attempt at teasing, and looked down at the floor in embarrassment. Rosie was crying softly and sniffling, and every so often, a whispered word of comfort could be heard from Angus. Tommy and Melinda Rose's children were so shocked to find themselves in a church with Indians, that they never so much as whispered, just stared and pointed! Amos and Amanda Culpepper sat side by side, her dainty hand enclosed within his large one. She dabbed at her eyes often during the ceremony, and when she did, Amos would pat her arm tenderly and smile at her.

Then, Reverend Higgins pronounced them man and wife, and Moses kissed Sarah—a kiss that even Cal Dunnevey doubted *he* could top, when he found a "lady-love" of his own. Everyone clapped and smiled happily, while Sarah and Moses rushed down the aisle. They stopped, only when Chief Standing Elk and the other Indians rose and walked— with heads held high—from the church and over to their waiting horses.

No one noticed the stricken look on Angus MacGregor's face and how he had fallen back against the pew, one hand upon his heart. Rosie, too, was half-way down the aisle when she realized he was not at her side. She turned, the color draining from her cheeks as she rushed back to him. "Angus, what is it? Oh, Lord, is it yer heart, my love? Angus, tell me what's wrong!" she cried.

Angus stared at her a moment as thoughts raced through his head, then he told her he'd had a wee shock, but not to worry. "Go run along, me angel," he said, his voice subdued as she had seldom heard it. "Go congratulate the lass and laddie. I'll be along shortly. Soon's I catch me breath. Go on now, go on." Rosie refused, at first, not wanting to leave his side, but he insisted, telling her he needed a moment to himself. She was hesitant, but finally did as he asked.

The townsfolk stood back, gawking and listening, as Chief Standing Elk spoke to the newlyweds. They looked surprised when Sarah answered him in his native tongue, and then reached out to embrace the two Indian women. Standing Elk presented the couple with a gift of two fine elk hides, and Howling Wolf handed Moses a tomahawk that he had made, while both Little Moon and Wind Runner each gave Sarah a lovely willow basket. Then the Indians mounted their horses, all except Howling Wolf, who stood by Moses, reaching out to shake his hand. "It was good to be here, my brother," he said, in perfect English, smiling at Moses. "May Wakantanka watch over you, Black Hawk, and give you and Red Bird many moons together." Then, with loud, sharp cries of joy, he leapt onto his horse and raced off with Chief Standing Elk and the others on the long journey back to their village. Moses and Sarah felt honored that their Indian friends had ridden for days to share this special time with them, but both felt great sadness to see them go, not knowing when they would see them again.

As the townsfolk wished them well, shaking their hands and kissing their cheeks, Moses grinned at Sarah. Bending close so only she could hear, he whispered: "Wedding night, at last, darlin'." Sarah blushed, and was about to whisper back a terse remark, when Cal Dunnevey approached.

"Congratulations," he said. "I guess now I'll have to keep looking for a beauty of my own."

"You can be sure of that," Moses replied, and Sarah was certain she blushed red, clear to her toes! Cal reached out his hand to her then, a smile upon his face. "I hope you don't take any offense to my teasing, Mrs. Gentry. Your husband is one lucky man...*and* a good friend of mine. I hope you will be, too."

Sarah took his hand, feeling the pulse in her temples pounding like crazy. "Then I needn't buy any more chewing tobacco, Mr. Dunnevey?" she asked, and both men burst out laughing.

"No, ma'am. You need not," he replied, adding, "but, from now on, please call me Cal."

It was at that moment Rosie appeared in the doorway of the church, wringing her hands, pale as the dress she wore.

"Rosie, what is it?" Sarah asked, as she saw how upset she looked.

Moses turned his attention to her, too, placing a hand upon her arm. "Rosie, what's wrong? Where's Angus?"

"He's in there," she replied, pointing back inside the church. "Oh, I'm afeared I'm goin' to lose him," she cried, clutching Sarah's hands, as Moses ran up the church steps and down the aisle.

When he reached the front pew, Angus was sitting there, leaning forward, his head in his hands. He looked up at Moses, studying him, it seemed. A strange look upon his face.

"Angus, what is it?" Moses asked, seeing how pale the old Scot looked. "Do you need the doctor? Doc Valentine's right outside."

"Nae... nae, laddie. 'Tis na' a doctor I be needin'."

"Then, what is it? You're pale as a ghost. What's wrong?"

"I've had me a bit o' a shock, lad, 'tis all. A *mighty* shock, 'tis true. I'll be all right in a wee bit."

Moses sat down beside him. He'd grown to treasure the old man's friendship, and knew that everyone who had met him felt the same, especially Rosie. "Do you want me to get Rosie, Angus? She's beside herself with worry."

"Nae, lad, I'm fine. Too ornery t' dee. Ye might say *'twas* a ghost I saw today. Aye, a...a ghost...an' I'll be tellin' ye aboot it, later, when the celebratin' is done."

"All right," Moses said. "If you're sure you're all right."

"Aye, lad. Tha' I am. Tha' I am."

Sarah had rushed in as he spoke, an anxious look upon her face. "Moses..." she began.

"He'll be all right, just...ah...saw a *ghost*" he said, one eyebrow raising, slightly. She looked at Angus, then at Moses. "Come on, darlin'. He wants to sit a bit," Moses said. And they went outside to calm Rosie, and talk with their guests.

CHAPTER 44

Folks gathered just down the road, at Lilly and Jonas' farm, to celebrate the Gentry wedding. Tables were piled high with food, and music spilled from the barn, filling the crisp night air.

Cal Dunnevey danced nearly every dance with the two gals from the Lucky Lady Saloon, managing to break in on Moses for a dance, or two, with Sarah. He was an excellent dancer, and Sarah had to admit she enjoyed dancing with him. Moses, on the other hand, stepped on her toes almost as often as he stepped down, causing her to beg out of most dances with him.

The celebration was in full swing when to most folk's surprise, Old Man Pearly arrived. He was unshaven, and clearly half-drunk, but there he was: not quite as mad at the world and as cantankerous as usual, but they were certain that would change before the night was through.

Sarah couldn't believe how happy she felt! It was certainly different, she thought, from her wedding to Gray Eagle! She thought of how they had been married in the bedroom of Silas and Nancy's house, just after Nancy had given birth to their baby, young Sarah. It made her smile, when she remembered how upset she had gotten with the preacher, Reverend Woods, because of all his loud and overly enthusiastic "caterwauling," as she had thought it. Yes, she thought, this is a much happier occasion, with all our friends attending and everyone laughing, and dancing. She thought of her dear friend, John Bruce, then. How she wished he could have been here to enjoy the festivities with her and Moses! And wouldn't Angus have been happy to see him! That would have been a reunion worth seeing! She would have had *him* walk her down the aisle, if only...she shook her head, her eyes filling with tears, then looked across the room at her new husband as he danced with Ophelia. Yes, John would have been happy for her, she knew that for a fact, and *that's* what she would "hang on to," whenever he came to mind!

Melinda Rose seemed on her best behavior, Sarah noticed, though Tommy didn't look all that happy. He had asked her to dance, once, but wasn't talkative, like he usually was. He seemed to have a lot on his mind. She wondered if they were having troubles, or if he was angry because she no longer shopped at his store. But this was not the time, or the place, to worry about that. Whatever the problem was, his children seemed unaffected. They ran amongst the dancing couples, squealing and carrying on, in their usual manner. Sarah noticed that many of the older women shook their heads in disgust at their wild, ill-mannered ways, whispering and nodding toward Melinda Rose, who seemed oblivious to it.

Though the night air was crisp, the dancers worked up a sweat as the music continued, long into the night. People helped themselves to the wide array of dishes and many of the men took seconds. It was a celebration to remember, and Sarah and Moses enjoyed themselves thoroughly, as did everyone else, it seemed. Except, perhaps, Old Man Pearly, who had been miserable so long that everyone *expected* him to be miserable!

As the night drew on and both the musicians and the dancers gradually became more and more tired, Moses finally pulled Sarah aside. "Darlin', it's about time we head for home, what do you say?"

She smiled up at him, happiness showing upon her face. "I agree, Mr. Gentry. My feet are killing me."

"I'm afraid you can blame that on me," he said.

"That's a fact!" she agreed, laughing.

"I promised Angus we'd stop at Rosie's for a few minutes, if you don't mind, so I guess we should go." They went and got their coats, thanking everyone for coming. Sarah hugged Lilly and thanked her for everything, while Moses thanked Jonas, who walked out with him to get their buckboard. Jonas had carried their wedding presents out earlier and put them into the back, covered with a heavy blanket. Another horsehair robe lay in front for the newlyweds to cover their feet and legs with. Moses shook Jonas' hand and told him to come visit soon. Then he drove to where Sarah stood, talking to Lilly.

Minutes later, they were on their way to Rosie's, snuggled close, Moses' arm around Sarah's shoulders. The moon was shining out across the snow, its silvery rays glistening like diamonds around the happy couple.

It was nearly ten o'clock when they arrived at Rosie's. "Let's see what Angus wants, and then go have that wedding night you've been promising me," Moses said, helping Sarah down from the buckboard.

She smiled, reaching up to touch his cheek with one hand. "I love you, Moses."

"And I, you," he replied, kissing her on the end of her nose.

The door opened slightly, then, and Rosie peeked out. They were surprised to see she still looked upset.

"What is it, Rosie? Is he all right?" they asked.

"It's worried, I am," she said, holding the door wide for them. "He went in to bed, soon as we got home. Said you had better things to do tonight than spend it here. Said he needed to do some more thinkin', before he talked to you." She wrung her hands, continuing, "I peeked in on him, just before you arrived, and he's snoring like a baby, so I don't know what to think."

"If he's asleep," Moses ventured, "why don't we let him rest, and we'll come by tomorrow and get to the bottom of this. We're…ah…*all* a bit tired."

"Yes, yes, I suppose it's best he rests," Rosie agreed. "Oh, it just sets a gal to worrying, to see a fellow so stricken."

"Especially if she loves him," Sarah said, squeezing Moses' hand, gently.

"Heaven sakes! It's your weddin' night, and here ya' stand, talkin' to an old woman! You children run along home. We'll be all right. I'll get Doc if…if…well, you know." Rosie reached out quickly, hugging first Sarah, then Moses. "Come for lunch tomorrow. You'll be all rested, by then."

Moses grinned, and Sarah poked him, then they told Rosie good night. They'd come by around two in the afternoon, they said. Then, at last, the Gentry's headed home. They had waited a *lifetime*, it seemed, to have their wedding night, and *nothing* was going to interfere any longer!

CHAPTER 45

It was nearly one in the afternoon when the newly married couple finally vacated their bed. It had been a night well worth waiting for, and they felt satisfied and content. Moses stroked Sarah's arm as she began to stir, and before long, they were—once again—passionately entwined.

"We'll be late," Sarah said, nibbling on one of Moses' ear lobes.

"I really could care...*oh!*...less, darlin'," he replied, once again exploring the beautiful curves and hollows of his bride. Sarah had responded to his love-making as passionately as ever he had dreamed! The heat of their bodies driving *both* on and on, to one explosive climax after another, 'till they lay back—exhausted and panting—drenched with sweat.

"Moses, we have to go," Sarah said, then laughed, "unless you think she really meant two o'clock *tomorrow* afternoon?" She giggled, running her hand across his chest, suggestively.

"I'd like to think so, darlin', but I'm afraid I wouldn't be *able* to get up, by then!"

"Well, we'd better be on our way, my love," she said, and slid over him and off the bed. He groaned, grinning seductively, as that old devilish grin of his stirred feelings once more within her.

She shook her head. "Let's save some of this for later," she teased, putting some water on to heat, so they could bathe.

"Sounds like a great idea," he replied, getting out of bed and picking up his pants. Sarah smiled at the sight of him, his bare backside so much whiter than the tanned skin on his neck and arms.

"You've got a cute backside, Mr. Gentry," she teased, unable to resist saying it.

"Not near as cute as *yours,* darlin'. Is that tub big enough for two?" he asked, grinning.

They arrived at Rosie's at three, Moses explaining that "chores" had taken a bit longer. Sarah felt her face grow hot with embarrassment at Moses' very obvious lie, but Rosie was still concerned with Angus, and didn't seem to notice.

Angus had gotten up early, assuring her that he was fine. After a hearty breakfast—his demeanor noticeably more cheerful—he told her he had some business to tend to in town and would be back shortly. He assured her he felt *absolutely fine! Better*, in fact, than he had in *years*! When she still protested that he wasn't up to a walk, he swung her around in his arms, then danced a lively jig, moving his arms like a chicken's wings, and humming a lively Scottish tune.

She couldn't help herself, and soon began to relax and laugh with him. Ah, how I love ya', she thought, and you love me, too, of that I have no doubt. "Angus MacGregor, you wrap up warm, you hear? I don't want to spend *all* my days nursin' ya' back to health."

He smiled at her, that twinkle that she treasured so dearly, once again in his big, blue eyes. "I'll be back soon, me lovely lass, and I'll be tellin' ye a tale tha' will bring bonnie tears o'joy t' yer heart!" And with those words, he wrapped his well-worn, red woolen capote around him and went out the door.

Sarah and Moses were getting a bit concerned about Angus, too, when he still hadn't returned by three. But just as Moses reached for his coat to go in search of him, he came through the door, his nose and cheeks red from the cold.

"Ah, here's the wedded couple," he said. "Me congratulations t' ye both!"

They thanked him, as Rosie began setting bowls of hearty rabbit stew and warm, buttered biscuits on the table. "Wash up, then come and eat," she ordered, glancing at Angus.

"Ah, me angel, if 'tis washin' ye want, 'tis washin' I'll du," he replied, winking at the younger couple, and went to wash his hands.

He had hung his wrap on a hook by the door, and they noticed a large envelope sticking out of his shirt pocket. When he was finished, they all sat down together, and after Rosie said a short prayer, ate their fill of her delicious stew.

When they were done, Angus bid them all come into the parlor. Moses and Sarah smiled at the old man's excited manner; both wondering what he could possibly have to tell them. Rosie sat across the room, asking if anyone wanted coffee, or a piece of cake. "Na' now, me angel, na' now," Angus said, looking at her and shaking his head. She sat quietly then, looking at him expectantly. Sarah sat down on the arm of the chair where Moses was sitting, also looking at the old Scot rather expectantly. There was a long moment of silence, and then Angus spoke: "First o' all, I need t' ask ye a question, er two, laddie," he said, looking at Moses.

"All right," Moses replied, gently running his hand back and forth across Sarah's back, and shifting a bit, to get more comfortable. He knew, first hand, how long some of Angus MacGregor's stories could be.

"I need t' ken—t' know—whaur ye got tha' thaur necklace ye have 'round yer neck."

"My mother gave it to me," Moses replied, wondering what on earth the old man had in mind.

"And wha' was her name?" Angus asked, watching Moses intently.

"She was an Indian," Moses answered. "It was Singing Raven—of the Blackfoot Nation." He expected a reaction from Angus, but there was none. Only a slight smile upon his lips.

"And yer father?"

"His name was Frank...Frank Gentry, the meanest son of a..." Moses caught himself before finishing, remembering that there were two ladies present. "Meanest fellow I ever met."

Angus rubbed his chin and thought a bit, before continuing. "Can I ask how auld ye are, lad?"

"I'm forty-four, be forty-five on July nineteenth."

Angus slapped his knee in delight, shouting, "I knew it! Saints be praised! I knew it!" causing his unsuspecting audience to jump in surprise. He laughed heartily then, while the others stared at him.

Then, he became serious again. "Can I see tha' thaur necklace... er... "medallion," as ye call it, laddie?"

"Sure can," Moses replied, and pulled it off and handed it to him.

Angus studied it a long time, turning it over in his hands as carefully as if it were extremely fragile. When he looked up, they saw that tears glistened in his eyes. He sniffled, more than once, pulling a large red hanky from his back pants pocket, wiping his eyes, and blowing his nose a resounding blow. Then he handed the medallion back to Moses. There was total silence throughout the room.

"Well, I guess I can tell ye 'boot the "ghost" I seen at church yesterday," he said, "'twas the ghost o' me friend, Johnny Bruce, t' be sure."

Moses patted Sarah's back lightly and smiled at her, wondering how long the old Scot's tale would last. He wished they could go home and resume their love-making. Sarah smiled back at him, and he was certain she had guessed what was on his mind. Rosie shifted in her chair, getting more comfortable, also knowing how long and drawn-out Angus' stories usually were.

"Ye see, laddie, years ago, as I told ye afore, Johnny fell in love wi' a lovely gal. An Indian lass. Oh! A pritty thing she was! Well, I told ye how she disappeared right after he give her a special gift. Give it t' her as a token o' his love fer both her, and the wee bairn she was carrying." Moses felt the hair on the back of his neck begin to prickle, and an uneasy feeling came over him. "Wha' I dinna tell ye, was tha' it was the Blackfeet we was staying wi' tha' winter, and the lasses' name was Singing Raven!" They stared at him, mouths agape, complete astonishment showing on all their faces. Moses said nothing, his thoughts running rampant. "'Tis a shock t' ye, laddie, tha' I know. Shocked me, too, when first I saw tha' thaur neckla... *medallion*, as ye call it. I watched Johnny carve tha' fer his babe, in me verra ain dwellin'. I du na' ken—du na' *know*—how yer mother come t' be wi' tha' man, Gentry... but as God is me witness, lad... yer the son o' me dear friend, Johnny Bruce."

Moses had a million thoughts running ramshackle through his head, while Sarah sat there looking stunned, and Rosie fidgeted in her chair. Then Moses spoke: "My mother told me she was taken from her people by some trappers, and later won in a card game by my fa...by Frank Gentry. She never told me he *wasn't* my father...I always just assumed he was. On the day I left home, she gave me this medallion and told me my father had carved it for me." He paused, thinking back to that day. "She said he was a good man, a kind man. I never could understand how Frank could treat her as he did, if he was so good and kind. I always blamed it on his heavy drinking. I guess now I finally understand."

They sat there in stunned silence. Moses tried to sort out the information Angus had revealed and connect it—in some fashion—to the facts, as *he* knew them. One thing was clear: He *did* have the medallion given him by his mother, and Angus had *seen* John Bruce carve it for his expected child. Moses found it hard to assimilate all this. It was a *handful* to digest, to put it mildly! All his life he had been ashamed of the man he *thought* was his father. Ashamed because he was a violent drunkard who had a serious mean streak—with or without provocation—and often took out that meanness on Moses' lovely, soft-spoken Indian mother. Moses had even grown to hate the fact that his skin was pale, like Frank Gentry's, and not more tawny, like his mother's. He sat there, lost in thought, trying to comprehend the truth as he *now* knew it. He was John Bruce's son. Old John: the trapper and mountain man who was said to have been brilliant! The kind and gentle loner who had taught Sarah so many skills, and cared for her from her childhood on, until the day he died, protecting her. Moses shook his head, his thoughts overwhelming him. "I'm John Bruce's son." he said aloud, trying to grasp the reality of it. He smiled as he said it, rubbing a hand over his eyes.

"Are you all right?" Sarah asked, softly. Angus and Rosie had retired to the kitchen to cut the cake and make a pot of coffee. Sarah remained in the parlor with Moses, sitting quietly at his side, deep into her own thoughts.

"I'm fine," he answered. "I feel sort of overwhelmed. I guess Angus could *never* top this!"

Sarah smiled at him, "I guess not. Oh, Moses, can you believe it? Old John was my *best* friend, and now I'm married to his...his *son!* I can't believe it! How wonderful!"

"I only wish I had gotten to know him better," Moses said, a sadness in his voice. "Wish I could have spent time with him. I know he was a bit of a loner. *You* were the only one he seemed to spend any time with."

"And I can tell you a lot of things about him! Oh, Moses, he was so kind, and I had such a wonderful childhood because of him! Like when he taught me to shoot: When I finally got the hang of it and hit my first target, he whooped and jumped around like a...like a...

"Like a wild Indian?" Moses asked, smiling tenderly at her.

"Well, yes," she replied, "and he hooted and hollered! You'd have thought I'd brought down my first buck!" They laughed together then, envisioning John as Sarah remembered him. "I loved him, Moses, *more* than a friend...more like a *father*. You would have loved him, too." He smiled at her, soothed, somewhat, by her words.

"Are ya' ready for a piece of cake and some fresh coffee?" Rosie asked, sticking her head in at the parlor door.

Moses winked at Sarah. "When have I *not* been ready for your cake, Rosie?" he teased. Sarah smiled at him, and they both rose and went into the kitchen.

As they began to eat, Angus looked at Moses and grinned, his blue eyes twinkling with delight or devilment—Moses wasn't sure which. "Well, how du ye like being a Scot, laddie? Du ye think thaur's room in Hastin's fer two o' us?"

Moses laughed, as did the others. "As long as you have no more tales to shock me with," Moses replied, taking a large bite of cake into his mouth.

Angus wiped his mouth, slapping his knee, and began to laugh so hard that his belly shook. He held his stomach and continued to laugh, and Moses got a funny feeling inside. "As a matter o' fact, I *du*," the older man said, when he could get control of himself. Moses put down his fork, trying to prepare himself for whatever might come next.

Angus got up from the table and fetched a ripped and soiled envelope from his pouch by the front door. Then he took the large, clean envelope out of his shirt pocket. He padded over to the table and sat back down, laying both envelopes on the table, side by side, with a flourish. Then he took out his red handkerchief and wiped at his eyes again. Sarah looked at Rosie, who shrugged, wondering—as they all did—what the fanfare was all about. Then, clearing his throat, he rubbed a gnarled hand through his fluff of white beard, and looked from one to the other, his eyes stopping at Moses. Moses eyed him steadily, feeling a bit wary.

"When I first met ye, I told ye the story o' me friend, Johnny. Told ye how I was lookin' fer him so's I could keep a promise." Moses shifted in his chair as Angus continued. "Well, when ye told me ye knew him, it's thrilled I was, knowin' I could keep tha' promise I'd made him nearly fifty year afore. Ye see, lad and lassies, when spring come and still nae sign o' yer dear mither, Johnny set oot again, t' look fer her. I tried t' tell him it was useless, but lovin' her like he did, he jist had t' go lookin'. Being his friend, and knowin' the dangers tha' could happen t' a lad in tha' thaur wilderness, o' course' I went along." He cleared his throat, then took a sip of his coffee, which had grown cold. "The second day oot, fer ye see, her friend had told us the way she was headin', we spotted a dark area in the side o' a rocky cliff. 'Twas a cave, lad, near hidden from sight by an o'ergrowth o' brush an' bramble. Well sir, Johnny lit oot like thaur be a fire 'neath his saddle! Callin' her name an' jumpin' from his horse! He scaled the side, as fast as a man could wi' oot failin'. I took me time, sure tha' I was, thaur'd be nuthin' but bones, if we did find her." He paused, taking another sip, as his listeners waited for him to go on. At last, he did. "Well, let's see…whaur was I?…Oh, aye, aye, the cave. Well, jist as I was aboot t' call oot t' him, I hear him yell—two, er three times—and I think, saints be praised, she's alive! And I go runnin' up t' the cave's entrance, fast as me legs can carry me! And thaur he sits, surrounded by the prettiest sight these auld eyes has e'er seen! 'Cept fer me angel, o' course," he said, smiling at Rosie. They had all leaned forward, so intent they were on not missing one word now, of his story. Angus looked at them, smiling, his eyes filling with joy. "*Gold*, laddie, we found *gold!* Enough o' it t' ne'er have t' worry again, aboot bein' poor! In tha' cave, we only found three or four good-sized nuggets, enough t' whet a man's appetite fer more! Woowie! I was excited aboot it, let me tell ye, but na' Johnny, his hopes lie in finding some trace o' tha' gal. Bein' a young lad, and havin' looked fer gold many a year afore tha' day, I weren't aboot t' give it up." He shook his head, and they could tell he was remembering that day. "Well, t' make a long story short, we went our separate ways tha' day. But, na' afore I had promised him tha' any gold I found, I would split, even up, wi' him when next we met." He stopped talking and reached down to pick up the torn and dirty envelope that lay in front of him on the table. "This here's the paper on our claim—Johnny's and mine—fer I put it in both our names, jist like I promised." He pulled out a piece of paper, declaring both Angus Charles MacGregor and John Bruce sole owners of the "Golden Lassie Mine," and dated, April 20,1810. He handed the paper to Moses, who studied it a few minutes, then handed it to Sarah. But Angus wasn't through yet. "Yer father, lad, was more a brother t' me than a friend. Our friendship meant far more t' me than I can tell ye." He paused, shaking his head, sadly. " Ye see, lad, the winter afore I found Johnny oot in tha' storm, I had lost me wife an' poor, sweet children, in a fire. The youngest a wee bain o' only three months. Me daughter," he said, and tears filled his eyes at the memory. Moses felt deep sorrow for the old Scot, understanding completely, the tragic loss he had been through. Both Rosie and Sarah looked about to cry, feeling the magnitude of his loss, and Rosie started to get up out of her chair to go to him. But he held up a hand, wiping his eyes, and sniffled loudly, blowing his nose a few times, then continued: "Ye see, I had decided I'd be better off *wi* ' me family. I was so powerful sad. Oot o' me mind, I was, fer sure. But, 'twas then, when I got t' feelin' I had nuthin' t' live fer, tha' I hears someone shootin', and finds this man, layin' in the snow, near froze t' death. Aye, a sad day it 'twas: me; wantin' t' end me life, and Johnny; near froze t' death an' hurting from the loss o' the lass in Scotland." He looked down at the floor, sniffling a few more times.

"Well, *somebody* had t' take care o' Johnny. Couldna' leave him oot thaur in the cold. A man shouldna' have t' go like tha', ye ken?" Everyone sat quietly, saddened by his words. "I reckon 'twas me dear mither, God bless her, and maybe God, Hisself, had looked doon from Heaven tha' day an' sent Johnny t' save me...and me, t' save him. Weren't only tha' it 'twas a *man* in trouble, ye see...'twas me friend, from tha' long boat ride o'er t' this beautiful land, so many year afore, when we were lads. Was me *friend*, Johnny Bruce," he said, and then wiped his eyes, shaking his head, sadly, at the memory.

Both women were crying softly, overwhelmed by all he had been through. Angus excused himself and went outside, the pain of remembering tearing at him. Moses sat still as stone, seeing in his mind, the events that superseded all manner of logic! First, not only to John Bruce and Angus meeting—first, on the boat, and again, that fateful day in the wilderness—but to Angus and *himself* John Bruce's *son*, meeting. He shook his head, solemnly, as the full wonder of it hit him. Maybe Sarah was right. This certainly seemed to prove it! Like him, she believed a person was led, by something, or someone: a "higher being," for lack of a better explanation. How many times, he thought, had he felt like that? Felt as if, though he had *choices,* they were choices that took him right to where he was *supposed to be*, all along! He got up and walked around, stretching his legs a bit, waiting for Angus to return.

When he came back into the house, Angus was his old, happy self. There was no trace of the sadness and grief he had gone through, only the jovial, old man they had all grown to love. He took his seat, as did Moses, rubbing his hands together to warm them. Then he picked up the large envelope. Opening it, he removed some crisp, white documents. "These are from the bank, laddie. I had me good friend, Johnathon Clark, make the necessary transfers t' Hastin's, this mornin', when me lovely angel sent me on me way, an' oot from under foot." He smiled at 'his angel,' then he continued: "As Johnny's son, Moses, you are his heir, and saints be praised, I can, at last, keep me promise!" With that, he handed Moses the papers. Moses took them, then gasped! He stared at them, and then at Angus, and back, again. His eyes widening in astonishment! His lips moved as he tried to speak, but no sounds came out. He shook his head, and reread the paper he held.

"Moses, what is it?" Sarah asked, seeing the stricken look upon his face.

He cleared his throat and tried again, his hand that held the paper, shaking a little. "We're rich," he said, at last. "There's more money than we could *ever* spend in our *lifetime,* Sarah! It's in the bank, darlin', and it's *all oursl"*

There was a long silence, as they all took in Moses' words, then everyone began to talk at once! Moses got up and grabbed Sarah, kissing her soundly, then excused himself and headed outside. Rosie's face was red from excitement, and she had said, "Oh, my," more times than Sarah could count! Sarah looked nearly as stunned as Moses, and picked up the documents, glancing at them in disbelief. Angus, smiling happily, went to the kitchen and poured himself another cup of coffee.

When Moses came back inside, they all pulled out chairs around the kitchen table, and sat down, still feeling the excitement in the air. Then, Moses reached out to Angus, shaking his hand, grand smiles on both their faces. "I don't know what to say, Angus, except of course, thank you! It seems so little to say, for all you've given us today. Not just the money, but what you've given to *me*...knowing I'm the son of a *decent* man. A man who loved both my mother, *and* me! I feel a sense of...of worth, that I've never had before. I can't thank you enough for it." He paused, looking at Sarah, Rosie, then Angus. "I thank you, not only for all you've given *me*, but, also, on behalf of my...my *father*, John Bruce! I will *always* be indebted to you."

Angus was greatly pleased by his words. "Yer welcome, lad. 'Tis happy I am t' be able t' keep me promise. I looked fer Johnny many a year. Always felt in me heart tha' someday our paths would cross again. Seemed "ordained," if ye understand wha' I mean. Canna' explain it. Now, at last, I'll be able t' shake his hand—man t' man—when we meet again, in tha' grand hereafter!" Both men had tears in their eyes as he spoke.

Rosie poured coffee into all their cups, and set a plate of cookies in the center of the table, smiling at Angus as she did so. She knew he could not resist her delicious cookies. Then they all sat there, enjoying the food and each others company.

Then, to their surprise, Angus said he had something else of importance to say. They looked at him, not really sure they could take any more stories that he had to tell. Almost as one, they set their cups down, giving him their full attention.

"Now, lad, and lassies, thaur's somethin' else I need t' say, if ye've still the patience t' hear me." They all laughed, and urged him to say his piece. Angus put down the cookie he held in his hand—his third—and began, turning to face Rosie. "Me bonnie lass," he said, addressing her, directly. "I've traveled far an' near most o' me life. Had a full life, filled wi' adventure and excitement. I've had me sad times and I've had me good times." He reached out, squeezing her hand, gently, as she smiled at him, her cheeks a delicate shade of pink. "I du na' have all the riches tha' Johnny's son has got, but I've a good heart and a decent nature. Nae man calls me his enemy, but many know me t' be a friend. A *true* friend, who'll stand beside 'em when needed." He cleared his throat, a moistness once again filling his old, blue eyes. "As I said, I'm na' rich."As he said this, both Moses and Sarah glanced at the worn red capote, hanging by the door, that he wore for a coat. Seeing—all too clearly—the threadbare places and holes in it. They looked away quickly, not wanting to embarrass him. "But, as God is me witness, I'm a good man, capable o' great tenderness and love, if the right lass was t' come along." He smiled at Rosie, patting her hand. "Point is, ye're tha' lass, me lovely angel. I've knowed it in me heart since first I set eyes on ye. And, if ye can find it in yer heart t' love me, too, I'd be *honored* t' have ye fer me wife."

Rosie smiled sweetly, a tear running down her cheek. She turned her hand over in his, taking a firm hold of his. Sarah and Moses watched the older couple, thoroughly enjoying what they were sharing. Then Rosie spoke, her words soft and tender: "I've no doubt you'll make a fine husband, Angus, for I've seen the goodness and caring ways you have about ya'. I've seen the joy and cheerfulness that seems so much a part of ya' and...I've come to love ya'. I don't care about riches. We've got riches *far beyond* what money can buy! For...if the truth be known..." she paused, wiping tears off her cheek, then reached out, touching his face and soft white beard, "for if the truth be known, Angus MacGregor, I, too, have felt since first we met—that you are the *love o 'my life*, and it's honored I'd be, to be your wife."

CHAPTER 46

Money—a great deal of it—especially more money than most men ever imagine, often changes a person. Some become reclusive, afraid they will be asked to share. Their reclusiveness grows, until they will stop at *nothing* to hide themselves and their money. Thus, they become misers, unable to enjoy their wealth, unable to build with it, a balanced life. They become a slave to it: guarding it, saving it, indeed, ultimately worshiping it.

Other men, of a more compassionate and caring nature, see the possibilities it can bring, and grow from having it. These men have the ability to look far ahead into the future: the entrepreneurs and positive thinkers, imagining all the gains to be made, not only for themselves and their loved ones, but also for their friends, neighbors, community and country! Fortunately for Hastings, Angus Charles MacGregor and Moses Gentry fell into this second category.

Going back to their cabin that night, Sarah and Moses were beside themselves with the realization that they were exceedingly rich. At one point Sarah gasped, "Oh, Moses, I can buy a new dress!"

Moses laughed, telling her, "Darlin', you can buy *all* the dresses in Hastings *and* Black Dog Lake, and have money left over!" They rode on in silence then, each immersed in their own private thoughts and imaginings.

"I've never thought about being rich," Moses said, after awhile. "It really changes a person's perspective about a whole lot of things."

Sarah nodded, in response, then asked, "I wonder why Angus has less money than we do, if he divided it evenly?"

"I asked him that, when we went out to hitch up the horse," Moses replied. "He said he's invested his—some of it, that is—in various enterprises. And, he bought a business, right here in Hastings," Moses replied.

"He did? Which business?" Sarah asked.

"The Mercantile. He says he has an idea that should bring more customers into it, and make it an excellent, money-making project, along with bringing more prosperity to the town."

"My goodness!" Sarah said, snuggling further down into her coat. The snow glistened in the light of the moon and a band of coyotes yipped, off to one side. They rode along at an easy pace, too lost in their thoughts, to hurry.

"I'm…having a hard time," Moses said, "realizing that I'm John Bruce's son, and not Frank Gentry's. I was always so ashamed of him, of the man he was, and the way he treated my mother. I always vowed I'd *never* grow up to be like him. Makes more sense to me, now. John Bruce! Whew! I guess he was peaceful enough. Might be I do take after him, somewhat."

"You're a good man, Moses: a man he would be proud to call son. In that respect, you *are* a lot like him. He was an honorable man who helped anyone who needed a hand. Though, for the most part, he was a loner. I guess it was because he was so smart. They say he was smart to the point of being stupid. Does that make any sense to you? I heard one of the old fellows talking, at Tommy's store—a long time ago—and that's what he said. Said you could be so smart, that simple things were hard for you to do." Sarah finished talking, watching a furry critter scurry across their path, though she couldn't tell what it was in the dark.

Moses rubbed his hands together, warming them, as he looked over at her, seeing that her eyes were closed. "Tired, darlin'?" he asked, reaching over to stroke her knee.

"Just resting my eyes. It's been a long day."

"That it has," he replied, "and a most surprising one!"

When they reached their cabin, Sarah put more wood on the fire, while Moses put up the horses. Then she slipped into her new gown, the one that Rosie had given her. When he came inside, Moses saw that she was already in bed. He blew out the light and stripped off his clothes. There was more than enough light to see by, from the moonlight streaming in soft golden tones through the window. He slipped into bed, snuggling close to Sarah, her back and buttocks pressed tightly against the front of him.

"Oh! You're cold!" she exclaimed, as she felt his body against hers.

He pulled her closer, breathing in the scent of her hair, which tickled his nose and cheek. "Not for long, sweetheart, not for long." Soon the night sounds were joined by the sounds of the couple inside the cozy cabin, as they made their own beautiful music, while thoroughly enjoying each other!

CHAPTER 47

Word spread quickly throughout Hastings of Angus MacGregor's acquisition of the Mercantile. Cal Dunnevey would stay on as manager, but had sold ownership of it at a substantial profit. He knew that the money he now had in the bank guaranteed him all the security he would have normally worked years to acquire. He agreed to continue managing the store in the same manner he always had, having shown Angus the financial gains he had made in just the year he had owned it. He liked Angus MacGregor. Liked the man's ideas, and liked him personally. The progress Angus hoped to accomplish, together with the bevy of ideas he had for expanding the business in the coming years, sounded more than a little feasible. If all went as Angus planned, Hastings would be a booming town in the not too distant future!

Dunnevey smiled as he stacked large bags of flour. As he worked, he whistled a tune and didn't hear Sarah enter the store. She looked around, hearing the lively tune he was whistling, then simply stood, watching him. He had on black pants and a white shirt, with a black and silver striped vest. His shirt sleeves were rolled-up to just above his elbows, and his wavy, brown hair looked soft as though he had just washed it. He turned, surprise showing on his face.

"Sarah...ah...Mrs. Gentry, what can I get for you today?" He looked handsome and happy, and so very pleased to see her.

Sarah felt her cheeks redden slightly. "I'd...ah...like a large bag of flour and some fine muslin, if you have it, please."

"Sure do, got some in, just this past week," he answered. She smiled, thinking that he was too strong to be a clerk, and too happy to be working at the Mercantile. She thought of Tommy Dawson. He had always felt "chained" to his father's store, after the elder Dawson died. Of course, Tommy had always had dreams of leading a wagon train west. Perhaps Dunnevey had always wanted to be a store clerk. She watched him, noticing the kindness in his eyes when he looked at her, and the softness of his voice when he spoke. It just doesn't seem right, somehow, that this is his profession, she thought. A man like Cal Dunnevey could do any number of things, but clerk in a store just doesn't seem right.

"Sarah, are you all right?" She was suddenly aware that he had spoken to her.

"What?" she asked, feeling terribly self-conscious. "I had my mind on other things. What did you say?"

"I asked how it feels to be back in Hastings. I'll bet it takes some getting used to, again."

"Yes, it does," she replied.

"It's always hard when you leave your home and then attempt to go back," he said. "At least I imagine it is." He spoke softly, his tone of voice having a mellowing affect on her.

"Are you happy here, Mr. Dunne...Cal?"

He smiled at her, wondering at her concern. "I suppose I am. I have a job I like, good friends, a comfortable room in the back of the store. Not much else a man could ask for."

"What about family?" she asked, and was certain she saw a fleeting look of sadness cross his features.

"My family is a long, long way from Hastings. I'd like to keep it that way."

She felt she had stepped out of line, by asking, and tried to apologize. "I'm sorry, Cal. I had no business asking such a personal question."

"No harm done," he answered, smiling once more. "Here, let me carry this out to your buckboard for you," he said, lifting the large bag of flour onto one shoulder.

She noticed he wore no gun, as most of the men in town did. A clerk with no gun, she thought, watching his long, lanky frame as he went out the door in front of her.

He caught the door with his foot, holding it for her. "Don't worry your pretty head about me, Miz Gentry. I've been on my own since I was a young boy. I'm used to it."

Sarah smiled at his words as he helped her up onto the buckboard seat, said to tell the Moses 'hello,' and stepped back as she urged Glory on. Funny, she thought, how a man so nice, and so handsome—for he was, she had to admit—could be so alone. Oh, well, it was none of her business, and unless she wanted him to think her a meddling, old busybody, she had better concentrate on her *own* concerns! She urged Glory on through the drifting snow, her curiosity temporarily held in check.

CHAPTER 48

Cal Dunnevey watched Sarah drive away, her auburn hair spreading across her back in a most fetching and familiar manner. He stood there, watching her, his thoughts rushing back through time to another woman with similar auburn tresses. Maggie. Maggie, who had cuddled him securely within her arms each night at bedtime, when he was a child. She had told him stories, filled with tales of kings, and queens, and magical places far beyond their town. Far beyond *any* town he could even imagine! It was she who had comforted him, when he skinned a knee, and cried with him when his heart was broken. Many a day she had sat with him, teaching him to read and write and count. Telling him how *special* he was, how wanted, how loved!

He squeezed his eyes shut, shaking his head. He still remembered, as clearly as if she stood beside him now, the scent of her perfume, and her "finery," as she had called it: dresses of bright red satin, and other shades, always bright and cheery. To this day, he couldn't look at a piece of satin fabric or the black lace like she had sported across her breasts and at her sleeves, without thinking of her. He had stared, in awe, as a child of eight, when she drew her skirt aside and pulled on a black silk stocking. A black, lace garter soon gracing her long, sleek leg.

She had never told him who his parents were, or how he came to be with her. All she had said was that he was an orphan, and she, his only living relative. And, she told him she loved him.

That was enough to know. He had never doubted her love. Not once, as long as he lived with her. Truth was, he *still* did not doubt it. But then, Victor Jalaco had come into the picture. Victor Jalaco: with his slicked-back, black hair, and diamond-studded cufflinks, his fancy, white, ruffle-fronted shirts, and tight, pin-stripe trousers. Victor Jalaco. Oh, yes, he thought, that was when the trouble first started.

Victor Jalaco bought the Hideaway Saloon where he and Maggie lived, and where Maggie worked, six nights a week, to support herself and Cal. Victor Jalaco, with his "pretty-boy" looks and clean hands. Clean, only in the respect that they did no work, other than stroke the silken skin of Maggie. And behind her back, more than one of the other gals who worked for him.

Cal was nine when he first saw Jalaco hit Maggie. Nine, when he grabbed a broom and slammed the handle of it against the back of Jalaco's head, before two of his thugs caught him and held him, while Jalaco pounded him: his fists hurting only half as much as the cruel words he had yelled. "You think you can hit *me*, boy? *Me*, Victor Jalaco? You tryin' to defend that *whore?* He had laughed uproariously, then, pulling Maggie by her hair over to his side. He made her kneel and watch as he continued to beat his fists into the boy's middle, till he vomited from the pain! Then, he forced Cal's face down into the vomit, holding him there till Cal thought he would surely die from lack of air! All the while, listening to Maggie beg and plead and cry and scream in the background. Finally, Jalaco's men hauled him up by his arms and shoved him against her! Against her favorite red satin dress, his vomit coating the front of it, as he shook violently and tried ever so desperately not to be sick again. Maggie grabbed out, putting her arms around him, trying to pull him away from Jalaco, and out of the hands of his men.

"Please! Don't hurt him! Please! *Please!* Vic! I'll do *anything* you want! Please don't hurt him anymore!" she had screamed. She let go of the boy, grabbing hold of Jalaco's leg. The boy's vomit—on the front of her dress—soiling his pin-striped pants, though in her fear for Cal she hadn't realized it.

Jalaco grabbed her by the hair, jerking her away from him, his eyes filled with a fury that would have frightened a grown man. He kicked her then, squarely in the stomach, and kept on kicking her, until blood ran—in rivulets—from *both* sides of her mouth! Kept kicking her, till a dark stain covered the red satin of her favorite dress, and Maggie no longer lay quivering upon the floor.

The thugs let him go then, so intent upon what they were witnessing. All was quiet in the saloon as onlookers stood frozen in place, too shocked to move, too afraid to go to the defense of the nine year old boy and the whore who lay in a bloody heap upon the floor. The other ladies of the Hideaway Saloon looked on in horror, wondering if they would be next. Younger ones wished they were still at home—on some farm—miles from there, safe under their parents' watchful eyes. No one saw the boy grab a gun from a nearby table, where a heated argument over cards had been brewing. But, *everyone* heard the gun fire, and saw Victor Jalaco grab at the dark hole that suddenly appeared on his forehead, seconds before he slumped to the floor, dead!

Cal Dunnevey rubbed the dampness from his eyes, stilling his thoughts. His large hands trembled, somewhat, from the pain of his memories. Sarah Gentry's lucky, he thought. She has a *man* to protect her, if ever needed. Unlike Maggie, who had only had a nine year old boy!

CHAPTER 49

The following Sunday, after services, with Amanda and Amos standing at their side, Angus MacGregor took one Rosie O'Day Mitchell Justus as his blushing bride. It was a quiet ceremony, with only the Culpeppers and Gentrys attending. The bride looked lovely in a pink cotton dress she had made herself, and the groom looked "spiffy" in a navy blue suit from the Mercantile. They held hands throughout the ceremony, both looking elated, but nervous.

The groom's snow-white hair and beard stood out against his navy blue suit and Sarah couldn't help thinking it looked like Saint Nicholas himself, about to be married. Angus winked at her as if reading her thoughts, and Rosie continued to squeeze his hand, her cheeks glowing a soft, pretty pink that nearly matched her dress. Sarah watched happily, her hand resting lightly within Moses' hand. When Reverend Higgins said "you may kiss your bride," Angus wasted no time in taking Rosie into his arms and kissing her a kiss that rivaled the one Moses had given Sarah on their wedding day!

Afterwards, everyone went to Rosie's house for a small celebration. There was Rosie's special chocolate cake, a bottle of the finest wine Hastings could provide, and a delicious dish of Apple Pan Dowdy that Amanda had brought. Sarah had cooked a large roast of bear meat that was smothered in its own succulent gravy, surrounded by carrots, potatoes, and onions, and everyone ate heartily.

Later they all retired to the parlor where they visited, with good-hearted teasing and plenty of laughter and comradery. When Angus began to yawn, exaggerating each yawn to get his message across, the other couples left: Amos and Amanda to their home next door, and Sarah and Moses to their buckboard and the long ride home.

Still later, as they settled in for the night—chores done and the day nearly over—Moses sat at the table, writing, and Sarah enjoyed the pleasure of a warm, soothing tub bath.

Breaking the peaceful silence, Moses asked her a question that he had asked himself, repeatedly, since they found out about the inheritance. "Darlin', what would you do to help Hastings grow, now that we have the money to do it?"

"Oh, love, I guess I'd leave that up to you. You think on a grander scale than I, when it comes to things like that. Look at how much better you made this place, while I was gone."

He smiled at her, his thoughts inconceivable, even to himself. "Did you know that Angus bought up fifteen hundred acres of timber land, to the east of town? Says when Hastings grows, there'll be a demand for lumber as more and more houses and buildings are built. Says there'll be a newspaper office here, someday, and a railroad station: things like that!" His voice was filled with excitement. "Sarah, we can do the same thing. Buy up land north of town—there's a fine expanse of timber there, too! Put more folks to work —you know, when the demand for more homes and such happens! Why, we could build a mill, down by Settler's Pond. That would make plenty of jobs for the new folks that come here!" His voice exuded the emotion that plans of this magnitude always brought to those able to conceive of them. "We could even build a hospital, someday, a *real* hospital, and add on to the school...why, hell...we could build a *new* school, bigger than what we have now! Maybe have *two* teachers: one for older students, one for the younger ones." Sarah giggled, hearing his excitement build as he spoke.

"I doubt anyone would want to hire *two* teachers at the same school," she laughed. "Not everyone is rich, you know."

"Then, *we'll* hire them!" he exclaimed, writing feverishly on yet another piece of paper. "Angus says the railroad will soon be heading this way. The railroad means a lot more people. It'll put Hastings on the map, darlin', and make it grow as fast as all git-out." As he spoke, she stood up in the tub, reaching for her towel. Moses looked at her, her smooth body outlined by the beam of moonlight shining in through the window: her small, firm breasts; her flat stomach; her skin, pale as the finest china, and smooth as silk. He felt his body respond to the sight of her loveliness. His papers, full of plans, quickly forgotten. "Oh, darlin'," he drawled, his voice deep, and filled with emotion.

He walked over to her, quickly removing his clothing. Then he lifted her out of the tub and carried her to their bed. "Moses, I'm all wet," she whispered, as she felt the coolness of the quilt beneath her.

"I aim to make you wetter, darlin'," he replied, nuzzling her neck and beginning to kiss a path to her already hardening nipples. She opened herself to him, a fire enveloping her.

That night, as snow fell around their small home, and winter's brisk winds whistled against the exterior, rattling the window, Moses took Sarah—again and again—at first demandingly, then gently, using all the skills he knew to pleasure her.

The next morning—though it was actually closer to noon when they managed to leave their bed—they shared a leisurely breakfast, discussing the idea of purchasing some land to the north of town. Sarah readily agreed that it made sense to get in on the ground-floor of any growth and expansion that might occur in Hastings, in the years to come.

"I'll talk to Johnathon, over at the bank, today," Moses said, thoughts and figures racing through his head.

Sarah placed her hand upon her stomach. She knew it was impossible to know if she was with child, but somehow she felt different this morning. Her whole being felt different. There was a glowing warmth deep within her, from head to toe. She felt almost satiated with those feelings. She looked over at Moses, whom she suddenly realized was watching her.

"What is it, darlin'?" he asked. "Are you okay?"

She smiled a timid smile. "I still feel full of you," she answered, a slight blush coming over her cheeks.

He got up, taking her hand, making her rise, then picked her up in his strong, muscular arms and carried her to her father's rocker. They sat quietly before the fire—Sarah curled against him in his lap—both of them knowing the bond of love between them had grown even stronger, and that now they were truly "one."

CHAPTER 50

The weeks passed quickly. Johnathon Clark was pleased to see Moses, and congratulated him on the wealth he had recently come into. He was even more pleased the more he learned of Moses' plans for the growth and development of Hastings. He, also, had once had dreams for such an endeavor, but never the capital to back up his ideas. Now he found himself handling the accounts of *both* Angus and Moses, not only as President of the bank, but as their personal advisor.

Each time Moses discussed plans with him, Johnathon took great pleasure in adding some perspectives of his own, and having them, also, considered. Both Gentry and MacGregor had more than enough capital to see their ideas come to fruition on a scale much grander than even *they* realized, he soon discovered, and their discussions often continued into the latter part of the afternoon.

Sarah, in the meantime, busied herself with everyday household chores and getting ready for Christmas, which would soon be upon them. Michael O'Leary came right on schedule to do the daily chores around the ranch, for it had, indeed, grown into a decent-sized ranch. Two younger O'Leary boys also helped on a regular basis—one tending to the chickens, and one helping Michael.

As she worked, Sarah thought of Glory, and how she had gotten on in years. How nice it would be, she thought, if she could be "put out to pasture," so to speak, to use as a brood mare. After all, she's a solid, sturdy-built animal, with a gentle disposition. And she's never given me any trouble. Wouldn't it be nice, she thought, to have a whole *herd* of her offspring to raise, and to sell someday. As she thought this, she realized that it would be even more profitable, she was sure, to raise Midnight's progeny. He was of sleeker lines, with a good temperament, hands higher, and who knows what bloodlines he might be from? Anyone could see he had an elegant bearing. She had read somewhere that most buyers from the South looked for that in a horse. Not being able to prove his lineage might prove a deterrent, however.

Visions of new barns and fences stretching across the land, as far as the eye could see, soon filled her thoughts. Yes, we could raise horses for all those folks that Moses said will be coming to Hastings, in the years to come. She rubbed a hand gently across her belly, a contented smile upon her face. And someday, our own children will ride the offspring of Glory and Midnight.

Just then, there was a knock on the door. "Yes?" she called out, opening it slightly. The youngest O'Leary boy stood at the door in a threadbare coat that barely buttoned around him, and his boots had holes in the toes that were filled with snow, his bare hands nearly blue from the cold.

"Come in," she offered, opening the door wider.

"Oh, no, Ma'am," he answered, wiping his runny nose on his coat sleeve, smiling sheepishly at her. "Miz MacGregor said you and the sheriff was to come to eat on Saturday, ifn you want to. Mr. Mac says he wants to talk to ya' 'bout Christmas!" As he talked, his face so red she could barely see the freckles that covered his nose, Sarah couldn't help notice that his trousers came only to the top of his boots, and he kept rubbing his hands together, to warm them.

"I'll tell the sheriff," she said, "and I thank you, but you must come in for some warm milk and cookies."

His eyes lit up at her words, but just as quickly he replied, "No thanks, Ma'am. Maw says we ain't to bother ya'. Just do our work and git back home." He looked wistfully toward the table where a plate of freshly baked cookies sat.

"I insist, as your...ah...*boss*, I insist you come in." A wonderful smile broke out across the small boy's face, and he grinned happily at her. "Now go get your brothers. Tell them it's time for a break," she ordered, feeling good inside because of the joy her simple offer had given the child.

Soon, all three boys sat at her table, drinking the warm milk and eating cookies, as though they hadn't had anything else to eat all that day! Sarah excused herself and went into her old room. There, she searched through an old trunk of her mother's, looking for the three pairs of mittens she had made, years before. As she found them, she heard the boys talking out in the other room, and couldn't help listening at the door. "Ain't she nice?" one said. *"Real* nice," the other replied. "Maw wouldn't like us being inside, eating her food," the third said, and she knew it was Michael who had spoken.

She hurried out, the mittens in her hands. "Here's some mittens I knitted a long time ago. I want you to wear these when it's cold." "No, Ma'am," Michael said. "The sheriff pays us enough for workin' here. It ain't fittin' we take yer "mitts," too."

"It's fittin', if I say it's fittin'," she said, her voice firm. "Besides, chores are easier to do, and done better, when hands aren't half-frozen!" She held out the mittens, a larger tan pair, and two smaller pairs: one red, one blue. Small hands reached out quickly, each grabbing the color they preferred. There were huge smiles upon their faces as they immediately pulled them on. She turned to Michael, holding the larger pair out to him. He hesitated, glancing at his younger brothers, seeing the radiant smiles upon their faces. Sarah laid his pair on the table in front of him, then asked them if they wanted another cookie. They reached out eagerly to take another, grinning from ear to ear.

"We best get back to work," Michael said, and the younger boys scrambled from their chairs, each wearing their new mittens. Michael walked to the door, then turned back, hesitantly, and picked up the pair of mittens that were for him. "Maw usually knits us mitts for Christmas, but she ain't been well since...our Paw died." He cleared his throat. "Thank you kindly, Miz Gentry. It's most appreciated."

Sarah smiled, as he walked away, happy with the thoughts that were running through her head. There was still time enough before Christmas to put her plan into effect! First, she would talk to Moses, though she already knew he would agree. Then, she would get busy, shopping for some new coats for the O'Leary boys, and—with Rosie's help—begin knitting them some warm socks and scarves. She'd also make some extra batches of cookies for their house, and try to find a small toy or book for each. Rosie would be more than happy, she knew, to make a few things for them, too. And, if Moses agreed—and she knew he would—they would also add a few things for their mother, Kathleen O'Leary, and their sister, Mary. Why they could even send some of the venison from the deer Moses had shot just the other day! Sarah was overjoyed with her plans, and hurried to check her sewing basket.

A month or so, earlier, Rosie had told her that Mrs. O'Leary had been having a real difficult time of it, due to a problem with her hands. It seemed they had become stiff and swollen in the joints, and caused her a great deal of pain. "Well," Sarah said, speaking aloud, "Christmas is the *most wonderful* time of year! A special time to "help Thy neighbor," and that's exactly what I intend to do!" She smiled, humming a little tune, delighted with the prospect of bringing some unexpected joy to the O'Leary family.

CHAPTER 51

One day in early January, Moses left Johnathon Clark's office feeling ten feet tall! Johnathon had agreed with most of his ideas, even improving on some of them. Up until Angus came to Hastings, Johnathon had been the richest man in town, and owned the biggest and most beautiful house.

He was a charming man, an elegant dresser and highly intelligent, Moses soon discovered, when it came to finances and investments. He was also well-respected, and kept up-to-date on all the news of the country, east and west of Hastings. Moses had heard that he had once been an advisor to the President, before coming to Hastings, but his wife's ill health had forced him to retire. When she passed away, a year later, he had come west—to Hastings—to begin anew. Moses judged him to be in his sixties, and knew he would be extremely proficient in the handling of any future business transactions they might decide upon.

I'll have to be getting me some fancy suits and shiny shoes, Moses thought, and a shave and hair-cut, too, I suppose. He laughed at the idea. If I don't watch out, I'll end up looking like one of those Eastern "dandies," that come to town by stage every so often. All fancied-up in pants too tight to sit a horse, and collars too stiff and tight to breathe. He laughed, feeling good about the changes that had come his way.

As he crossed the street to go to the jail, he heard Tom Dawson hail him. He stopped, waiting for him to catch up with him. "What can

I do for you?" Moses asked, his voice sounding stiffly official—even to him. Tommy looked at him, a troubled look upon his face.

Moses was still furious with Melinda Rose for the cruel remarks she had made to Sarah. In fact, if she had been a man, they probably would have had a confrontation, and somebody would have ended up getting punched! There was just no way Melinda Rose had any right to insult Sarah!

"Well?" he said, noticing how uncomfortable Tommy looked.

"Can I talk to you...ah...inside?" Tommy asked, looking toward the jail.

"Yup," Moses replied, a noticeable edge to his voice.

Once inside, Moses sat down at his desk, leaning back, stretching his legs under the desk. "Have a seat." Tommy sat down in the hard, straight-back chair opposite him. He glanced toward the cells, looking relieved to find them empty, then turned to look at the sheriff.

"Well, what's on your mind, Dawson?"

"I...ah...wondered why we haven't seen you or Sarah at our store in awhile? Saw her go into the Mercantile a couple times. Truth is, I wondered about it. She never used to go anywhere but Dawson's."

Moses laughed out loud. "So that's it! You thought you could come running over here, sniveling behind Sarah's back, and everything would be all right! Well, I'll tell you, you can *forget that!* As sheriff of Hastings, I'll protect your store and your family as best I can, just like any other family in town. But if you think Sarah will *ever* shop at Dawson's again, you've got another think coming!"

Tommy looked at him, a stricken expression upon his face. "I...I don't understand," he said, at last.

Moses stared at him, realizing the man truly had no idea how Melinda Rose had treated Sarah, or the cruel things she had said to her. "You *don't* know!" Moses exclaimed. "Well, I'll be! You *really don't know!"*

"Know what?" Tommy asked, his voice practically a whisper.

"Sarah stopped shopping at your store because of the cruel things your wife said to her!"

Tommy looked as if Moses had struck him. "I don't understand," he said, leaning forward.

Moses shook his head. "You really should be talking to Sarah," he said, "but since you asked, I'll tell you. Sarah went into your store when we came back to town. Melinda Rose met her at the door and asked if it was true she was going to marry *another* half-breed husband, and if she planned to have any *half-breed* children!"

Tommy gasped, and sat back in the chair. "I didn't know," he said. *"Why* would she say those things?"

"You tell me!" Moses said. "I'll tell you something else, for your own good, Dawson. If you don't put a muzzle on your wife's mouth, you're not gonna have a single customer, or friend left." Moses was angry as hell and couldn't resist adding, "and you should give her a lesson on raising children, too. Mrs. Carson, from the boardinghouse, was almost knocked down by your children when she shopped there last week, and another older gal was overheard saying how she can't stand to shop there, between the babies crying, and the older children running around like wild Indians! And just for the record, Indian children are respectful to their elders and *don't* run around like a bunch of wild critters!" Moses quit talking, his anger spent.

Tommy sat across from him, his head hanging down. He looked up at Moses, after a few moments. "I hope you will accept my sincere apology, Moses, for my wife's ugly comments and also, for... *everything*...my children's actions, and all. I'll make it a point to go see Sarah and apologize to her, too. I...I had *no idea* of any of this." He shook his head, a sad look upon his face. "I liked her being at the store...in the beginning. Liked having the children there, too. But, it's gotten out of hand. No one takes the time to stop and talk anymore...I guess they can't, with the children running wild." He stood up, slowly reaching out to Moses. "I appreciate your honesty, Moses. I'm *terribly* sorry about the whole thing, and I *will* apologize *personally* to Sarah. I hope we can still be friends."

Moses stood up, extending his hand, making no further comment.

"Melinda Rose had nothing when she moved to Hastings, you know? I think it all went to her head. She's really a good person...it... it just changed her, somehow." Tommy said, and he turned and left, his hands in his pockets and shoulders slumped. Moses watched him go, sorry to see his shame.

CHAPTER 52

Sarah was surprised when Tommy Dawson knocked on her door the day after he had gone to talk to Moses. She had not expected him to ride all the way out to her cabin to apologize. She knew him well enough to realize how sincerely contrite he was, and how it had shamed him to find his wife had been the cause of it. She accepted his apology, and even offered him a cup of coffee.

But he refused, saying he wanted to get home early to have a serious talk with Melinda Rose. She hugged him as he stood to leave, thanking him for coming all that way. However, she never did mention resuming her shopping at his store, and knew he realized it.

She was even more surprised, a few weeks later, when Rosie told her that 'Melinda Rose was no longer spending her days at the store, but was firmly ensconced at her mother-in-law's house with the children, and the elder Mrs. Dawson had gone east to visit her sister, and might not be returning for some time.' Rosie had also said, but she never disclosed how she knew, that 'Melinda Rose was no longer sharing her bed with Tommy, and was becoming more and more depressed. Sometimes *days* would go by, when she refused to leave the house or to even see anyone.' She feared that Melinda Rose would make herself ill, and Sarah had to agree.

On February sixth, Sarah had Michael hitch Glory to their new buggy, and she set off for town. She had decided to go see Melinda Rose and talk to her. She felt she owed it to her because they had long been friends. Truth was, Sarah felt sorry for the Dawson's; for all they were going through. She could not imagine being shut in a house, seven days a week, with such lively children and no adult companionship. Why, it was bound to make Melinda Rose ill, and possibly even the children! I'll just go talk to her and try to cheer her up, if I can, Sarah thought. Life is too short to go through it unhappy and depressed!

Arriving at Melinda Rose's, she tied Glory's reins to the hitching rail in front of the house and walked to the door. Moses had gone to the jail early that morning, and she had decided she would stop and see him when she was done visiting with Melinda Rose. She knocked, but no one answered. Again, she knocked. The sun had broken through the clouds, making it look warmer, but there was a sharp wind blowing, and she was glad she had worn her new, long, brown wool coat. The wind quickly bit into any exposed skin. She knocked a bit louder, and thought she heard a child running. She listened, putting her ear close to the door. Then, just as she raised her hand to knock a fourth time, the door was suddenly thrown open by a haggard-looking Melinda Rose. She stared at Sarah, not smiling, not saying anything. Her eyes seemed to be filled with an unfathomable sadness and she looked sullen and despondent. Her mouth was a colorless, thin line against her pale skin.

"May I come in?" Sarah asked, smiling at the children as they clustered around their mother's skirt, wide-eyed, but silent. Melinda Rose hesitated, staring calmly—too calmly—at Sarah, but stepped back, bowing her into the disheveled house. Sarah couldn't believe her eyes! All the curtains were drawn, letting in no light, and all through the house it looked dark and dreary. Dirty dishes with partially eaten food stuck to them covered the cluttered kitchen table. Even the cupboard that the elder Mrs. Dawson had always kept so clean, was hidden beneath an accumulation. Sarah felt sickened, and more than a little alarmed. Who could thrive in such dismal surroundings? Why she had only just arrived, and already she was touched by the melancholy atmosphere!

"I've come to help, Melinda Rose," Sarah said, brightly, taking off her coat and hanging it by the door, forcing herself to sound cheery.

"Did *Tom* send you?" Melinda Rose asked, looking at Sarah almost defiantly.

"No, I came because I heard you needed some company," Sarah replied, and began heating the water for dishes, and stacking and clearing the mess on the table and adjoining cupboard. "No, Tommy doesn't know I'm here, and neither does Moses."

There was a long silence, then Melinda Rose asked: "Why did you come? *Why*? To gloat? Why would you *want* to come, after what I said to you?"

Sarah filled a large pan with the hot water and set a stack of dirty dishes in it, to soak. "I came because we *all* need friends, Melinda Rose. And you and I have been friends a long time. I don't know why you spoke to me as you did, but I want us to stay friends." Melinda Rose sank down onto a hard-backed kitchen chair and began to cry. Holding her face between her hands, she literally sobbed. Sarah dried her hands and hurried over to her side, placing a hand on the despondent woman's shoulder.

"A good friend doesn't stand beside you only when everything's all right," Sarah said, "a good friend stands by when you need her. I've always felt we were friends, Melinda Rose."

Melinda Rose quit crying and blew her nose on a hanky from one of her pockets, then looked up at Sarah, a deep sadness showing in her eyes. "I was...jealous," she said at last. "Still am. Jealous because you have so much!"

"*Jealous?* Oh, Melinda Rose, *why* would you be jealous of *me*? Don't you see how much *you* have? With Tommy, and your family? Why, you have a man who loves you *so much!* And four *wonderful* children who all adore you! Why would you be jealous of *me*?"

Melinda Rose looked up at Sarah, studying her. Then she spoke, her voice sounding angry and harsh: "*You* never have to worry! That's why. You're *perfect!* 'Sarah can do this, Sarah can do that. Sarah can help you, *ask Sarah!* That's all I hear from Tom, how *perfect* you are... and always have been! I'm *sick of it! Sick of it! That's* why! You're the perfect *woman!* The perfect *daughter!* The perfect *wife!* And someday, you'll be the *perfect mother!* I'm *tired* of trying to be the *perfect* wife! The *perfect* Mother! I'm tired of trying to be *you!*"

Sarah gaped at her, stunned by her revelations. She stared at the woman before her, not at all certain how to reply. Then she knelt down in front of her distraught friend, taking her hands in hers. "Oh, Melinda Rose, I'm *so sorry* you feel this way! I...I never knew. I'm *not* perfect, far from it, in fact. I hurt my father deeply when I left with Gray Eagle. And, if I was so perfect, you would *know* we are friends—always have been—and you wouldn't feel so hurt." She spoke softly, trying to soothe the crying woman. "And if I was perfect, perhaps I wouldn't have lost my baby—Gray Eagle's and mine—maybe *both of them* would be alive today."

"You...lost a baby?"

"Yes," Sarah answered, softly. "I was injured, and lost our baby."

"I didn't know," Melinda Rose whispered. "I had no idea."

"Very few people know," Sarah replied, wiping her eyes and standing. "Why don't you put on a pot of coffee, Melinda Rose, while I do the dishes? All right?"

"All right," she answered, meekly.

Sarah spent three hours at the Dawson house: finishing the dishes, getting all the children washed and dressed, and sweeping the floors. She pulled back the heavy curtains, letting the sun shine in, lighting the rooms, and dispelling the darkness that had enveloped them. Then she put on a venison roast to cook and peeled potatoes and carrots from the root cellar, adding them to the meat, and quickly stirred up the dough for saleratus biscuits.

Melinda Rose watched her, for awhile, then she went upstairs to freshen up and put on a clean dress, as Sarah had suggested. When she came downstairs a while later, she looked a good deal better: her face washed and hair combed. She wore a pretty frock, and had tied her hair back with a matching ribbon, much the same way Sarah wore hers.

"You look pretty, Mother," Danny said, as he set the table for their noonday meal. She smiled at him, but made no reply.

With everything seemingly under control, and Tommy due home very soon for lunch, Sarah told Melinda Rose that she had to go. She laughed, saying she wanted to stop at the jail, for a bit, to steal a kiss from her favorite sheriff!

Melinda Rose thanked her for coming, smiled slightly, returned Sarah's hug, then shut the door behind her. Sarah could hear her telling the children to go wash their hands, their father would be home any minute.

Smiling happily, and feeling very good about the outcome of her visit, Sarah pulled her coat more securely around her, fastening it against the harsh winds, and walked out to her buggy.

That night, as Tommy and her children slept peacefully in their beds, Melinda Rose crept from her bed. She looked in at each of her sleeping children, with tears in her eyes and heavy heart.

Then she left the house, shutting the door quietly behind her. She walked through the drifted, frozen snow to the woods beyond their house: her feet bare, a thin, cotton gown her only covering. There, she lay down.

Amos Culpepper found her about noon the following day, just as more heavy snow began to fall, eventually blanketing the town under waist-high drifts.

CHAPTER 53

On February tenth, everyone turned out for the funeral of Melinda Rose Dawson. Tommy looked pale, and practically had to be supported by the reverend and Johnathon Clark as he walked down the isle to the front of the church. He looked drained of feelings, bereft, showing no emotion unless his young children spoke to him. They huddled close to him, holding tightly to him and to each other, their eyes red from crying. Tommy smiled a poignant smile at them and patted Polly's back gently, straightening Danny's stiff white shirt collar, as if unaware of doing so. He stood, when Sarah and Moses walked over to him, and nodded as they told him how sorry they were. Then Sarah bent, hugging each of the children, her heart breaking for them.

Angus and Rosie entered at the same time Amos and Amanda did, and whispered among themselves, quietly. Sarah was pleased to see Cal Dunnevey walk over to where Tommy sat and shake his hand, but she couldn't hear the words of comfort he offered. He nodded at them, his hat in hand, then sat down a couple rows behind them. Ruby Deegs and Jasmine LaRue came in, dressed all in black, with a respectable amount of make-up on, and high-necked dresses that were as decent as any the other women of Hastings wore. They shook Tommy's hand—adding their condolences—then shook each of the children's hands, before taking their seats in the row behind Cal Dunnevey. Lilly and Jonas arrived then, and Sarah couldn't help notice the healthy glow that seemed to exude from Lilly. She looked positively radiant! They came forward, shaking hands with Tommy, telling him how sorry they were. Then they smiled at Sarah and Moses, and took their seats in the row just behind them. Mrs. Carson, the boardinghouse proprietor, began to play the organ, and a silence came over the small church. Only a few sniffles were heard up front, and a few coughs in the rear.

The schoolmistress, Ophelia Denton, entered then, with an attractive woman at her side. She looked a slight bit younger than Miss Denton, with ash-blonde hair, done-up in a large bun. They took their seats across the aisle from Cal Dunnevey, who could not help but notice the beautiful woman who accompanied Ophelia Denton, and was, suddenly, very glad he had come. He couldn't seem to take his eyes off her; her long slim neck and soft, golden hair, her dainty hands and slim waist. A waist a man could easily wrap one arm around! The woman, whom her would later discover was Ophelia's sister, Lea, had arrived just that morning for an extended stay in town.

She glanced around, her smokey-gray eyes catching his, and for a moment the only thing he could hear was the intense pounding of his heart! She quickly looked away, her cheeks turning a slightly pinker shade of color.

Other than the many sniffles to be heard, everyone sat in stunned silence, each wondering what it was that could have driven a woman with so many blessings, to end her life. The answer seemed unfathomable.

Tommy's baby girl, Polly, began to cry loudly, and he reached to take her from Danny. Doing so seemed to bring some comfort to both of them, as he held her and whispered softly to her until she quieted. Danny sat stiffly, next to his father—a handsome boy with many features resembling those of his mother—as he tried hard not to cry. Tommy noticed a tear escape and run down his cheek and reached over, taking the boy's hand. Sarah heard him whisper. "We'll get through this son…somehow… don't you worry."

Sarah squeezed Moses' hand, her eyes welling up with tears. She had gone over and over, a hundred times, everything she had said to Melinda Rose, the day she visited her at her house. She could find nothing she might have said to have cause this most horrible tragedy. She nearly fainted, when Moses told her of Melinda Rose's death. She prayed that she had not, inadvertently, given her any cause to do something so terrible. She wiped her eyes with a hanky she took from inside her glove, her heart heavy with grief.

Moses sat beside her, looking down at his boots, one hand holding Sarah's and one holding on to his hat. He was unaware that he repeatedly rubbed his finger and thumb together at the edge of the brim. Unbidden, his mind conjured up memories that he thought his life with *this* Sarah had finally put to rest. But rest, they would not! He shook his head sadly, trying to focus on his present surroundings: on Sarah, so devastated as she sat crying, beside him, her small hand clutching his, her eyes brimming over with tears. He glanced at Tom Dawson and his young family: handsome sons and pretty baby daughter. All of them crying or sniffling, and pressing close to Tom for some remnant of security and normalcy to hold on to. The full extent of their loss too new and too tragic to be fully understood! Moses knew the shattering of their world was too horrific to be dealt with by an adult, let alone a child, and he wondered how they would fare in the years to come, because of it. He shifted in his seat, a fleeting vision of his own past losses darting once more across his mind: the pink dress 'his Sarah' had worn that day, and the bright red blood that spread so quickly across it, covering her stomach as she lay in his arms, dying. Her blood, and their baby's. He cleared his throat, feeling a lump in his throat, and dampness upon his lashes.

"Moses?" Sarah asked, knowing what he was thinking, with the innate perception of one who feels her loved-one's pain. "Are you all right?"

"Fine as can be expected, under the circumstances, darlin'," he replied. He squeezed her hand gently, then raised it to his lips and kissed it. The deep, mellow sound of his voice, brought her comfort, though she knew he was reliving the loss of his first wife and child. She leaned her head against his shoulder, momentarily, then straightened as Doc Valentine and his wife, Judith, approached, offering Tommy their condolences. They nodded at the Gentrys and took a seat in one of the back pews.

Reverend Higgins came down the aisle, stopping to speak with Tommy and his children. A stillness, broken only by a few coughs, was all to be heard in the small church, until the Dawson baby began to cry. It seemed that nothing would quiet her! Then, to Sarah's surprise, Mary O'Leary rose from where she had been sitting with her family, and walked to the pew where Tommy and his children sat. The reverend stepped back, allowing her to pass. She said something to Tommy, then slipped into the pew, quickly gathering the small child up into her arms. The baby's cries immediately subsided as she snuggled against young Mary, who continued to hold her and croon softly to her throughout the rest of the service.

Reverend Higgins stepped up to the podium and began the eulogy. Many people cried. Those who didn't, sniffled often, and wiped their eyes. Mary O'Leary continued to hold Polly, who slept peacefully, within her arms. Sarah was pleased to see the Dawson children comforted, to some extent, by Mary's presence. Why, even Tommy seemed to be consoled by her being there!

When the service was over, the assembly proceeded to the cemetery, then on to the Dawson house. Rosie and many of the other older women, had gone there earlier, bringing food and setting out plates and utensils that would be needed. They also had dusted, cleaned, and swept, so the house would be more presentable. As Rosie put the coffeepot to boil, Mrs. O'Leary shoved a mongrel dog out from under the kitchen table and out the door. It's dark, soulful eyes mirrored the sadness of all the Dawson family. Few words were exchanged as they went about their work. Most of the women had been at issue with Melinda Rose concerning her ways, never realizing she was, most likely, doing the best she could. Many had stopped frequenting the Dawson store as far back as the previous year, not wanting to be rundown by the unruly and undisciplined children. Others had found Melinda Rose's attitude snobbish and rude, and had avoided her, and the store, at all costs. They worked quietly now, each aware of their inability to reconcile her untimely death with the fact that they may have, in some small way, contributed to it. Without meaning to, of course, never dreaming it would come to this!

As the mourners began to stream into the house, Rosie poured coffee and ushered them all inside. Sarah noticed that the house seemed even more dreary and forlorn, if that were possible, than when Melinda Rose was alive. The Dawson children stayed close to Mary O'Leary, who proceeded to hang up their coats, wipe their noses, and dish them all up plates of the hot, delicious-smelling food. She seemed more at home in the Dawson house, Sarah noticed, than Melinda Rose ever had. Only Danny absented himself from her attentions. He stood off to the far side of the room, looking as lost and forlorn as a boy his age could look. Sarah noticed how sad he seemed as he stood there, staring out the window: his young, gangly, small-boned body and thin arms giving him an underfed look. He was fair-skinned, a handsome boy, with his mother's hair and eyes. Only in his body-build did he resemble his deceased father, Daniel.

Sarah put down her cup of coffee and walked over to where he stood, her heart breaking for the grief she knew he felt. "Danny, can I get you a plate of food?" she asked, noticing his hands clench tightly into fists, as she awaited his response. He said nothing. "I know how you must feel. We *all* feel deeply sad, but you must eat. Your mother would want you to," she added, speaking softly, hoping to comfort him. Still, he did not answer, though she noticed his lips begin to quiver and saw his thin body stiffen. "I'm *so sorry* about your mother, Danny. I *know* how bad you must feel..." she began, and she started to reach out to touch his arm. As she did, he whirled around to face her, his eyes blazing with a look of hatred so vile that she drew back in shocked surprise, feelings of trepidation enveloping her!

"You get away from me!" Danny screamed. "You *don't know* how I feel! You don't know *nuthin*'! You *killed* my Maw and I hate you! *I hate you!* Why don't you go back to the Indians *where you belong!*"

Stunned silence filled the room! Danny turned and raced from the house, tears running down his cheeks. Sarah stood there, unaware that her body was shaking. Unaware, too, of Moses hurrying to her side. Her heart pounded violently in her chest, and just as he reached her, she felt her knees buckle, and a blanket of darkness enfolded her within its soft embrace. Only a quick response on his part, saved her from hitting the floor; saved her from *physical* pain. But, *nothing* could lessen the emotional pain that flooded the very core of her being!

The smelling salts Doc held to her nose brought her back to awareness. Rosie and Angus stood at one end of the couch where she lay, anxious expressions upon their faces. Moses stood at her side, a mixed expression of worry and anger upon his. Doc Valentine smiled gently down at her, though she had to squint to make out his features.

"What happened? Oh, oh, Moses..." she began, as the memory of Danny's words rushed back to her. "Oh, Moses, oh, my goodness! He blames *me* for his mother's death! He blames *me*, Moses!" She began to cry, covering her mouth with one hand, and trying to push up to a sitting position with the other.

"Lie still, darlin'. I heard what the boy said. Don't think about it." His face contorted in anger. "Darn fool child!"

"He hates me," she whispered, tears running down her face.

Moses knelt beside her, gently brushing her hair back off her face. "There, there, darlin'. He's just hurtin', that's all. He's young and doesn't know how to handle so much pain. He had to blame *someone*, and you were a handy target." His voice was soft and gentle, though all the time worry filled him. Sarah had been through so much in her life, he kept thinking: adjusting to a new lifestyle when she married Gray Eagle, his death, and then being raped and the loss of their baby. She had survived all these things, and more. Survived, and stood tall and strong. Proud. And yet, today, a child's hateful words had caused her to faint! He had never known her to faint before, and it worried him immensely.

"How do you feel now, Sarah?" Doc asked, taking her hand and patting it gently. Sarah sniffled and looked up at him, her eyes betraying the depth of sadness she felt.

"I fainted, didn't I?" she asked, quietly.

"Yes, you did. Do you think you can sit up now?"

"I'll try," she said, and Moses stood, watching her as she did so. It was then that she saw all the others: the townsfolk who had come to pay their respects to Tommy and his family. They had heard every vicious, hate-filled word that Danny had flung at her, before she passed out. She hid her face in her hands and began to *cry*. A feeling of shame engulfing her. Moses sat down beside her, wrapping his arms around her, shielding her from the prying eyes, as Rosie ushered everyone out of the room and back into the kitchen. Doc Valentine excused himself, going to the kitchen for a cup of coffee, so they could have a few moments to themselves.

"Oh, Moses, he hates me," Sarah again stated, as fresh tears began to run down her cheeks.

"No, darlin', he's heard all the cruel things his mother said about you, over the years, and used them to give vent to his grief and anger at losing her. When he adjusts to her loss, he'll regret his words. You'll see."

"I doubt it," she said. "You didn't see the hatred in his eyes. I was... afraid he meant to hurt me."

"God help him if he had raised a hand to you, darlin'. He'd have answered to *me*, and answered *dearly!* Even if he *is* just a child!"

"Where did he go?" Sarah asked, wiping her eyes.

"I don't know," Moses replied. "Tommy went to find him, went to talk to him. He hasn't come back yet."

Sarah brushed some strands of hair back off her face, shaking her head sadly. "Would you mind if we went home now?" she asked. "I don't want to face everyone," she explained, nodding her head toward the kitchen.

"Can you stand up?" he asked, standing, and reaching to help her.

"I don't know why I fainted," she replied, as she got, shakily, to her feet. "That's not like me, at all. I *never* faint." And as she said this the room began, once more, to spin.

CHAPTER 54

They stayed the night at Rosie's. Moses had insisted when Sarah fainted for the second time. He was more than a little worried, and sat up half the night, watching her while she slept. Making silent promises to the Lord, and bargaining with God! Nothing helped to ease his troubled mind! Nothing helped ease his feeling of helplessness! He could not lose her! I can't imagine life without her, he thought, and prayed again that she was all right. That it was nothing serious, and God would "fix" whatever it was! I'll go to church *every* Sunday…if I'm not needed to do my job. I'll try to help Mrs. O'Leary and her children more. *Anything* You want, Lord, anything at all. You just show me what it is, and I'll do it! Just don't let her die. Please. It wouldn't be fair. I already had my whole world stop, once, when my first wife and baby died. It just wouldn't be fair to let it happen again! These thoughts raced through his mind, giving him no rest, nor comfort.

Sarah moaned in her sleep, and his mind swept him away to their wedding day and how beautiful she had looked, in her beaded buckskin dress, and moccasins. Then, at last, had come the night they had waited so long for: their wedding night. He felt his body warm as he thought of their love-making. Love-making like none he had ever experienced before! Her skin: smooth and white as the finest ivory, her breasts: peaking beneath his touch, her body: opening to him—whimpers of delight echoing in his ears as she arched to meet him, taking him deeper and deeper inside. They had been consumed by the love they felt for each other, surrendering themselves to it until they lay in each other's arms, blissfully content and exhausted!

She moaned again, calling out to him. "Moses?"

He quickly undressed and slid into the bed beside her, holding her close against him. "I'm right here, darlin'. What is it?" He wrapped his arms around her, stroking her side gently.

"Was I wrong to come back? Was I wrong to think they'd ever accept me again?"

Moses pulled his arm back and gently turned her toward him, his heart growing heavy at her words. He caressed her gently, carefully choosing his reply.

"Sarah, you belong here, with me. This is your home...Hastings. This is where your family and your friends are. Where *I* am. I love you, Sarah, more every day. You can't beat yourself up over the hurtful words of a child. Especially a child who got those words right from his mother. Melinda Rose, God rest her soul, was *sick*, honey. Sick in her mind. Sick with jealousy where you were concerned, and nothing you ever said—or did—caused her sickness. You've got to believe that."

She lay there, listening to him, her hand resting softly against his chest, her hair spreading across his shoulder. Her eyes were shut, his body warm against hers.

He went on..."Remember when you helped the baby to turn, the night Danny was born? If you hadn't been there darlin', he would have died, sure as anything. Isn't that right?"

"It may be right, Moses, but now he hates me."

"No. I don't believe that. He's just a little boy with a whole lot of pain on his plate. *Too much* pain for a child his age. He lashed out at you because of all the crap he's heard spew from his mother's mouth. Because she was *sick!* Do you think a woman who was well would have put her children through all the grief and sorrow the Dawson children are going through now? *No!* No *sane* woman would have, and you know it! You're *not* to blame, Sarah, and Danny will come to see that, too, when he gets older."

Sarah snuggled deeper into his arms, comforted by his words, and by his closeness. They kissed then, a kiss not of passion—though each might have welcomed it—but a kiss that embraced the love they felt in their hearts for each other. "I love you, Moses Gentry," she whispered.

"And I love you, darlin'," he replied, hoping with all his heart he would never lose her. Hoping with all his heart that God had heard his earlier pleas, and had accepted all his offered bargains. Hoping with all his heart that Doc Valentine would find her completely healthy when he examined her the following day. He heard her sigh and felt her body relax against his, knowing she was asleep. "Asleep and safe," he whispered into the silence, as he watched the moon slide behind a dark cloud beyond the room's only window. He prayed she would always remain so.

The next morning, the smell of Rosie's good cooking woke them. Sarah stretched as she lay beside her husband, playfully brushing his hair from his eyes. He kissed her, first on the lips, then on the side of her slender neck.

"Moses...Rosie will hear us if we get...you know...rambunctious," she whispered, running her fingers across his chest, then lower and lower.

"You'd better stop *that*, my love, or she'll hear *plenty!* She giggled and rolled away from him. Placing a kiss on her shoulder, he reveled in the sleek, smoothness of her back and the tantalizing swell of her buttocks. "Um-m-m, you take my breath away, lady," he drawled, bracing himself up on one elbow and trailing his hand along her backbone. She inhaled sharply as he touched her buttocks, and moaned as he fondled her, no longer wanting him to stop.

Reaching back, her hand touched his muscular stomach. He held his breath as she moved her hand lower, slowly tracing the outline of him until he could stand it no more. "Oh, darlin'," he whispered softly, rolling her onto her back and positioning himself between her welcoming thighs. She closed her eyes, her senses reeling as he entered her, thrusting slow and easy so as not to squeak the old bed. She wrapped her legs tightly around him, taking him deep inside, all the while trying to be as quiet as possible. She knew Rosie and Angus, were probably in the kitchen just below, having a coffee together and she had no wish to entertain them, she thought, with squeaks and moans and unholy groans! As she thought this, she began to giggle and could not stop! Moses "shushed"her once, a pained expression upon his face, causing her to dissolve into further peels of laughter. And though he tried to keep his mind on the job at hand, it quickly became apparent that was impossible. As tears ran down her cheeks—her hands covering her mouth to stifle the sound of her laughter—his passion dissolved into a limp and useless mass. He groaned, rolling away from her, knowing beyond a doubt that it was useless to try to proceed. She looked at him, a look of pure devilment dancing in her eyes. He grimaced, rubbing his stomach. "You wait till I get you home," he whispered, grinning at her.

"Promises, promises," she replied, grinning back at him, knowing it would be a wonderful homecoming—well worth waiting for.

CHAPTER 55

Angus had already left for his daily walk through town when Sarah and Moses came downstairs. Rosie was busy straightening up in the parlor, at the moment, so Moses stole a quick and very discreet kiss. "How do you feel, darlin'?" he asked, watching her closely.

"Fine...just fine...really, you can stop worrying," she replied, smiling at him. "I think it's because I didn't eat much yesterday, with the funeral and all, you know. Maybe I've become a ninny, like all the other women in Hastings," she added. "Next, I'll be screaming at the sight of a snake." She hoped making light of what had happened would erase his worried look, but it didn't.

He smiled, but it was an uneasy smile, and she knew it.

"Children! I didn't hear ya' come down...sit! sit!" Rosie ordered, cheerfully. "I'll fix ya' some breakfast." She bustled around, filling their cups with coffee and breaking eggs into a large skillet, as bacon fried in another smaller pan. "How are you feeling this monin'?" she asked, trying to sound alot more unconcerned than she felt.

"I'm fine," Sarah replied, "really I am. With you two fussing over me, I have to be!" Rosie laughed softly in response, but she saw her glance quickly in Moses direction, as if to confirm it. "I'm fine, *please* stop worrying...*both* of you," Sarah stated, and rose to pour them all a second cup of coffee. Both Rosie and Moses saw her suddenly grab the side of the table, trying to regain her balance.

Moses nearly tipped his chair over in his rush to reach her, as she swayed unsteadily, the color draining from his face as he lifted her up into his arms. "Get her coat, Rosie. I'm taking her to Doc's, now!" His voice was filled with concern bordering on fear.

"Oh, dear," Rosie said, hurrying to drape Sarah's coat over her as best she could, while Moses held her. "Oh, dear, I do wish Angus was here," Rosie said, her cheeks flushed.

"I can walk," Sarah said, her tone less them pleasant. "Moses, *please*... what will people think? What if someone sees us?" "Someone be damned!" he stated, hurrying even faster. "Now be still, so we don't fall on the ice."

Sarah knew he was frightened, so she buried her face in the fabric of his shirt and remained silent. I've always been a hardy sort, she thought, able to walk and run long distances without even tiring. Now something *must* be wrong. *Decidedly wrong!* And she had to admit, at least to herself, that *she* was frightened, too!

Moses fairly kicked open the door at the doc's office, in his haste to enter. Doc Valentine came running at the resounding bang of the door as it hit the wall. Not to mention, in response to Moses' yells.

"Put her down on the examining table, over there, and tell me what happened," Doc ordered, calmly.

"She nearly passed out again! What is it, Doc? What do you think's wrong?" Moses asked, his voice raising as he continued to explain. "I caught her, Doc, but this ain't right. Maybe the boy, Danny, upset her too badly yesterday. Maybe..."

The doctor interrupted. "Moses! Moses! Calm down, calm down. Go out in the kitchen with Judith, while I examine Sarah. Go! Go on, now. She'll be all right."

"Don't let her stand up, Doc, or she'll fall. Maybe I should stay here and be ready to catch her, in case...?"

"Moses, I won't let her stand. You have my word. Now go talk to Judith, so I can examine your wife."

Moses shook his head, in response, but did as the doctor requested. Thoughts raced through his head as he waited for the doctor's prognosis, a feeling of dread squeezing his heart until he thought *he* might pass out! "I can't lose her, I can't," he kept saying to Judith, who had given up on having a normal conversation with him.

"I'm certain she'll be all right, Moses," Judith replied, trying to calm the sheriff. Twice, he nearly upset his glass of water, when even the slightest noise had been heard from the doctor's examining room. After that, it was useless to try to carry on *any* conversation with him as he paced back and forth across the floor! When he heard Sarah squeal he could take it no more! He rushed down the hall, throwing open the door, trying to deduce the seriousness of her condition from the looks on Doc and Sarah's faces. His heart nearly stopped when he realized she was crying! Drawing on all the reserve he had, he hurried to her side, determined to be a veritable pillar of strength for her, no matter how serious the situation!

Doc Valentine saw Moses muster every ounce of courage he could as he rushed to her side. Saw him steady himself and draw on all his reserves. It warmed his heart to see the depth of love the sheriff had for his wife. He smiled, knowing that such love was a rare and true blessing from God, a love like he also felt for *his* wife.

"What is it, Doc? We can take it! Don't hold anything back. Just tell me right out!" Moses implored, his hand gently kneading Sarah's shoulder, as he spoke.

Doc Valentine looked at Sarah, and then at him, noticing that—even though it was cold outside—the sheriff was sweating. "Do you want to tell him, Sarah? Or would you rather I did?"

"Perhaps you should," she said, reaching over to grasp Moses' hand tightly.

"Well, it's like this…" Doc Valentine was enjoying himself now, and couldn't help prolonging the news, just a bit.

"What is it? Just tell me, Doc. We'll get through it, whatever it is," Moses stated, looking at him with a look of impending doom upon his face.

"It's just this, my friend," the doctor said, "and I'm certain you and Sarah *will* get through it just fine…because…you're going to have a baby!"

Moses looked at the doctor, then at Sarah, not expecting good news. For just a moment, he looked totally confused, then the truth began to sink in.

"A *baby?* We're gonna have a…a *baby?* But, why were you crying?" he asked Sarah. "I don't understand. And why do you keep fainting?"

"I'm crying because I'm happy. Women cry sometimes, when they're happy," she said.

"Then you're all right? *Really* all right?"

"Yes, *really* all right. Right, Doc?" she asked, smiling happily.

"Absolutely!" he replied, "though I want you to take it easy for awhile, till your body has a chance to adjust, and the fainting spells stop."

Moses walked over to a chair and sat down, looking as if the wind had gone out of him. He looked down at the floor, covering his eyes with one hand. It was a moment or two before he got up and walked back over to her, a moment or two, before she noticed that his eyes were damp with unshed tears.

"A baby, darlin'," he said, too choked up to say more. He held her to him, silently thanking God for hearing his pleas and answering them. He couldn't remember, at the moment, the promises and bargains he had made with God, but knew he owed his Maker a "big one"!

CHAPTER 56

Rosie wrung her hands and paced back and forth in her kitchen. What on earth could be taking Moses and Sarah so long at the doctor's? Why, in her day, fainting—unless something like an accident or bad fright had taken place—was usually a sign that a woman was going to have a baby, and her body was adjusting, that's all. She stopped in her tracks! "Oh, Angus!" she cried, "How foolish I am! I *know* why Sarah fainted, I'm certain of it!"

Angus had just returned from town, and nearly upset the cup of coffee she had poured for him when she shouted. "And why is tha', me angel?" he asked, taking her plump hand within his own, and enjoying the radiant smile that shone like the morning sun across her lovely face.

"A baby!" she proclaimed. "Sarah's going to have a baby. I'm certain of it!"

He pushed his chair back from the table, pulling her onto his lap, his arms wrapped tightly around her middle. "A wee bairn, me angel, and us... gran'parents!"

Rosie rubbed her cheek against his soft white beard, wrapping her arms around his neck. "And a fine grandfather you'll be," she said, kissing him on the tip of his nose.

He nestled his head against hers, enjoying immensely the precious love they had found in each other. "'Tis blessed, I am, me sweet Rosie. 'Tis so happy ye've made me," he whispered, nuzzling her neck.

She giggled, like a young schoolgirl, as his beard tickled her. "No, Angus MacGregor, it's I who have been blessed—as surely as I'm sittin' here—for I love ya' as no other before ya', and I can't imagine a day without ya'!"

Angus held her close until he heard Moses and Sarah's voices, as they approached the house. "Me legs have gone fast asleep, dear angel," he teased, "and the children are comin', so off ye go." And he grinned at Rosie, helping her get to her feet.

She rose and rushed to open the door, just as Moses reached to knock. The beautiful smiles on the young couple's faces, confirming, at first glance, her predictions.

"We're gonna have a baby!" Moses exclaimed, before she could ask.

Angus rose and gripped Moses' hand, as Rosie helped Sarah off with her coat. "Why, we knew tha', laddie. We'd already figured it oot," Angus replied, his eyes twinkling with delight.

"Come sit, both of ya'," Rosie ordered. "I'll get us all some breakfast now, and ya' can tell us what Doc said."

Moses pulled out a chair for Sarah, taking her by the arm until she was safely seated. She smiled at him, her cheeks reddening in embarrassment at his over-protectiveness. "Moses, you don't have to guard my every move. I'm fine! I just have to eat regular meals and take it easy for awhile."

He grinned at her, hearing her words, still unconvinced of their validity. "I know, darlin', but, I intend to see that you don't overdue it." Rosie and Angus exchanged smiles, enjoying the young folk's discussion.

"Let me get us another cup of cof..." Sarah began, starting to rise from her chair.

"I'll get it!" Moses exclaimed, nearly upsetting his chair, in his hurry to do so.

"Moses," Sarah pleaded, "please..."

He grinned sheepishly at her as he filled all their cups. "I can't help it," he stated, and they all had to laugh at the look of utter helplessness upon his face.

Sarah knew that she had to get these fainting spells behind her, somehow, or her husband would *never* let her resume *any* of her normal activities! It pleased her, how overjoyed he was about the baby, but she had always been a completely capable person, and she felt bothered to think she was somewhat less than that now, due to the fainting spells.

As Rosie dished up their food and passed each their plates, Angus spoke: "I've a favor t' ask ye, lad."

"Name it!" Moses replied, feeling immensely beneficent.

"I know ye have enough money t' buy the wee bairn a cradle, laddie. But, if ye would let me, I'd be pleased t' make him his first one," Angus offered. They all looked at him in surprise.

"'Tis a skill I took up t' pass the long hours, when Johnny and me were holed-up, tha' long ago winter." He got a faraway look in his eyes. "I was carvin' yer verra ain cradle, lad, when yer mither disappeared."

Moses stared at him in shocked surprise, saying nothing, as thoughts assailed him. At last he replied, "I'd be proud to have you make the baby a cradle, Angus. *More* than proud." There were smiles all around as they commenced to eat. Moses had not gotten used to the idea, yet, that he was going to be a father. Nor had he thought of the ties this child had, not only to his mother—Singing Raven—but also to John Bruce. Why, this baby was the grandchild of *both*, he realized, smiling. He shook his head in amazement. All those years after his first wife had been killed, he had wandered from place to place. Drunk and filled with anger and grief, beside himself with tormented feelings as burning as hell, itself. Some days, he had slept off his drinking bouts in strangers' barns, or in livery stables, waking to the startling realization of not knowing where he was, or how he had gotten there. His mind was clouded back then, from too much whiskey and too much pain. His sober moments, few. His soul had been filled with rage! A rage that spread all through him, ripping at his guts and clawing at his mind, deadening his heart till he felt nothing! Nothing, but the hellish surcease of all that was good and decent. He had lived with the rage. Rage so black that all sense of goodness and decency had left him. Had drifted through one day to the next, thinking only of his loss, his intended revenge, and his next drink! He had not cared, or prayed, or even cried, after awhile. No tears were left inside him. Just a hate so vile that he wanted only to die! A hate so vicious, that he felt totally *consumed* by it! Suddenly, overcome by these thoughts, he told Sarah to stay off her feet, rose from the table, quickly grabbed his coat, and went out the door.

Sarah began to rise... to follow him, not understanding the expression that she had seen on his face. But Angus stopped her. "Let him go, lass, let him go. He's a few things t' think oot, is all. 'Tis best you let him be."

She sat back down, feeling confused. Angus chewed another bite of food, and then put down his fork and looked at her, a tender expression upon his face. "T' some men, lass, being a father is nae big thing. Jist anither day, at best. Anither mouth t' feed. Yer Moses is na' like tha'. The gravity o' this new blessin' has given the lad a fair shakin'. Ye see, lass, unless I be mistakin', 'tis given him pause t' consider a few things he's na' considered afore."

"I don't understand," she replied.

"Well, lass, sometimes a man has t' look *back* at his past deeds, and put them righ...er bury them, if he can, afore he can look ahead. Aye, awareness of a new bairn t' be born, can cause a man—a good man—t' recollect on how he's lived his life...and how he can be the kind o' father the new babe will need. A father who can raise-up the wee babe on a righteous path. I reckon yer husband's been through a lot in his life, lass. Now, 'tis time fer him t' du some soul-searchin': t' "settle accounts," so t' speak, wi' in hisself. I reckon tha's wha' he's doing right this verra minute."

"How do you know that?" Sarah asked, as Rosie quietly cleared the table.

"Been through it, meself, lass," he stated, and sat back, a faraway look in his eyes. "Aye, lass, been through it meself."

She remembered then that he had been married, and lost his wife and young children in a fire. She reached over and squeezed his hand. "Thank you, Mac. I know old John would be *so very proud* to have *you* be our baby's grandfather."

CHAPTER 57

Lea Denton liked the town of Hastings. It was small and peaceful, with friendly people who seemed to sincerely care about each other. She had hesitated, at first, to go to the Dawson woman's funeral, but her sister, Ophelia, had assured her that it would be quite proper, and an appreciated gesture.

"We're all friends here," she had told her, "and no one will think it odd if you go with me."

So she had changed from her traveling clothes, washed the dust and grime of the stagecoach trip from her body, fixed her hair, and accompanied Ophelia. She was quite nervous as they entered the small church, somewhat self-conscious, but after a few introductions, she realized that none of the townsfolk—or the mourning family— seemed to think she was out of place, being there. In fact, she was quite impressed with the town's inhabitants! Especially, one in particular. The handsome, dark-haired man who occupied the pew directly across the aisle from her and Ophelia. She couldn't help noticing that he seemed more than a little interested in her, too! She noticed how often he had glanced her way, and it pleased her, but it also reminded her of the futility of garnering any hopes where he was concerned. After all, she *was* married, though she wore no ring, and was using her maiden name now.

Yes, she was well aware of the man's attractiveness: taller by a head than she, nice build, a pleasant smile, and eyes that held a look of tenderness. Cal was his name, Ophelia had told her, Cal Dunnevey. He was fairly new in Hastings, having arrived there about a year ago.

He was the owner of the Mercantile where Ophelia often shopped, and she had said he was considerate, well-read, and laughed easily. If it hadn't been for Johnathon Clark—the banker—and their on-going, comfortable friendship, she said she would have entertained the possibility of a friendship with Mr. Dunnevey, herself.

Lea had laughed at her sister, teasing her. "You've been in an "on-going" friendship with Mr. Clark ever since you arrived in Hastings, practically! When is he ever going to propose?"

Ophelia smiled at her younger sister, shaking her head, slightly. "He has proposed. He does so quite often, in fact."

"Then, why aren't you married?" Lea asked, taken aback by learning this.

Ophelia was making up the small bed in the spare room, for Lea, and did not answer immediately. When she finished, she returned to the small sitting room and sat down on the couch beside Lea. "You know what Mother went through, Lea. How Father was when he drank. How he raged at her, and... and threw things. You know how sad she was, and frightened. And you know what *you've* endured. I can't bring myself to accept Johnathon's proposal because of these things. *You* should be the *first* to understand," she explained.

"I *do* understand, Ophelia, but are you happy by yourself?" Ophelia measured her words carefully, before speaking.

"What is happiness, Lea? Can you tell me? Happiness is different for each person. Some women want a grand house and an affluent, hard-working husband. Some are content to live in a more usual manner: a home full of children, a dog, and the everyday blessings and burdens of such a life. *Or*, perhaps they're *not* that content.

Perhaps they married the man they loved, expecting a successful husband, and little by little, their expectations became nothing more than a harsh reality." She straightened her skirt, frowning. "I define happiness differently...a "peaceful contentment." That's what I want, and have: peaceful contentment. I may live alone, but it has its benefits. I can grade papers in the middle of the night, if I feel like it, without riling a husband by doing so. I can sleep late when school is not in session, or wake early, to do whatever it is I please. Oh, Lea, I don't suppose you can understand, being younger, but I enjoy my life as it is! Johnathon enjoys my company, and I, his. We're considered a "couple," I suppose, but, still we are free to enjoy our own pursuits, our own lives! We don't have to explain our relationship to anyone, since we're older, except to say we're "friends." I've given it a lot of thought, Lea. Johnathon is an extremely nice person: kind, considerate, and not hard on the eyes. He's also very intelligent, worldly, and well-read. He dresses nicely, is quite well-to-do—though we've never discussed it—and is well thought of. All traits I want in a man." She sat quietly, then, looking toward the window, hearing a buckboard pass on the street below. "Lea, those are *all* great attributes, but I can't help remembering how deceiving those qualities can be. How quickly they can change to cruel words, and even crueler actions." She shuddered, as she thought back in time, then rose, walking across the room to stand before the mirror. She looked at her reflection a long time, without speaking, and saw the few wisps of gray hair, the small wrinkles at the corner of her eyes, and more, above her lips. Worst of all, she was still able, after all this time, to see the pain that lingered there, from so long ago. She turned to face her sister. "I used to want children: a boy and a girl, preferably. And a husband, not unlike Johnathon. Even wanted a large, elegant home like his, with flowers in the yard and a pond we could sit beside on warm summer days. And I...oh, I *like* my life, as it is, Lea. I've grown to like it. Grown to accept it. It brings me satisfaction and a sense of worth when even one child at school learns something I've taught him, or her." She walked over and sat back down beside Lea. "Happiness is not always as we wish it. Circumstances tend to dictate what it is, Lea."

Lea looked at her, not understanding how Ophelia felt, so immersed was she in her own thoughts and feelings. "I'd say happiness is...being loved by a wonderful man," Lea said. "A man who *wouldn't* change! *And* having a home where both the children—*and the* mother—felt safe." She rose from the couch, taking up the oil lamp. "I can't keep my eyes open another minute, Ophelia, and I'll need to be rested if I'm to look for work in the morning. We'll talk more, then, all right?"

Ophelia stood, giving Lea a quick hug. "I'm glad you're here, Lea. I hope you'll stay."

"I hope I *can*" Lea replied, and for only a second, Ophelia saw the fear in her eyes.

CHAPTER 58

Cal Dunnevey was having a bad day! A shipment of goods he had ordered had arrived on the stage the day before. But, to his chagrin, it was *extremely* larger than what he had wanted! He sat at his desk in the back of the store, his shirt sleeves rolled up to his elbows, order sheets and receipts spread out in front of him. Inventory records and statements lay to one side, checked and rechecked for mistakes. Should have been on hand to get the delivery, myself, he thought. Should have made it my business to check the merchandise, instead of going to Melinda Rose's funeral. Instead, I had Patrick O'Leary tend to things while I was gone, and now I've got a mess on my hands. He added the long list of figures for the third time, then sorted through the stack of invoices, again. His hair hung down as he leaned forward and he reached up, absentmindedly, to brush it back, while trying to make sense of the task at hand.

"Of all the darn fool mistakes!" he exclaimed, as he began to figure out what had caused the problem. "Why any fool with decent eyesight can see that's 100, and not 700!" he exclaimed, angrily. He had not heard the front door open as he spoke, nor noticed the slim, young woman that entered. "Time I get this mess sorted out, I'll *never* have time to get the wagon unloaded, and the supplies in," he mumbled aloud, "let alone, price everything. I swear, a man needs *four* hands to get everything done, in this business!" He shook his head, then realized he was not alone. Looking up, he was more than a little surprised—and pleased—to see Ophelia Denton's sister, standing in front of his desk. "Hello," he said, reaching out to shake her hand.

Lea smiled, extending her hand. His was warm and covered her small one. Cal began rolling down his shirt sleeves, and reaching for his suit coat. "I apologize for the mess," he said, "and my unsuitable attire. I didn't hear you come in."

"Don't trouble yourself, please," she replied. "I can see you're hard at work. And I don't mind shirt sleeves." She laughed softly, and Cal smiled back.

"Can I help you, Miss ...?"

"It's Lea," she replied. "Please...just call me, Lea."

"Yes, Ma'am," he said, taking in her lovely ivory skin and extremely small waist, not to mention, her soft ash-blonde ringlets and those incredible smokey-gray eyes!

She turned and walked slowly through the store, with Cal following closely behind, his heart beating so loudly he was afraid she'd hear it. Suddenly, she turned to face him, and he nearly bumped into her. "Oh! Sorry," he said, feeling like a lumbering idiot.

She looked up at him, then demurely lowered her eyes, before speaking. "I heard what you said."

"Said?" he questioned. He felt so dazzled by her that it seemed his mind had turned to mush. "I beg your..." he began, then words failed him as he gazed at the ruffled lace at her graceful neck, and at the dainty locket that lay against the fabric of her blouse above her small breasts.

She moved her hand up to her neck, her cheeks turning a soft shade of pink, as she noticed the expression on his face. "You said a man needs four hands to get everything done," she replied, thinking how soft his lips looked: kissable, she thought. She felt soothed, somehow, by the mere nearness of him.

They stood there, staring into each other's eyes, hearts pounding, and senses tingling with awareness. Cal had never seen another woman as beautiful. Never wanted to touch one, or hold one, like he wanted to hold her. He thought her *exquisite*! No one had ever had this effect on him!

Lea broke the spell that seemed to bind them. She closed her eyes, for just a moment—to get control of herself—then, once again, looked down at the floor.

Cal cleared his throat, not certain if he had understood...or not. "You're...you're looking for a *job?*" he asked, wondering if he could *be* so lucky.

"Yes," she answered, softly. "If I'm to stay here, Mr. Dunnevey, I must find work."

Cal felt like jumping over his desk and shouting at the top of his lungs! "How soon can you start?" he asked, hardly able to believe his good fortune!

"Immediately," she replied. "If you'll just tell me what I'm to do."

Cal looked around the store, trying to think of all the things he had planned to get done before he closed for the day, but his mind had become a total blank. He shook his head, trying to think of something—*anything*—but ideas failed him. He grinned, then, exclaiming, "You're hired!" And they both had to laugh.

CHAPTER 59

Lea was positively glowing when she entered her sister's rooms at the boarding house that evening. Her cheeks were flushed and her eyes seemed to sparkle, Ophelia noticed. "Why Lea, what have you been up to?" she asked, putting down her sewing, as Lea shut the door and danced happily across the room.

"Oh, Ophelia, you'll never believe the day I've had!"she said, removing her coat and hat.

"Well, I've never seen you so happy. Come sit here beside me, and tell me all about it." Lea dropped down beside her sister on the couch and told her—practically word for word—all the details of what had occurred.

Ophelia said nothing, not wanting to cloud the happiness she saw on Lea's face.

"Oh, Ophelia, he's so wonderful. He's kind and gentle, and has the sweetest smile." She noticed the disapproving look upon Ophelia's face, but continued talking: "He hired me to work at the store—can you believe it?—starting when I went in to apply. I dusted shelves and organized some things on them, and later, folded yards and yards of fabric that had just come in. It wasn't hard at all, and he's going to pay me *two* dollars a week!" She bent down to unbuckle her boots. "Well, say something!" she demanded, as Ophelia continued to sit still, not commenting.

"Did you tell him you're married?" she asked at last, seeing the joy disappear from Lea's face, as she knew it would.

"No! No, I did not," Lea replied. "I…I just couldn't. You didn't see the nice way he kept looking at me, Ophelia, like I was…*special.* Like he …*cared* for me."

"All the more reason to tell him," Ophelia stated. "If he gets feelings for you, you'll hurt him deeply when you *do* tell him. That's not right. Cal Dunnevy is too decent a man, Lea, to play for a fool."

Lea sat there, thinking over what Ophelia had said, though just the tiniest bit angry. She knew Ophelia was right. She had no business ignoring the facts! She *was* married, and whether she liked it, or not, Cal Dunnevey had a right to know. He was, after all, her boss. And because of it, *he* was in danger now, too!

CHAPTER 60

The weeks passed quickly as winter storms abated and buds began to appear on all the trees. Lea had worked at the Mercantile for seven weeks now, and at Ophelia's insistence, she had finally garnered all her courage, and had—at the end of her first month of employment—told Cal she was married. How deeply she regretted having to do so, but she had realized Ophelia was right, and knew she had no choice.

Cal had looked stunned, at first, then deeply disappointed. She could read his feelings in his eyes, without him saying a word. She nearly cried while telling him, but managed, somehow, to keep her composure. If only he knew how hard it is for me to tell him, she remembered thinking, as she turned away, walking to the back of the store to where a box of fabric sat that needed folding.

She had stood there, her back to him, hoping he would say something, *anything*! Hoping he would not tell her to leave. After awhile, she slowly turned to face him, raising her head to look up at him.

"Lea..." he began, but stopped, and only stood looking at her, his eyes betraying the emotion he was feeling.

"I'm sorry," she whispered. "I should have told you right away."

He watched her as she spoke, and saw her eyes well up with tears. He cleared his throat and slowly reached out to touch her cheek, where first one tear, and then another, began to fall. "I wish you weren't married," he said. "I never would have..." he paused, as she looked up at him, "let myself...fall in love with you." His voice choked up.

Lea couldn't believe her ears! She stared at him, her heart doing leaps and bounds, at his words. Then he pulled her gently into his arms and kissed her!

Time seemed to stand still as they embraced. Lea felt weak, as his lips pressed softly against hers. Felt faint, as her body began to respond to the fire that suddenly enveloped her. She couldn't help herself, and began to cry, causing Cal to quickly end the embrace.

"Oh, Lea, I'm sorry. I didn't mean to...please forgive me." He had only meant to give her a kiss. A quick kiss. A kiss that meant nothing, he told himself, but he knew that was not the truth. He had told her the truth: told her he loved her, and then...his feelings for her had gotten out of hand. He reached out to touch her arm, but she turned away, no longer crying, but looking helpless and hurt. "I'm so sorry, Lea. I was out of line. I...I can only hope you'll forgive me," he said.

"Do you want me to...go?" she asked then, her voice a mere whisper.

"Go?" he questioned. He groaned as he continued, "If you must... I'll understand." She did not move. "Lea?" he said, as she continued to stand there.

"Do you want me to *stay*?" she asked then, much to his surprise.

It took him only a moment to reply, "Oh, God, I wish you would!"

He never touched her after that, never held her or kissed her, but only the very strongest willpower kept him from doing so. Just to enjoy her presence, was enough for him. Better to see her, to hear her voice as she hummed or sang as she worked, or when she talked with him. Better to glance up and see her as she came through the door every morning, her smile as radiant as the sun, her hair shining like fine spun-gold. He was hopelessly in love with her, and that was enough, if that was all he could have! He had never loved anyone before as he loved her, and knew he never would.

Lea became more indispensable with each passing day. She had gotten adept at tending to not only cleaning, stocking, and sorting, but often keeping the books up-to-date, if he had to be out of the store for the day. She was good at math, she found, and often made out the orders, figuring how quickly an item usually ran low, and how often they could expect delivery. The townsfolk liked her, Cal noticed, and more ladies were starting to shop at the Mercantile, he realized. Often they sought her advice concerning the products, or the quality of a certain fabric. Like him, he was sure everyone appreciated her effervescent personality. He was certain that *she* was the main reason more and more folks had begun coming in. A lot of his customers had been regulars at Dawson's store, and he often wondered how Tom Dawson was making out since his wife's death. Someone—he couldn't remember who— said that Mary O'Leary went daily to the Dawson house to stay with the children, and they mentioned how clean she kept both the children and the house. They had wondered if Tom was paying her. Cal hoped all was well with them, and when he didn't have what a customer wanted, always encouraged them to look for it over at Dawson's. He felt sorry for the kids, and even sorrier for their father. It was hard having no one to care about you, and no one you cared about. How many years had he been alone? How many days had he said his morning prayers, praying that someone would come along that he could love? How many nights had he tossed and turned, his needs as a man going unmet? Oh yes, he thought, I know how lonely and hurting Tom Dawson must feel. I used to feel the same way, before Lea. Before Lea. Before Lea. Had *anything* ever really mattered, before Lea?

CHAPTER 61

Hastings was alive with flowers the latter part of the month of May. Everywhere the eye looked, there were flowers. Birds sang and soared in flight, and knobby-kneed baby calves stayed close to their mothers, as did all the other newborn animals.

Moses Gentry rolled out of bed and began to dress. Sarah was already up, he saw, and the aroma of fresh coffee beckoned to him. "Good morning, darlin'," he said, as she greeted him with a kiss. She was aglow with the fullness and beauty women have when they are with child, and he felt an inner contentment and a wealth of happiness every time he looked at her.

Sarah had experienced only one more fainting spell since that first visit to Doc Valentine, and after a couple weeks of bed rest, she seemed fine. Gradually, she resumed her usual routine.

Except, of course, for lifting, walking far, riding Glory, or hanging out clothes to dry. Moses saw to it that she did none of those things— and a few more—always warning her she must be careful. She had been angry, at first, trying to explain to him that she was not sick, simply with child, but it did no good. Rosie and Angus came to stay with her the two weeks that she was in bed, at Moses' insistence, and he was grateful. There was no way he could be in town—doing his job—and home, watching over her. When he was at the jail, he worried about her constantly, and had a hard time keeping his mind on his work. Gradually, however, their old routines re-established.

Sarah had to laugh the day Rosie and Angus had first arrived. There was Moses hanging out wash on a line he had run between two trees, his hair disheveled, and an apron of Sarah's tied haphazardly around his waist, covering his gun and holster.

"Mornin'," Angus had greeted him. "Are ye fixin't' go t' the jail in tha' thaur git-up?"

Moses had grinned, his eyes getting that devilish look she knew so well. "Think anyone would notice?" he countered. They had all laughed, and Sarah felt proud of him. Prouder than words could say, too, at how attentive he was. She had never felt so protected and cared for. She had never dreamed he would be such a wonderful husband, and relished every moment of it. But, as time wore on, it tried her patience! *Every time* she made a move to do even the smallest task, he rushed to her side! He was treating her like an invalid, one at death's door, and she began to resent it!

At last, she could stand it no more! "Moses, I'm *not* sick! And I'm *not* an invalid!" she snapped at him one day, when she could not take his constant fretting any longer. *"Stop suffocating me!* Please! I'm *not* fragile and frail like the ninnys' in town, and you're *not* going to lose me! I'm *not* your *other* Sarah!" She was dreadfully sorry the minute the words were spoken and gasped, clamping her hand over her mouth in shocked surprise.

Moses stared at her as though she had slapped him, and she saw, in his eyes, the gravity of the wound she had inflicted. "Oh, God! I'm sorry, Moses, I didn't mean..." but he turned and walked outside, slamming the door behind him! Sarah sat down in her rocker, hearing the sound of hoof-beats, knowing he had ridden away.

It was quite late when he returned. She lay in bed, waiting for him, praying he would forgive her. He came in, after unsaddling Midnight, a dispirited look upon his face. Sarah began to get up to go to him. "Stay in bed," he said. "It's chilly in here." He walked over and sat down on the edge of their bed. "I'm sorry," he said at last. "You're right. About everything." Sarah tried to speak, to tell him how sorry she was, but he put a finger to her lips, continuing: "I know you're a strong woman, Sarah. I know you're not an invalid. It's...it's like you said. My world *ended* when...the other Sarah was killed. I lost...everything that day. My past, my future, *everything*! I *died* that day as surely as she and the baby did." He paused, momentarily closing his eyes. "Then I ended up in Hastings, sober...*finally* sober...and...well, life went on." He gave a half-hearted laugh, shaking his head. "Life went on, but I was empty inside, do you understand? A man going through the *motions* of living, but still dead inside! Then, I met you. At first the resemblance pulled me to you." He sniffled and cleared his throat, then continued: "Later, when we delivered Danny, I saw how strong you were. I knew that night that something had changed for me, changed inside of me. I also knew that I loved you. I didn't admit it to myself. *Couldn't,* then. But, I knew. I felt *alive!* Alive, and filled with hope, again! Then, you told me about Gray Eagle and...well, you know the rest: your marriage to him, and later, your marriage to me. I loved you even more by then. Loved you more than I ever dreamed it was possible to love someone! When you fainted at the Dawson's, and those other times, I was terrified! I had learned through our love to live again. To hope, and trust, and *believe*, again! Then it seemed like all those things were going to be taken from me—a second time—and that's why I guess I 'suffocated you' and treated you like I did!" He rubbed his hand across his eyes, then turned to look at her. "You're my *everything*, Sarah. A second chance at life, *and* love! I can't bear the thought of losing you. You, or our baby!"

She began to cry as he spoke and reached out to him, her tears wetting his cheeks as she kissed him. He wrapped his arms around her, his own eyes damp with tears. Then he laid down next to her, his heart overflowing with the love he felt for her. "I'm so sorry, Moses," she whispered, as he kissed away her words.

Peaceful sounds filled the air around the cabin that night as they slept, wrapped in each other's arms. And the child growing within her kicked, now and then, and sucked its thumb. The Gentrys had had their first fight as a married couple and were none the worse for it.

CHAPTER 62

It hadn't been easy for Cal the last six months, working side by side with Lea. He always had to hold in his feelings for her. It wasn't just the fact that he loved her—he had known that almost from the moment he first set eyes on her—and it wasn't his body's response to her as he spent each day with her. It wasn't even the effect her beauty and loveliness had on him whenever he looked at her. He wanted her. Lord, how he wanted her! How many times had he thought of what their life together could be? No, the worst part of his imaginings was his fear that she would walk away, if he told her what he had done, long ago, to Victor Jalaco! Would she stay, if he told her he had killed a man? He had never had any regrets concerning Jalaco's death. He deserved it, plain and simple. But, how could a woman as sweet and gentle as Lea understand? He wracked his brain many sleepless nights, pacing back and forth in the small room at the back of the store where he stayed. He was not a man who could hide his feelings. Maggie had often told him that. She had also told him that the eyes were a window into a person's soul, and that's how *she* knew when he was sad, angry, or hurting, without him telling her. If Lea could read him like a book, too, would she know what he had done—someday—without him telling her? He couldn't bear the fact that she might turn away from him, if so. He paced back and forth, his thoughts tormenting him.

He walked through the store, aware that the changes he saw all around him were because of her. The mercantile positively shone! She had, in her spare time when no customers were about, polished all the furniture and cleaned the large window. Even the glass fronts of the counters were sparkling clean, thanks to her. Not a smudge, smear, or fingerprint on *any* of them. Also, she had devised a new way to draw in the womenfolk of Hastings, by setting a display of goods in the large front window. He had thought it a bit foolish, at first, but she seemed so certain it would work, that he had finally agreed. He had hesitated when she told him it would look like the inside of a cozy and comfortable cabin. But, her enthusiasm—and the look of happiness in her eyes—had won him over. When he nodded in agreement, she reached up on tiptoes and kissed him quickly on his cheek. He was putty in her hands, then, and knew he would have agreed to just about anything.

Together, they set up the scene in the large front window, and passerby's stopped to watch: some waving, some laughing. When they finished, Lea was delighted! On a table centered before the window, sat a display of dishes, utensils, and the newest graniteware coffeepots to come from back East. Red checkered material hung across the top of the window and down each side. She had taken it from some bolts of fabric he had not been able to sell, draping it to look like curtains. Then she put a rocker to one side, laying some new fabric he had just gotten in, across it. On the table, she also sat a vase of flowers and cast iron skillets and other pots and pans, arranging them so they all could be seen easily, from outside the window. Then she draped more fabric across the back of the chairs around the table: linens on one, plain cotton on another, and over on another, brightly colored calico fabrics. "That'll bring in the gals!" she said, clapping her hands, her eyes filled with excited anticipation!

On the floor in front of the table, she had Cal sit a bag of flour, a bag of sugar, and a large bag of rice. She told him it was "good business." It would remind folks if they were running low, so they could buy a bag before they left town. It would also show folks that The Mercantile had a good supply on hand. He liked the way she thought, and gladly carried all the bags to the front, placing them where she wanted them. She hummed, he noticed, as she worked, and often ran outside to check the effect of her display. Cal was glad he had agreed to her idea, just because it made her so happy. After all, he thought, if it made no difference in sales, what harm had it done? If it *did* improve sales—

though he doubted it would—that would be even better! He was sure he'd get plenty of razing from some of the fellows' in town—especially the ranch hands from over in the valley—but seeing Lea's happiness made it all worthwhile. He balked a bit when she had him set an old trunk to one side of the table, wondering how that could possibly help business. But she told him it made a lot of sense, and he would soon understand why. He shrugged his shoulders, smiling at her, and went to wait on some customers. When he had a free moment, about a half-hour later, she took him by the hand and led him outside. He was amazed at the scene she had managed to put together, seeing all the items arranged so precisely, and clearly visible to all who passed by. Well, he thought, it might just be a good idea, after all. It was then that he noticed the old trunk. It was no longer sitting there, looking drab and shabby. Instead, a beautiful quilt filled it, cascading from inside it and down its front. It was rich in color: a tiny floral print and dark blue, against a white background. The design was a series of scallop-edged circles, each piece made from the floral or blue fabric. Cal thought it was nice, but it wasn't part of his inventory, and he wondered why she wanted it in her display. He was soon to find out!

Lea knew he had noticed the quilt. You couldn't help but notice it. It stood out. She bit her lip, wondering if he would make her take it back out of the window. Well, she thought, there's only one way to find out! She followed him back to his desk, hoping he would not be mad. "Cal, I guess you're wondering about the quilt in the display," her voice was soft. "You see, I thought...well, I thought it would be a good thing, putting it there." She looked up at him, a little afraid to speak her mind. "If you don't like it there, since we don't actually sell quilts at the store, well...I guess I should explain." She cleared her throat and straightened her shoulders, looking him squarely in the eye. "It's an idea I had," she said. "A really good idea, I think."

He smiled at her, aware that she was nervous. He wanted to reach out and pull her to him. To hold her and kiss her and tell her to put anything she wanted in the window! But after all, merchandise they actually sold is what rightly belonged in the window. She should understand that. She looked so pretty standing there, however. What harm could one quilt do? "Tell me what you have in mind, Lea," he said, and couldn't miss the bright smile that appeared upon her face.

"Well, you know the folks around here. You know that some of them have it rough. Some can barely get by, due to one thing or another." She paused, "Well, I was talking to a lady the other day, after church, and she's a real nice lady. A widow with a lot of kids. She hasn't been too well since her husband died, Cal. And her hands are all swollen and bent, but her children do the chores and tend to most things around their place, and she stays in where it's warm and…well, she makes the most beautiful quilts. She's been making them since she was a young girl. Doesn't know how much longer she'll be *able* to make 'em, with her hands the way they are, and all. The quilt in the window is just one of them. I went to visit her last week, and I couldn't believe all the beautiful quilts she's made." Her cheeks had flushed to a bright pink as she talked, and Cal wasn't sure if it was from excitement, or enthusiasm. "Anyway, I asked her if she would let me take the quilt I have in the window, to see if we could sell it. It would really help her, and when that one sells, we could get another from her. We could give *her* most of the money we get for it, but keep a little for displaying it, I guess. That way the store would make a little from it, too. For our time and trouble, I guess you could say. What do you think?"

He couldn't miss the look of hope and anticipation on her face. Never in a thousand years had he expected her to come up with such an idea! Why, he could have been knocked down by a feather! Not only was she beautiful, she had brains! He couldn't have been prouder of her than he was at that very minute! "I think that's the *best* idea I've *ever* heard, Lea! I wish I had thought of it, myself," he said. She let out a squeal and looked happier than he had ever seen her.

That evening, after she had left for the day, he walked through the store. His thoughts prevented him from sleeping, and he felt restless and sort of sentimental. He walked to the front of the store, to where he could see the window display. It looked like the inside of an actual cabin. Warm and inviting. Homey. Like the rooms he hoped to have someday, when he built his house. A house he now hoped, somehow, to share with Lea.

He stood there, thinking back to the past spring when he had purchased a piece of land to the west of town. It was in June, when he had been in Hastings about six months. Out riding one day, he had found a beautiful spot, with a stream that flowed into a large lake just below a hill. A hill just perfect to build a house on! There was an enormous outcropping of rock behind the planned building sight, and everywhere—as far as the eye could see—were tall, stately trees! Maples, elders, cottonwood, scrub-oaks, and ash. And even two thick stands of pine.

He had often taken rides, when he wasn't working. Not being a drinking man, or interested in games of chance, he had few other forms of entertainment. Few he enjoyed as much as heading out of town, going along at a leisurely pace, soaking up the sun and the view.

Right from the first day he arrived in the area, he had been taken with the beauty of that piece of land, and felt an intense longing deep in his soul, to own it! To belong! He had never felt that way before, though he had traveled far and wide, putting mile after mile between himself, and the memories that could so quickly bring pain: memories of Maggie. Of her laughter and her bright satin dresses. Of her love for him. And always, memories of the day she had died.

He shook his head, glancing once more at the display in the window, a smile upon his face. He knew what his house would look like. Many a long, lonely night he had sat on his bed in the rear of the store, drawing out the plans for it. He wanted it more than ever, now. For himself, and Lea. Every time he thought of it, or looked at the drawings, he saw—in his mind's eye—her lovely face, her golden hair, and tiny waist. Everything he saw, or touched, or imagined, reminded him of her. However, it wasn't long before reality would set in. Stark reality! She belonged to another, and was not his. And would *never* be his, in all probability! His heart sank at these thoughts, and he wrestled with a sense of despair, the magnitude of which he had felt at only one other time in his life: the day Victor Jalaco beat his mother to death! He walked back into his room at the back of the store and lay down upon his bed. There was no use getting his hopes up. They only crashed down again. He lay there, his eyes closed, listening to the sounds of night in Hastings. Listening...to life passing him by. Lea was not his. He had to accept that.

CHAPTER 63

To Cal's surprise, more and more folks began coming into the Mercantile to shop. A few ladies from as far away as Black Dog Lake had their husbands bring them along with them when they had to come to Hastings, just to see the display in the Mercantile window. One lady actually bought all the checkered fabric that Lea had draped the window with! Fabric that Cal had not been able to sell the whole previous year. Men Cal had never seen before—ruffians and city-slickers, alike—who were simply passing through town, drifted into the store to ask about the guns in the display, or the fancy holsters. Often, they purchased them. Cal was amazed! Never before had he had so many customers! And positive reactions were heard, left and right!

Cal had never asked Lea why she was in Hastings, and not with her husband. He gathered up the courage on more than one occasion, but got an uneasy feeling each time and changed his mind. He was afraid what her answer might be. Afraid he might, somehow, push her away by asking.

As the months passed, however, his need to know grew more and more difficult to brush aside. So when he closed the door and locked it, at the end of a particularly prosperous day, seeing that they were *both* in high spirits, he asked her. He had to know, had to know if there was even a *smidgen* of hope for him to hold on to. Or, if there was none. He could not go on, any longer, in a state of oblivion.

Lea paled at his question, looking at him a long time, before walking over to where her shawl hung. "I can't tell you," she said, not looking at him.

"Can't, or won't?" he asked, feeling pushed to the breaking point by his need to know. To him, she had become an indelible part of his life. Though he had not kissed her since that one day when she had first begun working for him, he could not imagine—a moment—that she was not a part of him! His heart teemed with love for her. Love that he had never felt for anyone before. Love that he had never shared. A love as virginal and pure, as he was. It filled him with a deep sense of futility, when she pulled the shawl around her slim shoulders. "Lea, I *need* to know! I love you! You *must* know that!" He watched her closely. "I can't go on like this…if there's no hope for us." He looked at her pleadingly, his heart filling with fear as she turned her face away from him. "Lea, please. *Please!*"

She turned to look at him then, seeing the anguish he was feeling, and began to cry. "I'm sorry. I'm so sorry," she said, at last. "I never meant to hurt you like this, Cal," and she hid her face in her hands, her shoulders shaking, as sobs emanated from her.

He gathered her into his arms then, holding her tightly against him, and felt his heart pounding wildly in his chest as she continued to cry. When she finally gained control, he realized her arms were also around him, and he took what comfort he could, in that. He could smell her perfume and feel the silky strands of her hair against his cheek as they stood there. He held her, willing his heart to calm, willing her to explain.

Not moving from within his embrace, Lea began to speak. Quietly, hesitantly, her words faltering, now and then, she began to tell him what he wanted to know.

"I married young," she said, "to a man much older than I. A man who had sons my age. He was extremely well-to-do. A widower who had always been kind to Ophelia and me whenever we happened to encounter him around the town where we lived. Right from the start, he was always more attentive to me, and Ophelia and I used to laugh about it. We joked that someday he and I would marry and I'd go to live on his large ranch." She shuddered, as she said this, and moved to one of a pair of chairs nearby, before continuing. "I guess that furthered the idea, talking with Ophelia about him that way; how I'd be the mistress of his beautiful house, with servants at my constant beck and call." She paused, pulling the shawl more tightly around her, as if she was cold. "We lived in a small cabin to the west of his land, on five acres: Father,

Mother, Ophelia, and I." She looked at Cal, as he sat down in the other chair—pulling it to the side of hers—his love for her visible in his eyes. "I'm going to tell you…going to tell you *everything*," she said, at last. "I owe you that because of the feelings you have for me." Cal reached out to take her hand, but she pulled it away. Taking a deep breath, she soon continued: "My father worked as foreman and trail boss for my husband. Worked from dawn to dusk. Mother tended our place—doing whatever she could—to keep it going, and make things better for our family. Then, my father got hurt. He fell, injuring his head and back. It was a serious injury, Mother told us, and it laid him up for over a year. Ophelia and I did what we could to help Mother. But we weren't used to the really difficult jobs—like mending fences and things like that—and eventually, we fell behind." She shifted in her chair, sitting back, her eyes taking on the faraway look of remembering. Cal remained as he was, sitting very still, knowing that his future with her—if any—hung on what she was telling him. She stared, unseeing, toward the front of the store, seeing only the past.

"Father began to drink, then, because of the pain of his injuries, Mother said. First, only when the weather changed, and then, when we didn't do things exactly as he wanted around our place. He began going into town, more and more, and when he returned he was even more somber and depressed. He began to curse and rail at us, and one day he hit Mother." Cal reached out, again, as he heard the sorrow in her voice, but she folded her hands tightly together and he realized she was composing herself, so she could go on. He sat quietly, then, time seeming to stand still as he waited for her to continue.

"Ophelia was eighteen, then. I was sixteen. She drew into herself, as things got worse and worse. She worked, yes, hard as a workhorse. But, in quiet times, when Father was gone—or passed out—she buried herself in books and read till we teased her that she would ruin her eyes. She spurned all the attentions of any of the fellows who came 'round, asking to take her to barn dances, or the church socials. We had never been to church except for special events: weddings and such, and funerals. It seemed more important to try to do the chores the way Father demanded, so he wouldn't…so he wouldn't…be angry. We'd become afraid of him, you see, afraid of his drunken outbursts and irrational behavior." She grew quiet then, staring dejectedly, down at the floor. Cal rose and went to get her a glass of water to soothe her throat. She remained still, though she stirred from her reveries long enough to drink all of it and thank him. Then she continued: "We felt we couldn't leave Mother. Poor Mother! She had been so sweet-natured, always smiling and happy. She found such pleasure in just simple things. In the evenings, when he was gone, she would sit with us—sewing or reading—teaching us things. We enjoyed those times so very much! She liked to feed the birds, and would sneak some crumbs into her apron pocket as she cleared the table after we had finished eating. Later she would slip outside, and here they would come: birds of all sizes, shapes, and colors! One even got brave enough to eat from her hand." Her eyes filled with tears at the memory, and she sniffled and shook her head.

"You don't have to go on, Lea," Cal said, feeling sorry for what she had been through.

"Yes, I do," she replied, inhaling deeply. "You need to know... *everything.* " He could see her resolve strengthening, unaware that what she now told him would change his life, forever!

"We stayed there, with Mother, two more years. All Mother's gaiety ceased, as she grew to fear him. To fear his angry outbursts and drunken fury, as much as we did! One day when Ophelia and I went to town to get some supplies, my...my husband..." she shuddered, again, at the mere mention of him, Cal noticed. "My husband approached us. Of course, he wasn't my husband, then. Yet. He asked to speak to me, privately. Ophelia excused herself and went into the store to begin shopping. He was a handsome man, though he was older. Soft-spoken. A fine, up-standing fellow, a gentleman, I thought, being young and so very inexperienced where men were concerned. When he asked me to marry him that day, standing in front of the store...I...agreed. I didn't know...she stopped speaking, and looked down at the floor, a long while, before continuing. "I thought Ophelia and I—and Mother, too—would have a place to...to go...to be *safe* from Father's continual drunken rages, *if I* accepted." Cal noticed the look of raw pain upon her face, and wished he had not questioned her.

"We rode home that day, Ophelia and I, filled with mixed emotions. It seems, Ophelia had heard many things about my...my "intended." Terrible things that I refused to believe when she told me! She was concerned for me, and pleaded with me to tell him I had changed my mind. I, on the other hand, saw only his kindness to me...never believing he would be anything *but* kind, believing I would grow to love him, in time. Foolishly, I also believed that if some of what she had heard was true, my love for him would change him." She stared down at the floor, then looked at Cal, clearly organizing her thoughts and carefully choosing her words.

"When my father came home that night, he had already heard the news. He was quiet, at first, saying very little, but I noticed he watched me, constantly. He told me to do the milking that night, though usually Ophelia did it, and after supper I walked to the barn." She moved suddenly, surprising Cal, jumping up from where she had been sitting, pacing back and forth in front of his desk. She did not look at him, or speak, for the longest time. When she did, he wished she hadn't!

"He was waiting for me in the barn...my father! My *father*!" her voice rose, as she continued. "He had a bottle of whiskey in his hand, and he...he reeked of it!" Her words were coming faster and faster now, and tears were coursing down her cheeks. Cal rose to go to her, but she held up a hand, motioning him to stay where he was. He sat back down, his heart hammering in his chest, his hands gripping the arms of his chair. He felt her pain stabbing into him like a knife!

"He called me names. Said I was a...a *whore*, if a man like that, wanted me. That I must have encouraged him...as any whore would." She was shuddering violently now, yet she continued. "He grabbed me, tearing my dress, his whiskers rubbing the skin raw on my face and neck!" She paused, taking a deep breath, then continued: "Ophelia heard my screams from inside the house, and she and Mother raced outside and found us, found him trying to..."

Cal groaned aloud, and Lea grew silent, closing her eyes, her body shaking uncontrollably. "He hadn't hurt me…that way…but he had *tried,* and I'll *never* forget the look on Mother's face!" She grew calm: a calmness that made Cal uneasy. He said nothing, watching her, feeling her pain.

"We left that night, Ophelia and I, to go stay with my mother's sister, Aunt Hilda. Mother stayed behind. A week later, a passing salesman found her. She had been beaten to death. Our father was gone." Tears welled up in her eyes. "His body washed-up by the ferry crossing outside of town, a few weeks later."

Cal could not believe his ears! He shut his eyes, stunned by all the horrific events Lea and Ophelia had been through. His heart felt an overwhelming amount of compassion for both. He glanced up, surprised to see it was nearly dark outside. He rose and lit the oil lamp that sat on his desk. "Lea, let's go into the back, all right? It's warmer back there and I can heat us something to eat, if you like." She nodded, saying nothing, and followed him. Her face was startlingly pale in the light from the lamp. He pulled the curtain aside that separated his room in the back from the rest of the store. She entered, glancing at his unmade bed. He had forgotten to make it that morning, as he usually did, and felt a stab of embarrassment. Sitting the lamp on the small table in front of the bed, he picked up the quilt from the foot of the bed, and with a flick of his wrist, it fell into place. He smoothed it quickly, then turned, surprised to see that she still stood by the doorway. "Lea, would you like to sit down?" She glanced timidly at the bed, then at the table. There was only one chair beside the table, so she walked over and sat silently at the far end of the narrow bed. She looked as sad and as totally dispirited as a person could look, and it was all he could do not to take her into his arms to comfort her. Instead, he asked if she was hungry, but she shook her head in answer. Cal pulled the chair up, facing her where she sat on the bed, not sure what to do or say. If her own father could hurt her so badly, what in God's name had her husband done, he wondered, to make her run away?

After a few moments, she spoke: "There's more," she said, with whispered breath. He sat across from her, leaning forward, his arms resting on his upper thighs, wondering how she could possibly have endured more! "I married the following summer, still too distraught over all that had happened to think straight. Or, perhaps I was…merely greedy, as I have often thought. At any rate, I knew Ophelia was safe and settled in at Aunt Hilda's, but it was a small house. Even with the few things we had taken from our parents' house, it was quite cramped. Neither of us could face the possibility of returning home to live, however. The pain of all that had happened there was too fresh in our minds." She shifted a bit, looking at Cal, then resumed speaking.

"So, I married. His name doesn't matter…I pray I never hear it again!" She was kneading the folds of her skirt nervously as she continued. "We were happy the first couple of years. His sons lived at the ranch, in another wing. It was a spacious house, you see, with many rooms and a wide veranda encircling it." She saw his questioning look, and as if reading his mind, said simply, "near the Mexican border." He smiled a momentary smile, not at all surprised that she had known what he was thinking, without him saying it. That had happened often, the longer they worked together, and he had come to expect it.

"One day in late spring, my husband's foreman was caught stealing from our herd. My husband and his sons raced off into the night in pursuit, along with others who worked for us. The man was caught red-handed, they claimed, in an arroyo...in a gully, changing the brand on one of our cattle. They had shot his companions, but brought him back to the ranch. I had always been polite to any of the men who worked for us; speaking to them in greeting... though my knowledge of Spanish was very limited. They were always polite, in return." She took a deep breath, before continuing. "When they brought Miguel back that day, he *denied* any wrongdoing, but my husband ordered everyone— myself included—to go outside. There, under the blazing sun, he made us watch what they did to him. He said it was a good lesson for all the others, to see what happened to *anyone* who dared to rustle *his* cattle!" She grew still, though her hands still twisted the fabric of her skirt nervously. "They tore off his shirt, and chained him to a section of the corral fence. His arms spread wide on either side of him. Then my...my husband ..." she shuddered, and Cal could see the horror in her eyes as she remembered. "My husband whipped Miguel until blood covered his back. Then, laughing loudly all the while, he loosened one of the chains, letting him fall on his back, so the sand stuck to his open wounds." She hung her head, taking a few deep breaths, her small body shaking. "I did nothing! *Nothing!* I walked into the house...though I don't remember doing so, and did *nothing* to help him! *All that night* I heard his cries, and lay in my bed ...doing *nothing!*" Tears ran down her cheeks, her small body shaking with sobs as she raised a hand to stop Cal from reaching out to comfort her.

When she quieted, he knew by her facial expression there was more. "In the morning I took a pan of water, a cloth and some ointment, and walked to where he still lay. I whispered as I cleaned his wounds, 'Lo siento, Miguel. Lo siento,' telling him I was sorry. He never said a word, but his eyes looked into mine." She hesitated, and Cal saw her hands kneading the fabric of her skirt as she remembered. "My husband found me there, cleaning his wounds. He was furious! He called his sons, telling them to pick Miguel up and hold him. Then he ordered them to break his arms, and then his legs, and when they had, he shot him, holding the gun against his forehead. I...fainted...couldn't watch. I felt the blood spatter all over me—over my face and dress—and everything began to spin. When I came to, he was carrying me into the house. He raped me then, over and over, laughing crazily, and when he was done, he... hurt me." A groan escaped from deep within Cal, and he closed his eyes—feeling tears fill them—his hands tightening into fists as he tried to control the rage he felt!

Lea continued, her voice now a monotone, her eyes staring at a button on his shirt, though not seeing it. "After that day, he never let me out of his sight. If he had to be away on business, his sons watched me. This went on for six months, or so. I've lost count. I tried to escape, more than once. But each time I tried, they caught me. The punishment...was...always the same. He told me he would kill me, if I ever told anyone about Miguel, or what he'd done to me. I plotted and planned, all the while, waiting my chance. Then, a fence broke and the cattle got out. They were running all around the house, even up onto the veranda. My husband and his sons all ran outside to help round them up. It was after sunset, and I saw my chance! I gathered up all the jewelry he had given me during our earlier years together, filling my pockets. Then I piled all the clothes I could gather upon our bed, and lit them afire. I prayed the fire would occupy them long enough for me to get away. I also hoped he might think I had died! Then I escaped down the back stairway!" She was shaking as she finished talking, and Cal was surprised to realize that he was, too.

A knock at the door, just then, startled both of them! Cal told Lea to stay where she was, and he went to answer it. It was Ophelia. She took one look at Cal's face and knew that *he* knew.

"Where is she?" she asked. Cal said nothing, but locked the door behind her, then led the way to his room at the back of the store. "Lea, when you didn't come home, I got worried," Ophelia said. Lea looked up at her, her eyes empty of tears, a haunted look filling them. Ophelia sat down beside her, turning toward her sister, brushing her hair back from her face. "So you know?" she said, turning to look back at Cal.

"Yes," he replied, his voice sounding strangely unfamiliar, even to himself.

"I'm glad," Ophelia said. "I hope this doesn't change your feelings for my sister."

Cal stared at her. At first, he didn't understand, then he realized Lea must have told her how he felt. "I love Lea. I guess she told you. *Nothing's* changed that! *Nothing can!* But, they'll *never* hurt her again...I can promise you that!"

"Would you come by the house tomorrow, Cal? We've managed to keep Lea hidden since she escaped, but I know her husband. He'll never quit looking for her. It's just a matter of time until he finds her. We'll need your help, I'm afraid."

"You've got it," he said. "You can count on it!"

She hugged Lea, quickly. "I'll go now. I'm certain she's perfectly safe here. Thank you, Cal." Cal stood, then walked her to the door, locking it securely behind her.

"It'll be all right, Lea. I promise you that, honey," he said, when he was back in his room with her, again. "No one will *ever* lay a hand on you. I give you my word. It's all over now."

She pulled away from him to his surprise. Then stood and walked over by the table. "It's *not* over," she said. He started to walk over to her, but she motioned him to remain sitting where he was. He did so, watching her, wondering what she meant. As he watched, she began to unbutton her blouse.

"Lea, what...?" he began, but she hushed him, and continued undoing the buttons—one by one—a look of shame upon her face. "Lea..." he intoned, totally confused by her actions.

She kept her arms across her breasts, as she undid her undergarments; his body warming at the sight of her. He wanted her more than ever before. But, not now, not here, he thought, and he started to tell her so. It was then, that she finished disrobing. From the waist up, she was naked! She stood before him, her arms, all that covered her breasts, her shoulders smooth as silk and the color of finest porcelain! He stared at her, taking a deep breath, aching to touch her.

"It's *not* over, Cal," she said, her voice a mere whisper, and slowly turned her back to him.

Cal stared in horror at the sight before him! Red and purple welts and scars crisscrossed her back! *Whip marks!* He wasn't a man who shocked easily, but he gasped at the appalling sight! Stunned beyond words!

Lea stood silently, her head bowed. Then, without a word, she began to dress. When she was again properly attired, she turned to face him, her eyes looking sadly into his. "I'm sorry," she said, as tears ran down her cheeks. He reached out to take her hand. " No," she said, "that's why I didn't tell you before. I didn't want to see the look of revulsion on your face. It's...it's all right," she stated, hurriedly. "I understand."

"You *don't understand*!" he replied, anger rising up inside of him. "I don't care what your back looks like, Lea. I care about *you!* Dear God, Lea! My sweet, sweet Lea. Did you think I would stop loving you because of *that*? Any revulsion you see, honey, is because of what you've had to go through. Not because of any scars." He shook his head, "How could he *do this* to you? How could he *hurt you* like that?" He gathered her to him, speaking softly now. "I love you, Lea. I can't even imagine my life without you. I want you to be my wife, honey...a wife I will love and cherish! Oh, Lea, I promise you, you'll *never* be hurt again, *as long as I live!"*

Lea cried softly, her tears falling against his chest. She found it hard to believe that he could still love her. Could still want her. She clung to him, feeling protected and safe, for the first time in a long time, praying silently that that would never change!

CHAPTER 64

When Ophelia opened the door, the following morning, she was more than a little surprised to find the sheriff standing there, beside Cal. "Sheriff Gentry," she said, hesitantly, stepping back so the men could enter.

"Mornin', Ophelia," Moses said.

Cal walked quickly over to Lea, as she entered the room. "I hope you don't mind, but I asked Moses to join us today," he said. Both women looked uncomfortable, but said nothing. "I couldn't sleep last night," Cal continued. "I kept thinking about everything Lea told me. Kept trying to figure the best way to keep you both safe." He paused, looking at Lea. It was impossible to miss seeing the depth of his feelings for her. "You can trust Moses to be discreet," he stated. Ophelia asked them to be seated, then offered rolls and coffee. The men refused. "I went to see Moses, first thing this morning. Told him everything. He agrees that these men won't stop looking for you, Lea, so he needs to ask you some questions."

Lea looked pale and anxious, but Ophelia straightened in her chair, obviously the stronger of the two sisters. "Go on," she said, her voice firm, as she looked directly at the sheriff.

"First of all, Lea never told Cal her husband's name. If he can be so brutal where his wife and hired hand are concerned, I'm sure there may have been other such incidences. Some rewards out for him, something I can lock him up for, if he comes to town."

Ophelia glanced at Lea, who rose from where she had been sitting and began to pace back and forth, across the room. "Lea?" Ophelia said, "You *must* tell them. The sheriff is right."

Lea stopped pacing and sat back down, shaking her head, sadly. "I was such a little fool!" she said, and started to cry. "A stubborn, foolish child! If only I had listened to you, Ophelia."

She shook her head, gathering her courage, then looked up… first at Cal, and then at Moses. "My husband is…his name is…Don Diego Santiago."

A hushed silence fell over the room. Cal spoke first, his voice faltering slightly, in disbelief. "Your husband is "El Carnicero"…*The Butcher*? You're married to the man they call *The Butcher?*"

"Yes," she replied, her voice a mere whisper.

Moses whistled, shaking his head. Now he knew for certain that her husband would not stop searching for her! They sat there in silence, each realizing the gravity of the situation. Then Moses spoke: "How did you manage to get away, Lea? I already know about the fire, and the cattle, but how did you get to Hastings?"

Lea cleared her throat, sniffling and wiping tears from her cheeks, then proceeded to answer. Moses was glad to see Cal reach out and take her hand within his. "I took a horse from the stable that night: hiding in arroyos… gullies…crossing some streams. Twice, I crossed the nearby river, where it was shallow, backtracking. I didn't go directly to Aunt Hilda's that night. I knew he would look for me there. Instead, I lay nearby, huddled in a small cave; a hollow, really, where Ophelia and I used to play whenever we visited our aunt." She paused, looking down at the braided rug. Then she continued: "Diego arrived at Aunt Hilda's the next morning, looking none the worse for wear. He told her we had a terrible fight—a lover's quarrel—I believe he called it, and that he wished to speak to me. When she told him she hadn't seen me, he pushed by her and rushed through her house, uttering all sorts of threats! My aunt ordered him to leave, at once, or she would get the sheriff! He did leave, of course, but not before threatening her life if she, *in any way*, tried to help me. Meanwhile, I changed into other clothes—some of *his*, actually—tying my hair up and wrapping it in a bandana. I sent the horse toward home, then I waited. I was afraid that he could have me hung as a horse thief if I was caught with it. That,

295

or *worse.*" She looked at Cal, shuddering slightly, and he squeezed her hand, to give her comfort. She smiled at him, then she continued: "The next night, I walked into town, cutting through alleys and slipping through the livery stable. I was so terrified that someone would see me! When I got to Aunt Hilda's, she was sitting in the dark, waiting for me. She knew I would come to her, if at all possible. She hid me for two days, selling the jewelry I had taken, to a traveling salesman, and getting quite a substantial sum for it! The next day we noticed a man we had never seen in town before, watching the house. He stayed across the street, smoking and talking to people that went by, but always his gaze shifted back to my Aunt Hilda's. That afternoon, Aunt Hilda left the house, going to her friend's. He's a widowed doctor whom she often sees, not only for ailments, but as a suitor. She told him of my plight, then returned home. That night he arrived in his buggy to, supposedly, take her for a ride. It was something they often did. However, it was I—dressed in one of her dresses and a veiled bonnet—who blew out the light and left with him. The man was obviously fooled, and did not follow." She held tightly to Cal's hand, pausing to get her thoughts in order, then she continued: "The next day, done up in another disguise, I made my way east with a friend of the doctor. I was certain Diego would head north. I continued east for two days, then turned north, then back east. I was always careful to cover my tracks. I was sure, by then, if he caught me he'd kill me." She shivered as she said this, and continued: "We have a childhood friend who lived near Fort Smith, in Arkansas. A second cousin, by marriage, isn't she, Ophelia? Anyway, she hid me for many days, at which time she and her husband were leaving to go north, to meet up with a wagon train heading west. They gladly offered to take me as far as I wanted to go, but I was afraid to stay with them any longer. Afraid of what he'd do to *them*, if he caught me with them. We went our separate ways at St. Louis. Once there, I stayed at a boardinghouse, off the main street. I rested there for two days, not going out. I was delighted to be able to bathe again, and sleep in a comfortable bed! Then I caught a number of stagecoaches, still zig-zagging to cover my tracks, until I finally got to Hastings."

Moses listened intently, then asked Lea a question that had been troubling him. "Your husband doesn't know Ophelia lives in Hastings? Seems that's the first place he would check, after your aunt's."

"No," Ophelia cut in, her voice rising. "I was aware of the kind of man Diego was. I had warned Lea about him. At least I *tried* to warn her, but she wouldn't listen. When word got to me, soon after their marriage, that I was no longer welcome to visit the ranch—or to see Lea—I rode out there at once! She *is,* after all, my sister! Diego was *furious* to think I would dare to challenge him!

So furious, in fact, that I was afraid he was going to hit me, and I drew back quickly when he approached." She was twisting her handkerchief in her hands, and both men did not have any doubt how upset she was. "He ordered me off the ranch, laughing maniacally, telling me I should be 'very careful,' that women could so easily meet with an accident in those parts, so far from town! I ran to my buggy and raced back to town. I had no idea that he had begun to…to mistreat Lea, as he did. However, as I got into my buggy, Miguel slipped a note into my hand from her. She said I was not to worry about her, that all was well, and she would explain later. At that time, she was still trying to make excuses for his strange behavior…blaming herself for somehow causing it. She didn't understand why he insisted upon us having no visits, but said we should do as he said. She said Miguel would see to it she and I were able to exchange letters. He would stop at Aunt Hilda's whenever he came to town alone, to pick up supplies. It's obvious to me, now, that that could be the *real* reason Miguel was killed." She shook her head, looking first at Lea, then at the floor. "I was angry at Lea for being so foolish," she said, "never realizing that she was afraid that he would hurt her if I refused to stay away. I left my aunt's soon after and looked for work, finding jobs in different towns, and eventually arrived in Hastings. I had hoped to find work as a seamstress, but there was none. I liked it here: its friendly people and quiet peacefulness. When I realized there was a position available as a teacher, I applied, and was hired. I continued to correspond with Lea, through our aunt, but not often I hate to admit, and Aunt Hilda made certain none of my letters revealed my whereabouts. Just in case he …well, you know."

Moses shook his head. "Well, I'm sure your husband won't rest till he finds you, Lea. And I'm afraid it won't be long before he knows you're here. I'm surprised he hasn't *already* found out, in fact. I'd have thought he would have *forced* your aunt into telling by now."

"Aunt Hilda is a strong woman, sheriff, not very easily frightened. I've no doubt she'd *die*, before telling!" Lea shuddered at her own words, and Cal patted her hand, tenderly. "Can you do something, Sheriff Gentry? Something to protect us, I mean?"

"You can count on it," he replied. "I give you my word." Both women sighed in response, as the men stood to leave.

"Thank you for that," Ophelia said, reaching out to shake his hand. "Thank you for...for *everything*. I do hope..." she stammered.

"It'll be all right," Moses replied. "You're not alone against him, anymore."

"But, he has two sons...they'll come with him, I'm sure," Lea said.

"Then, *we'll* meet them," Cal stated. "They'll *never* hurt you again, Lea. I promise you that!" It was a promise he would be hard-pressed to keep!

CHAPTER 65

Sarah walked through the woods near her cabin, enjoying the warm sunshine and fresh air. She basked in the happiness that seemed so much a part of her life now. The closeness she shared with Moses and the anticipation of their child's birth filled her with feelings of joy, love and goodwill. She hummed as she walked, certain that she was the luckiest woman in the whole world! In less than a month, if she and Doc had figured right, she would give birth to the baby. A child whose very presence would heal the emptiness she felt whenever she thought of Gray Eagle's baby. The baby she had lost, before it could even be born. This child would also heal the loss that Moses felt, whenever he thought of his first wife, and their baby. Also, a baby who had died before it could be born. How similar our losses, she thought, as she walked along. She rubbed one hand gently over her stomach and felt the child within kick, in response. She smiled, feeling happy.

As she neared the cabin, she saw a buggy parked in the yard, and recognized the horse that pulled it as one belonging to Lilly and Jonas. She hurried across the yard, seeing them talking to Michael O'Leary, out by the barn. Little Eli, the boy Lilly's sister, Lydia, had given birth to and asked them to raise, ran over to hug Sarah. He was a sweet-natured child, tall and thin, with at least a million freckles adorning his cheeks and bridge of his nose. His eyes were a deep brown, and his shock of red hair shone in the sun like red-gold. "Hello," she called out, especially pleased that they had come to visit. She hugged the boy to her, as she walked over to where his parents stood.

Lilly hugged Sarah, as Jonas nodded in greeting and continued his conversation. "How are you?" Lilly asked, smiling happily, noticing the look of contentment on her friend's face.

"I'm just fine," Sarah replied, "and I'm so glad to see you!" The women walked into the cabin. "Coffee, or milk?" Sarah asked. "Eli, come get a cookie."

"Whatever you're having will be fine," Lilly answered.

Sarah put the coffeepot on to boil and placed a plate of cookies—baked that morning—on the table, then sat down across from Lilly. "So...what's new?"

"Well...let's see...there's some surprising news from town."

"What is it?" Sarah asked, excitedly, and Lilly laughed at her expression.

"Reverend Higgins stopped by to ask Jonas about mending a harness the other day, and he just happened to mention that Tom Dawson and Mary O'Leary had gotten married."

"Oh! Why, he's twenty years older than Mary," Sarah said, not believing her ears.

"Twenty, if he's a day," Lilly added. "But, that's not all! Reverend Higgins said he's selling the store! Already *has,* in fact! To some fellow from back East: Boston, I think it was. He and Mary and the children are going west. To California!"

Sarah was stunned. "Why, I'm speechless! Tommy has wanted to go west for as long as I've known him. I can't believe he's finally getting his dream. After all these years!"

Lilly smiled. "The good Lord does work in mysterious ways, doesn't He? I thought he would *never* get over Melinda Rose's death, and then along came Mary, and now here he is, starting a whole new life with her. It's great for the children, of course. They absolutely adore her. I've seen her in town a few times, and she seems so grown-up, so mature. And she's so patient with the children! Never raises her voice. You know how wild they were, before, when...well, you know."

A million thoughts raced through Sarah's head. "I wonder what her mother thinks of her marrying him, not to mention her moving so far away?"

"Oh, I can't imagine she likes it at all, but I haven't heard. A lot has changed for her, you know, since she began selling her quilts at the Mercantile. I heard she's sold *five*, already! In just a short period of time. Can you imagine?"

"I've seen them," Sarah replied. "In fact, I have one! Moses brought a beautiful blue and white one home, just the other day. Remind me to show you before you leave." She walked over to the door, then called to Eli, and handed him two more cookies. "Can you stay to supper? Moses tries to get home by six o'clock...and there's plenty to go around."

"No, but, thank you. It was hard enough to get Jonas away from the farm, as it was. I know he'll want to get back soon."

"So...is that all that's new? I don't hear much news, way out here, unless Rosie and Angus come to visit."

"Well, there is...something else I wanted to tell you," Lilly said, teasingly.

"Tell me!" Sarah ordered. "Don't keep me in suspense!"

"Well...I'm going to have a baby!"

"Oh, Lilly, how wonderful! I'm so happy for you! Have you told Jonas, yet?"

"No, I plan to tell him tonight." Both women smiled, as they visualized how happy he would be. "Sarah...do you think...you know, that it will be all right? Mother was ill, remember."

Sarah saw the worried expression on her face and reached out, taking her friend's hand in hers. "Oh, Lilly, I'm sure everything will be all right! I *know* it will be!" And she hoped that she was right. They hugged then, and talked of other things, until Jonas was ready to leave.

CHAPTER 66

On her way to the Mercantile, a few weeks later, Lea spotted the Santiago brand on three horses, tied to the rail, in front of the Lucky Lady Saloon! She stopped in her tracks, her heart pounding so hard within her that she was afraid she would swoon. Turning back the way she had just come, she lifted her skirt so she wouldn't trip, and raced back to the rooms she and Ophelia shared at the boardinghouse. Ophelia was fixing her hair as Lea burst into the room, shutting and locking the door behind her. "Did they see you?" Ophelia asked. She didn't bother to ask *if* Lea's husband and two sons were in town. One look at the terror in Lea's eyes, and she knew that their worst nightmare had been confirmed!

Lea dropped down into a chair, her whole body shaking in fear! "Oh, Ophelia! They're here! They're here!"

Ophelia hurried to the window, to see if Lea had been followed.

"What will we do?" Lea asked, her voice shrill.

"Be quiet!" Ophelia ordered, as she watched the street below. There was no sign of the Santiagos. Ophelia hurried to her sister's side. "We have to stay calm, Lea. Stop crying, and let me think!" She noticed her own hands were shaking, and she rose, hurrying back to the window, hoping Lea hadn't noticed. "You stay here. I'll go tell the sheriff. He can let Cal know."

"No! I don't want you to go!" Lea cried. "What if they see you?"

"I'll be careful," Ophelia answered, keeping her voice as calm as she could. She drew the curtains closed, then walked quickly into her bedroom. In the top drawer of her dresser lay a small handgun she had purchased long before she came to Hastings. She picked it up, made sure it was loaded, then slipped it into her bag. Then, wrapping her shawl around her shoulders, she spoke. "Stay here, Lea. Stay out of sight. I'll be right back."

Lea looked at Ophelia, a frightened expression upon her face. "I'm sorry I didn't listen to you, Ophelia, when you warned me not to marry Diego."

"I know you are," Ophelia replied. "Now try not to worry! The sheriff will see to it we're safe."

"I hope so," Lea answered, adding, "tell Cal to be careful."

"I'll tell the sheriff to tell him. Now lock the door, Lea, and don't open it, unless you know it's me!" She opened the door, peered out cautiously, and pulled it shut behind her.

Moses was sitting at his desk at the jail, going through some wanted posters, when Ophelia rushed in. One look at her face, and he knew what she had come to tell him. "Sheriff!" she exclaimed, then hesitated, realizing he was not alone.

"Ophelia," Moses replied, as Amos Culpepper turned to look at the young schoolmistress. Moses had told Amos of the trouble he expected concerning the Santiagos, and Amos stood, offering Ophelia his chair.

"They're here!" she exclaimed. "Lea saw the Santiago brand on three horses in front of the saloon, when she was on her way to the Mercantile. I don't think they saw her."

"Where is she now?" Moses asked, laying aside the papers and checking his gun.

"She's in our rooms. I told her to lock the door and not open it for anyone but me."

Amos interrupted, "Want me to go get Cal?"

"Yup, good idea. They'll be watching for Ophelia and Lea. Shouldn't pay much attention to a man on the street."

Amos nodded at Ophelia and left the jail, heading toward the Mercantile. Moses walked to the window, watching for any sign of trouble. He had heard of Diego Santiago over the years: nothing good. He hoped he was not as skilled with a gun as most folks claimed. "Ophelia, why don't we go out the back door. Then we can cross the street farther down." Ophelia nodded. Moses slid his gun back out of his holster and stepped out the back door, looking first one way, and then the other. All was still, no one in sight. As they crossed the street, he spoke. "If anything should happen to me, Ophelia, I'd be grateful if you would take a message to Sarah. Tell her I love her. Tell her...I'll always be with her...and the baby."

Ophelia's heart ached at his words. She knew how deeply he loved Sarah and was aware of how much danger he was being put in, by helping her and Lea. "I'm so sorry for involving you in this, Moses," she told him.

"It's my *job*, Ophelia, and I'd *want* to be involved if it *wasn't*," he replied. She smiled at him, grateful to him for his kindness and compassion.

They entered the boardinghouse, climbing the stairs to her rooms. Ophelia knocked, whispering to Lea to unlock the door. Immediately, the door flew open! "Oh, Ophelia, I was so afraid!" Lea whispered, pulling her sister inside.

Moses halted, just outside the door. "You stay inside," he ordered. "Don't open the door till Cal or I return." The women agreed, and quickly shut the door, locking it behind him.

Cal Dunnevey looked up as Amos entered the store. It took him only a second to read the expression on the old gunfighter's face. "They're here, aren't they?" he asked, already certain of the answer.

Amos nodded, noticing the guns Cal wore. He was well aware of the fact that Cal had never worn them until recently, and was concerned for the younger man. "Know how to use those?" he asked, motioning with his head toward them.

"I've been practicing," Cal replied. "I've got a lot of broken bottles out on my land now."

"Broken bottles don't shoot back," Amos replied.

Cal looked at the gunfighter-turned-deputy. "Ever heard of the Santiagos?"

"More than heard of 'em; tangled with 'em down near the Mexican border, years back. There were *four* of them then."

Cal shook his head. "I'm glad you're on our side," he said, smiling at the older man.

"Thank you, son," Amos replied. "I hope you can say the same when this day's over."

At that moment, Moses entered. "They're still at the Lucky Lady. Getting meaner by the minute, by the sound of things. Time to go?" The three men stood there, just long enough for Moses to deputize Cal, then they walked outside. With their backs to the sun, they headed for the saloon, and their appointment...with destiny!

CHAPTER 67

Sarah was sitting on the fallen log beside the barn shelling peas, when she heard the large wagon approaching. She brushed a wisp of unruly hair back from her face and sat the bowl of peas aside. She was surprised to see Tommy Dawson and Mary.

"Hello, Sarah," Tommy called out.

"Hello. Hi, Mary."

"Hello, Mrs. Gentry," Mary replied. "How are you?"

"Oh, I'm just fine, anxious for the baby to arrive."

Tommy helped Mary down from the high seat of the wagon as the Dawson children poured from the rear of it. "We're getting ready to leave, but I wanted to stop and see you before we left," Tommy said, looking happier than Sarah could ever remember him looking.

"I heard you were going to California," Sarah replied. "Heard you got married, too."

"Sure did," Tommy answered, and Mary blushed pretti-ly, in response.

"I'm happy for you, Tommy. For *all* of you! I know how much the children love you, Mary. And how good you are for them." "She's good for *all of us*," Tommy replied, and Sarah could not get over how different he seemed: more open, more contented. "We *all* love her," Tommy stated, and Mary beamed at his words.

"I heard you're selling the store?" Sarah questioned.

"Store *and* house," he replied. "Already sold both, to a family from Boston."

"Well, well. And now you get to live your dream."

Tommy's face brightened at her words. "You remember that?" he asked.

"Yup, I sure do," she replied, laughing.

"And you're living your dream, too, by the looks of it. You sure look happy."

"That I am," Sarah replied. "Good thing we never gave up on those dreams, isn't it? Come on in, all of you, I'll make some coffee ... and there's some cookies for the children."

Mary ushered the younger children inside, and told the others not to go far, then sat down with Sarah and Tommy, at the table. "I like your home, Mrs. Gentry. It's so warm and inviting. I hope Tom and I have one a lot like it, when we get to California."

"Thank you. Tommy, what will your mother do when she comes back? Where will she live, now that you've sold the house?" Sarah asked.

He laughed aloud. "She's not coming back! She lives with her sister, over in Destiny, *teaching school!* Can you imagine? *At her age!* Says she's happier than she's *ever been!*"

"I'll bet she's good at it, too," Sarah replied.

"Not only is she good at it," Mary said, "but she said it's been *her* dream since way before she married Tom's father!"

"That's wonderful! Looks like we're *all* getting our dreams," Sarah stated, pouring them a coffee and setting out a plate of cookies for all to enjoy.

The Dawson's stayed about an hour, then Tommy said they should be getting on their way. Sarah packed up the rest of the cookies for the children to take, to eat along the way, and handed Mary a book of poetry, and a cookbook, she seldom used. She kept her favorite, one that had been her mother's. "These are for you, Mary, to take to your new home in California. I hope you have a safe journey and are very happy there," she said, her eyes misting with tears.

Mary clutched the books to her and hugged Sarah, then climbed up onto the seat of the wagon. The children climbed into the back, amid peels of laughter and cheerful chatter! All but one, that is. To Sarah's surprise, Danny walked over to her, a shy look upon his young face.

"Mrs. Gentry, I'm…ah…I'm sorry…ah…for what I said to you, *before*. I know now that you…ah…did what you could to help my Maw. Mary talked to me…about it. I was wrong to blame you. Don't, anymore."

Sarah hugged him to her then, smiling warmly. "Oh, Danny, I knew you didn't mean it," she replied, "but thank you *so much* for being so kind as to tell me." He grinned at her then, and turned, running to the back of the wagon, and climbing in amongst his siblings. Sarah felt a great sense of peace, at his words.

Then Tommy approached. "Well, time to head for that "dream" I always told you about, Sarah. I guess this is good-by; probably won't get back this way," he said, sounding a bit unsure of himself.

"You'll do *just fine*, Tom Dawson," Sarah stated. "I *know* you will! Enjoy your dream, my friend. You deserve it!" And with that, he kissed her on the forehead, gave her a quick hug, and climbed up onto the wagon seat beside Mary. With a flick of the reins, they were off.

It's about time! Sarah thought. *Chase that dream*, Tommy! You've carried it within your heart for *so very long!* Good luck, my old friend!

CHAPTER 68

On August 24th, 1855, Sarah Gentry watched her lifelong friend, Tommy Dawson, leave for California with his new wife, Mary, and his children. He was, at last, in pursuit of the dream he had carried in his heart most of his life. Sarah smiled happily, thinking how wonderful it was that—as in the books her mother had read to her, so long ago— dreams *really did* come true. Hers had, and now Tommy's was, too. She was concerned about how late he was leaving, due to the terrible storms that occurred in the mountains, but he assured her he knew what he was doing. She turned, walking toward her cabin. I'll just keep them in my prayers, she thought, and then they'll be all right.

As she reached the cabin door, a terrible pain suddenly ripped through her! She cried out, grabbing her stomach, as another—even stronger—followed! Leaning against the door frame, she steadied herself until it passed, unable to do anything more.

Michael O'Leary was in the barn when Sarah screamed, and dropped what he was doing, vaulting over the rail of Pet's stall! He raced out of the barn, his heart pounding like a drum. When he saw Sarah, her face pale and contorted with pain, he knew she was in trouble. "Miz Gentry, what is it? Here...lean on me. Let me help ya'!"

Sarah tried to answer, but another pain, worse than the first ones, made her gasp and double forward! Michael had seen his mother have "birthin' pains" but, *never* like this! Never so fierce! He was sure something was wrong, and knew he had to get her inside and off her feet.

"I'm gonna carry ya', Miz Gentry...don't worry, I won't drop ya'. Here, put yer arm around my neck. That's it, that's it, easy. Just...there... don't worry now, Ma'am, yer gonna be all right!" He laid her on the bed, more frightened than he'd ever been before.

"Go...get Moses," Sarah pleaded. "Get...*help!*" she said, through clenched teeth. "It's the baby...Michael...*get help!*" She cried out again as another pain tore through her.

"I'll get Doc...*and the sheriff*" the boy said, already running out the door. He hurriedly put Glory's halter on, his hands trembling so he could hardly fasten it, and led her out of the stall, jumping onto her back. There was no time to saddle her, but he had ridden bareback before, so he lay close along her neck, his legs gripping her sides! He breathed a silent prayer for Miz Gentry and the baby, wishing town was a whole lot closer. Hoping he'd get there and back, before disaster struck! He knew it was nearly 5 o'clock. What if Doc's out somewhere, and can't be reached? he thought, but he put the thought out of his mind. He *had to* be there! He *had to be!* He clung to the old horse, laying low against her neck, urging her on! The pounding of her hooves matching the pounding of his heart!

At the same time, Rosie MacGregor was taking a cake from the oven. It was her favorite chocolate cake from her Irish Grandmother's special recipe, and it filled the kitchen with a wonderful aroma. She had made it especially for her husband, Angus, who would be home any moment. Today was his birthday, the first they would celebrate together, and she wanted to surprise him. She smiled, humming softly, as she stirred up a creamy, white frosting for the cake. She had never been happier than since Angus MacGregor had come into her life, and she couldn't help but think how blessed she was. She brushed a wisp of hair back from her face, glancing out the window. Must be about 5 o'clock, she thought. He'll be home soon, and she walked to the stove to stir the kettle of vegetable soup that bubbled there, feeling blissfully content!

Angus MacGregor stood at the grave of his friend, John Bruce: telling him—if indeed, the dead could hear—how the cradle was coming along, that he was making for Moses' baby. "Won't be long, Johnny, afore the wee bairn is here. A fine lad, or lassie, 'twill be! 'Tis sure I am o' tha'! And ye should see the cradle I'm makin'. The finest oak, she is, t' last *all* the young'ns Sarah and Moses bring into the world!" He looked back toward his house, noticing Cal Dunnevey and Amos Culpepper walking on either side of the sheriff, heading toward the Lucky Lady Saloon. He turned back, looking down at the cross that marked John Bruce's grave. "I carved a medallion, Johnny, like the one ye carved fer yer son. Carved it on the head o' the cradle. And painted it t' match! Know they'll understand, when they see it." He coughed, then looked out at the setting sun that just graced the tree tops on the far side of the cemetery. "Must be gettin' on t' 5 o'clock," he said. "Time I be headin' fer home. Rosie'll have supper 'boot ready. God bless ye, Johnny. Rest in peace, me auld friend." Then he turned and ambled down the road toward home.

At Mrs. Carson's boardinghouse, Lea sat on the small couch beside her sister, Ophelia. Both young women were pale, as they listened, intently, for any sound of footsteps outside their door. Ophelia thought again of the message the sheriff had asked her to give Sarah, if anything should happen to him. She was to tell Sarah that he loved her, and would *always* be with her and their baby. She shivered slightly, wondering how she would *ever* face Sarah Gentry, if Moses was terribly hurt, or worse, killed. She shook her head sadly, saying a silent prayer that both he, and Cal, would be safe. Lea held tightly to Ophelia's hand, fidgeting slightly, as each second passed. She thought, for just a fleeting moment, of her wedding night to Diego Santiago. He had been a most tender and loving bridegroom, stirring her senses to a fevered pitch. She remembered the way he had lifted her up against him, his body smooth and muscular. He had been so handsome, then, before he changed. She *still* could not understand *why* he had changed. She had never given him any reason to go from a loving husband, to a brutally cruel stranger! How she feared him, now! She thought then, of Cal. She remembered the first time she had seen him, at the Dawson funeral. He had kept glancing over at her, and she could not help looking back. He was so kind and gentle! She remembered the first time he had kissed her, his lips soft upon hers, not bruising and forceful. He was a good man, tall, ruggedly-built, and soft-spoken, but his greatest attribute seemed to be his innate sense of understanding and compassion. She shut her eyes as tears threatened to flow, remembering his words of love. Remembering, too, how his face had looked when she showed him the whip marks on her back. He had been too angry to speak, at first. But when he did, he had told her it made no difference, that he wanted her for his wife, and couldn't imagine his life without her. She glanced at the small pocket watch lying on the table beside the couch. It read 5 o'clock and she wondered *when*, *if ever*, this nightmare would end! More importantly, she wondered if Cal would be alive when it was over. Praying silently, she asked God to please keep him safe. Asked, too, that they have a chance at the happiness they *both* had lived *so long* without! She squeezed Ophelia's hand, feeling sick with fear as she sat there watching the clock.

Moses walked slightly ahead of his deputies as they approached the Lucky Lady Saloon. He wondered what Sarah was doing. Getting supper, he thought. Must be just about 5 o'clock. She'll be expectin' me around 6. He thought of how pretty she had looked that morning as she got out of bed. Her gown sheer against her body. Her stomach was a sight to behold in it's fullness! He thought her *even more beautiful*, if that was possible, with her stomach rounded: the skin taut, a pattern of tiny, blue marks on each side, at it stretched to accommodate the child growing inside: *their* child! *His* and *Sarah's!* I wonder if John Bruce felt this same pride and joy when my mother was carrying me? He smiled, at the thought. Then he felt the cold butt of his gun and a weight crushed down upon his heart as worry filled him. What if I die today? he thought. How will Sarah manage? How will she get through it? He remembered what had happened to Melinda Rose, and felt sick at heart! Would Sarah suffer the same?

He straightened his shoulders, hearing the sounds of music and laughter coming from the saloon. He had a job to do, didn't get a choice, as sheriff! The Santiagos weren't gonna stop in their quest to get Lea back, and it was his duty to protect her. Not just my duty as sheriff, he thought, but my duty as a decent human being! He had heard stories of "The Butcher," Diego Santiago. Heard that most men died when they confronted him and his sons. Many of those men hadn't had a chance! Amos had told him that. Amos knew them, had faced them, long ago, he remembered him saying. He had killed the youngest Santiago son, before he even had time to draw his gun! Moses wondered if he would be as fortunate today. He knew Amos was still fast, but he was older, and time had dimmed his sight, somewhat, he had once remarked.

He thought, then, of Cal Dunnevey. Cal had been his friend ever since his arrival in town, a year earlier. He smiled, remembering how Cal had looked at Lea that day at Ophelia's. There wasn't any doubt that he loved her! Hell, Moses thought, he'd be in his store, working as usual, if he didn't love her. And *safe* from the likes of the Santiagos! Moses halted as the three men came out of the saloon, his thoughts turning from Cal, to the job at hand!

Cal Dunnevey kept pace with the sheriff and Amos, as they walked toward the Lucky Lady. He felt empowered, somehow, by both the guns he wore and the deputy's badge on his shirt. It was as though some unseen power surged through him, making him feel invincible. If this was what it took to keep Lea safe, he thought, then he was ready! He didn't go to church regularly, true: didn't even say his prayers very often, but *nothing* would stop him from doing his best to protect her! He smiled, thinking of the first time he had seen her as she entered the pew across from his, during Melinda Rose's funeral service. His heart had skipped more than one beat, it seemed, he was so in awe of her loveliness and beauty! He hadn't been able to keep his eyes off of her!

Across his mind, flashed the memory of the welts on her back. *Whip Mark!* Whip marks that had ripped into her tender flesh, *again and again*! Put there by her husband, Diego Santiago!

His hands tightened into fists! She had looked so small and defenseless, so *ashamed*, when she showed him. He stifled a groan, as he relived the moment, anger blazing through him! An anger like he had felt at only one other time in his life: the day he killed Victor Jalaco! The day his childhood ended, and Maggie lay dead upon the floor of Jalaco's saloon.

He glanced at the front of the bank, his mind taking in what he saw, as though it was a series of scenes, flashing across his consciousness: lights lit, Johnathon Clark at the window, dust cloud swirling past bank doors, bank sign-above door…rocking in the wind. Must be after 5, he thought, Johnathon's working late.

He wondered, then, if he would die. As Amos had said, shooting bottles wasn't the same as shooting a man. He already knew that, though. Had known it since he was nine. Confronting these Santiagos wouldn't be easy for *any* man, let alone one who hadn't worn a gun up until a week ago! Well, he thought, if dying was what it would take to free Lea from the vile bastard that had hurt her, then *die he would*, and *gladly!* She was the only woman he had ever loved, besides Maggie. The only woman he had ever wanted to marry. He saw the Santiagos walk out of the saloon. A surge of excitement coursed through him. He squared his shoulders, sizing up the one in front of him: brash, young, cocky, smiling, nervous. He held his hands steady, just above his guns.

Amos Culpepper straightened his shoulders as he walked down the street beside the sheriff. There was a stone in his boot that made every step painful. But he ignored the pain, determined to see the pending confrontation through to the end. How many times had he faced guns, he wondered, including those of these same Santiagos? Well, this time it was necessary, he knew, if he was to honor the deputy's badge he wore upon his shirt. A deputy, he thought. Strange, how a man's life can turn about! All the years he had walked on the other side of the law, enjoying the excitement and adventure of it. Enjoying, too, the pride he'd felt when younger, as his reputation grew. Amos *Pepper*, he mused, famous gunfighter. He smiled at the thought.

Amanda never acknowledged those years. Never let him reminisce when those memories came. He understood: their memories of those years were very different. Indeed, *world's apart!* He knew they had been difficult for her. Not the kind of memories most young wives had. Oh, he'd sent her money, and always looked forward to the occasional letter from her, when she knew where to send them. But, often as not, he hadn't been able to let her know where to write. Had to keep on the move, or keep undercover. Long periods of time would pass before he heard from her, or her, him. He grimaced as the stone pressed deeper into the sole of his foot.

Amanda: how she had surprised him that day by the water, when she told him she loved him! He hadn't even known she existed then. He had been full of Sarah, Sarah Mathews: the girl who had stolen his heart right from the first moment he laid eyes on her. Sarah Mathews, with her sweet smile and special ways! With her sleek, firm body, and fiery-red hair! Oh, how I loved her, he thought, feeling the weight of his gun and holster against his hip. But, had he loved her? He wondered, now. Age had taught him a thing or two about love. Love wasn't whispered words and stolen kisses. Wasn't timid touching that left a pain inside a man. No...love was *so much more* than those things, he realized, things like loyalty and patience. Amanda had shown him that. He shook his head as he thought of the many long years she had been patient and true. The many long years she had waited for him. *Trusted* him. *Knew* he'd come back. He felt a rush of love at those thoughts. Amanda had told him she loved him, the very first day they met! The day Sarah Mathews had destroyed his world by leaving with Moses Gentry!

He saw Johnathon Clark step up to the window of the bank. Saw the questioning look upon his face. Any other time, he would have waved—or at least, nodded—but, there was business to tend to today. *Serious business*!

He saw three figures come out of the Lucky Lady. The three gunfighters he had faced, once before. He hoped time had dimmed *their* eyesight, as it had his. Hoped the sun would do so, if not. He knew it was nearing 5 o'clock. The sun was still bright and shining warm against his back. Shining into their eyes! He came to a halt at the same time Moses did. Yes, he thought, I killed one of the Santiago sons, years before, and I'll do the same today if it becomes necessary.

He eased the heel of his foot up a slight bit, inside his boot, as he began to silently pray: "Well, Lord, things don't look good here, today. I'd be right grateful if You'd put Your hand over the men at my side. They're good men, Lord. Young. As for me, You know I've made my peace with You. All I ask, Lord, is…if it's Your will… I have more time with my dear wife, Amanda. Amen."

Johnathon Clark was rummaging through a stack of papers, looking for a deed that he had misplaced, when he happened to glance out the bank window and see Sheriff Gentry, Amos Culpepper, and Cal Dunnevey walk past. He wondered what was going on, seeing the serious expressions on their faces. He walked over to the window to see where they were headed. He was especially surprised to see Cal Dunnevey wearing a gun! As long as Cal had lived in Hastings, he could not remember seeing him wear one! "Must be some serious trouble," he said aloud. "I hope Ophelia's gotten home by now." He looked at his watch, surprised to see that it was already 5 o'clock. She'll be safely home, having supper with her sister now, he thought, smiling. He glanced down the street, once more, surprised to see three strangers come out of the saloon and walk to the middle of the street, facing Moses, Amos, and Cal. Well, whatever's going on? He wondered, seeing the angry expressions on the strangers' faces. He had no idea they were connected, in any way, to Lea or Ophelia. No idea that in a matter of minutes a stray bullet would ricochet off the sign above the door of the bank, hitting him in the chest, killing him instantly!

If he *had* known, he would have been *even happier* that *only five days earlier* he had made a new will, leaving everything he owned—including his grand home just outside Hastings—to Ophelia! He had never convinced her to marry him, and did not understand why she seemed so reluctant to do so. But it was enough that *he loved her*, and *this* was his way of showing it!

CHAPTER 69

All was still except for the clanking of spurs, as Diego Santiago and his sons walked out of the Lucky Lady Saloon and into the street. Carlos and Ruben Santiago flanked their father, Diego, feeling a rush of excitement! Many times before, they had faced tougher-looking men, and walked away. Today would be easy! An old man, looking too confident, stood before Ruben Santiago. A younger one, looking unsure of himself, faced Carlos. It looked as though only their father would have an opponent to reckon with, in the sheriff, whom he faced. They grinned at the lawmen, their hands close above their guns, their fingers twitching! They were anxious to be done with these men, and this town of Hastings. Anxious to find their father's "gringa bitch," and head back home.

Carlos shifted his body a slight bit to one side. Damn sun, he thought. It's right in my eyes! Ruben, too, moved a bit, squinting at the old man before him. Didn't he look a bit familiar? he wondered. Hadn't they faced the old one, a long time ago, down near the border? He grinned at the old man, trying to remember.

Diego Santiago swaggered as he walked toward Moses. So this was Sheriff Gentry! He'd heard of him, and knew of his reputation with a gun. He'd heard that Gentry had built that reputation, long ago, when he was a drunk. Maybe his hands shake, he thought. Maybe the sheriff wants a drink *bad,* right now. Or *needs* one! He smiled at the thought, standing eye to eye with Moses, feeling no fear.

"Senior Sheriff, my sons and I were just coming to find you," he said. " I see you have saved us the trouble!"

"There's a wanted poster in my office, on you, Santiago, and a couple on your sons. I'm here to arrest you," Moses said, never breaking eye contact.

"Si! Si, Senior," the elder Santiago stated, smiling. "And how do you plan to do that?"

"Peaceably," Moses replied. "If you want it that way."

Diego Santiago's dark eyes flashed as he looked at Moses, and a muscle in his cheek twitched. "I've come to get my wife," he stated, his voice steady. "I know she is here. I've come to take her back to my hacienda. Do you want to die, Senor, over a stupid, gringa whore?"

Out of the corner of his eye, Moses saw Cal flinch at the words of Diego Santiago, and then all hell broke loose!

Thinking Cal was going to go for his gun, the Santiago in front of him started to reach for his! Amos saw *him* start to move, and drew his gun, firing rapidly, still lightening fast! Ruben Santiago dropped where he stood—his gun still in its holster—at the *very same time* Diego's shirt turned crimson and he pitched forward, firing as he fell!

Moses drew and fired as soon as he saw Cal flinch, hearing Amos fire, and then further explosions as he and Cal fired! Cal saw the Santiago across from him grin at him just before a bullet tore into the Mexican's chest, his grin becoming a grimace as he fell, blood quickly pooling on the ground beside him. Cal felt a moment of relief, then suddenly a searing fire—hotter than hell itself—cut a path along the side of his head, just above his temple! He grasped his head, crying out in pain! Then he felt his knees begin to buckle, and everything turned black!

Amos knew his shots had hit their mark! He saw the man across from him jerk and fall as soon as he fired, Ruben Santiago's gun still in his holster! And he saw the blood spreading across Diego Santiago's shirt as his second shot tore into him. Then he felt his body jerk back as the ground rushed up to meet him ... the stone in his boot no longer causing him any pain!

CHAPTER 70

Amanda Culpepper sat in her small rocker, mending a tear in the shirt Amos had worn the day before. She smiled happily, enjoying how she always felt when she did things for him. Yes, she thought, I like taking care of my tall, handsome husband. It's so nice to be needed, in some small way, by him. Amos Culpepper, she mused. The famous gunfighter, Amos Pepper! She giggled, softly. "If only he knew how "famous" I've *always* thought him to be! He doesn't have to be, or do, *anything* to be *special* to me," she said aloud.

She laid his shirt in her lap, then leaned her head back against the tapestry headrest of the rocker. Closing her eyes, memories filled her mind. She saw him walk toward her the day Sarah Mathews left him for Moses Gentry. Saw, again, the anger that had flashed across his handsome, yet boyish, face. She saw, too, his surprise, when she let him kiss her. It was the only way she had known to help ease his pain! She smiled, remembering his shocked expression when she told him she loved him. He was so smitten with Sarah Mathews, that he hadn't even realized *she* existed!

As she sat there in their cozy home, she looked at the old wall clock above his chair. He had bought it for her when they married. "5 o'clock," she said. "I'd better set the table." She stayed where she was, though, a tiredness suddenly enveloping her. Laying her hand on the shirt that lay across her lap, her thoughts drifted back to the day she had answered a knock on the door, expecting it to be someone from town:

Rosie, perhaps, or Tom Dawson. But to her amazement Amos had stood there. An old Amos, yet still as handsome as ever. He had stood there, his blue eyes looking at her in that special way of his. She had been too surprised to speak at first, she remembered, her heart not believing what her eyes saw! She smiled as she remembered how he had unhooked his gun belt, handing her his guns; asking her if he could come home. Tears filled her eyes at the memory. Yes, I still wanted him, she thought. Haven't I always?

The sound of gunfire rang out down toward the saloon, causing her to jump. She opened her eyes, wondering what all the commotion was about, and started to rise, to go see. But as she did, a terrible pain tore through her chest causing her to fall back into the rocker. The shirt she was mending for Amos, falling to the floor at her feet! She sat there, her hands gripping the arms of the rocker, her eyes squeezed shut, as another pain coursed across her chest and down her arms!

She wasn't sure how long it lasted—couldn't remember opening her eyes—but, suddenly, she looked up and her heart filled with the *greatest joy* she had *ever* felt! Amos stood before her, his hand outstretched to her! And though she never saw his lips move, she clearly heard him say: "I'll never leave you, again, my love," and she rose up, taking his hand, *knowing* it *was forever!*

CHAPTER 71

Events that occurred in Hastings on August 24th would be talked about for years to come! When the shooting was done, four men lay dead in the street, and another lay seriously wounded. A ricocheting bullet claimed another victim at the bank down the street!

Moses Gentry holstered his gun, amazed that he was still standing. He knew—without a doubt—how lucky he was! He also knew—without a doubt—that his deputy, Amos Culpepper, was dead. Culpepper's body lay sprawled, face up, eyes staring, a long, thin line of blood running from one side of his mouth. "Damn!" Moses exclaimed, hurrying to his other deputy, Cal Dunnevey. Cal, too, lay sprawled, but was groaning and moving about, both hands clutching his head!

"Cal! Cal, let me take a look!" he ordered. A crowd began to gather 'round the men, all talking at once, and craning their necks to see. He heard them whispering questions: "Who is it? Oh, it's Amos Culpepper. Oh, his poor wife. Hey, Amos Pepper's been killed." Moses ordered someone to get Doc Valentine, and one of the "gawkers" from the Lucky Lady rushed off down the street. He knelt on one knee, talking softly to Cal, assuring him that everything would be all right. Assuring him, but not believing it! He had seen head wounds before. Seen the damage they could do. A man could lose his speech, or his ability to balance, or his ability to think! All because of a head wound.

He glanced around, ordering two of the patrons from the saloon to get the bodies over to the livery stable. Told them to take Amos

Culpepper's to Doc's, to the back room. That was where the long, wooden boxes were stored, standing on end against the wall, awaiting their dead. He saw a young boy kick the leg of Carlos Santiago, then race off with his friends as they applauded his act of bravado.

A scream tore through the crowd then, at the same time Doc reached Cal's side. Moses stood quickly to grasp a frantic Lea within his arms, as Doc knelt to see to Cal. Over the crowd, Ophelia looked at Moses, the look in her eyes questioning. He shook his head and looked away.

"Take it easy, Lea...he's alive! He's *alive!* Give Doc a chance to look at him...easy...easy." Lea's body shook violently as she stood there. She saw the blood on Cal's head and hands. Saw the way he clenched his fists and grimaced as Doc worked on him. Her heart felt as though it would burst, it was beating so hard! Then she glanced to where the men were lifting up the dead bodies into the back of a waiting buckboard. As she did, she saw the man they carried. Saw his head fall back, saw his long, black hair, his sombrero dangling from his neck. She stared in horror, seeing his arms hanging limp, one hand dragging on the ground, his dark eyes staring vacantly in her direction! Her knees buckled then, and her world turned black! Moses felt her start to sway and caught her before she could hit the ground.

"Take her to my office," Doc said, to one of the men nearby. "Tell Judith to see to her. She'll know what to do." Then he signaled to the two men who stood nearest him and motioned toward Cal. "Let's get him to my office. Take it easy! Don't jar him!" They lifted Cal, one holding his legs, one holding him under the arms, and moved him as gently as they could, down the street to Doc's.

Moses stood, surveying the aftermath. A few onlookers still congregated: mulling around and talking excitedly. They shook their heads and pointed to the darkly stained areas in the street, giving *their* version of what had occurred. Anyone arriving in town at this moment would be curious as to why people stood around, here and there, in small groups. Otherwise, they would be unaware of the tragic events that had recently transpired. He saw Jasmine LaRue and Ruby Deegs talking to Jay Bullard as they walked back into the Lucky Lady. Three young boys ran down the street. One of them pointed his finger and made a sound. Another clasped his chest and fell to the ground, rolling over and over, then lay still, playing dead! Moses shook his head, and bent to pick up his hat, then turned and hurried to Doc's to see how Cal was.

Angus MacGregor hurried along the street after leaving the cemetery and his usual visit to his friend, John Bruce. He knew Rosie would be awaiting his return. The sudden burst of gunfire startled him, and he saw, in the distance, one man standing in the center of the street. All around that man lay bodies. Only one appeared to still be alive and moving!

"Saints preserve us…oh, Lord, 'tis na' good," he said, under his breath, as he hurried on. He realized the man still standing was Moses, and knew the two on the ground were Amos and Cal. He rushed down the street, nearly colliding with Doc Valentine as he ran from his house, bag in hand, a worried look upon his face. He wondered who the other men were that lay in the street.

As he passed the bank, he glanced inside, noticing the small hole in the large window. "Oh, Johnathon's na' goin't' be happy aboot tha'," he said, and then his eyes caught sight of the figure lying in a crumpled heap upon the floor of the bank! His heart gave a lurch that took his breath away and he stopped, bracing himself against the wall, staring through the glass, his heart racing! "Ah-h, nae Lord," he said aloud, then turned and hurried into the bank.

He knew, even before he knelt at the side of his friend, that Johnathon Clark was dead. A small hole, directly above his heart, showed in the dark blue material of his suit, positioned neatly between two of the thin, white pinstripes of the fabric. Angus reached out, closing Johnathon's unseeing eyes. "Ah-h," he moaned, patting the arm of his friend. He rose then, with a good deal of difficulty, his legs strained from kneeling. He felt shaken and rubbed his eyes, realizing they were damp. Filled with great sadness, he turned and left the bank, going to tell the sheriff of their friend's death. He knew in his heart that it was, indeed, a sad day for Hastings!

Entering Doc's, where he had just seen Moses go, he pushed through the crowd that had gathered there, looking for the sheriff. He saw a trail of blood running across the floor, heading to a room off to his right, and called out for Moses. Voices buzzed all around him, and he wished he could sit down for just a moment to catch his breath. His pulse was pounding in his ears, and he hoped he wouldn't collapse and die from all the excitement.

Just then the door opened and Moses came toward him. "Angus, what is it? Are you all right?"

"Aye, laddie," he answered, "an' yerself?" He placed a gnarled hand upon the sheriff's arm.

"I'm fine," Moses replied. "Can't say the same for Cal, though. He's head-shot," Moses added, and Angus noticed the silence all around them as the others listened intently, anxious for any news. "Amos is dead," Moses stated. "Got two of them before he fell. Saved my life."

Angus shook his head. "'Tis sad news, laddie, and I've more t' tell ye: Johnathon is dead, too, I'm sorry t' say. He was hit by a stray bullet, straight t' the heart."

There was a muffled cry off to the side as he finished speaking, and to his dismay, he saw Ophelia Denton hurrying through the crowd of onlookers who filled the hallway. "Johnathon?" she questioned, staring at him. Her face noticeably paling as she looked at him.

"Aye, lass," Angus replied, reaching out to take her arm. "I dinna ken ...dinna *know* you were here. 'Tis sorry I am, lass, so sorry."

"Where is he?" she asked, looking from Angus to Moses. "Please, I must go to him. Tell me where he is."

"At the bank," Angus replied, feeling deeply sorry he had caused her pain.

"I'll go with you, Ma'am," Kevin Landford said, from where he stood, off to one side. He took her arm, gently guiding her through the crowd and out the door.

"Angus, could you...are you up to telling Miz Culpepper about Amos? I've got to clear up some things around here. Want to stay with Cal, too, and see what Doc says."

Angus nodded, "Aye, laddie, tha' I am. Best we *both* go tell her: Rosie and me. I'll go now and tell Rosie, then we'll go right over." He wished more than anything that Moses hadn't asked this of him. He knew how upset Rosie would be, and how devastating the news would be for Amanda! He turned, slipping through the crowd, though many had left now, returning to the normalcy of their own lives! Walking slowly down the street, he shook his head, attempting to sort out his thoughts and find the words he would say to tell his wife of the tragedy that had befallen her best friend's husband!

Rosie rushed to the door as Angus entered. She couldn't help noticing how upset he looked. "Angus, what is it? I heard gunshots… are ya' all right?"

He took her hand in his, his heart racing. "Aye, me sweet Rosie. 'Twas gunshots ye heard, and I've some verra sad news t' tell ye."

"Oh, Angus. It wasn't the sheriff, was it?" she asked, fearing the worst.

"Nae, lass, nae. Na' the sheriff, but equally as bad," he said, pulling out a chair for her and then his own. She clutched his hands, seeing the terrible sadness that filled his eyes, then sat there, quietly waiting, knowing he needed a moment to compose himself.

At last, he cleared his throat, brushed a hand over his eyes, and then began to speak. When he finished, Rosie held her face in her hands and cried at the news. News far more terrible than she had expected… Amos and Johnathon both dead, and Mr. Dunnevey seriously wounded! It was just too dreadful!

When she gained control and quit crying, she wiped her eyes and blew her nose, then reached out, running her hand along the side of his face. "We've got to go tell Amanda," she said, "before she hears it from someone else."

He smiled at her, proud of how strong she was being. "Aye, me love, tha' we du." And they rose from their chairs and headed out the door.

CHAPTER 72

"Knock louder," Rosie said, wondering why Amanda wasn't coming to the door. Angus did as she said, and still got no response. "Might be in the back," she said, "working in her garden." She looked anxiously toward the back.

"We'll go see," Angus replied, and they walked quickly around to the back. Still there was no sign of Amanda. Angus knocked on the back door, then knocked again.

"Oh, dear. Ya' don't suppose she heard the commotion and went to see what it was all about, do ya'?" Rosie asked, wringing her hands, concerned for her friend.

"I'm hoping na'," he replied, and tried the back door. It opened immediately.

"Door's open, lass. Let's look inside...if she's na' here, we'll go find her." Rosie shook her head in agreement, one plump hand upon her chest, as she entered her friend's immaculately clean kitchen. Angus went on in before her, suggesting she sit, while he have a look-see. She sat down at the kitchen table, as he suggested, seeing the large Bible laying open upon it and the dainty blue and white cup and saucer beside it. She remembered the cup of tea they had shared just the day before... how they had laughed together over something, though she couldn't remember now what it was.

"Rosie," Angus said, as he reentered the kitchen, his voice soft, and brimming with sadness. "She's..." he began, his voice failing him.

Rosie looked at him, hearing the way his voice faltered. "What is it, love?" she asked, and felt chills break out across her skin.

"Ah-h, me sweet angel," he replied, reaching out to take her hand. "She's...*gone,* Rosie. She's wi' Amos."

Rosie stared at him, then rose, too astonished to speak. Angus patted her hand, watching her closely. To his surprise, she pulled her hand from his and wiped her eyes, then smiled at him. A sweet smile, full of tenderness. "It's God's will, my husband. As sure as I'm standin' here, it's God's will that she be with him! Now show me where she is, Angus, and I'll be seein' to her," she said, sniffling, once or twice. A small tear ran down her cheek, followed by another.

He smiled at her, thinking how proud he was of her. A strong woman she is, he thought, strong...like an angel! "'Tis only fittin', Rosie, her waitin' so long," he said. "'Tis only fittin' they be together."

They walked into the room where Amanda was, her small body resting peacefully in her rocker, her hands lying in her lap as if she were asleep. On the floor, by her feet, they saw the mended shirt that belonged to her husband. No, there was no doubt in either of their minds: Amanda Culpepper had gone to spend *eternity* with her beloved husband, Amos!

CHAPTER 73

Moses left the room as Doc continued to tend Cal. He felt overwhelmed by the emotions inside him. Feelings of bitterness and grief, all rolled into one, surged through him! Their intensity nearly numbed him! Cal Dunnevey was blind! He'd live, Doc said, would live a good, long life. If the wound didn't get infected, that is! Moses had seen the wound: a deep gash. It hadn't looked all that bad, once Doc got it cleaned up. Only a gash, Moses thought, and a man's life would forever be changed! He realized he was clenching his fists—and stopped—flexing his fingers, then walked out into the hall. A few folks remained there, and he looked from face to face, seeing their looks of concern. Lea rose from where she was sitting, hurrying toward him, anxious for any news of Cal.

"How is he, sheriff?" someone asked, off to one side, but he kept his eyes on her.

"He's..alive," he replied, searching his mind for some way to blunt the rest of the facts. There was none. "He's alive…but…he's blind," he said, in a whispered tone. A moan rose up from the onlookers as Lea reached out, gripping his hand. He was afraid she would faint, again, and reached to support her. She stared at him, and he wondered if she had understood. Then, she seemed to pull herself together. She cleared her throat. "I *must* go to him," she said, at last, her voice soft, but steady. Moses nodded, then led her into the room where Cal lay. His head was all wrapped in bandages, his hands clenched at his sides. Lea squared her shoulders, released her hold on Moses' hand, and walked quickly to Cal's side.

As she did, there was a loud commotion in the hall. Moses' head jerked up as he heard Michael O'Leary's extremely excited voice, calling his name! He turned, throwing open the door, his heart catching in his throat as he saw the frightened look on the young man's face!

"Sheriff! You gotta hurry! *Somethin's wrong!* Miz Gentry needs ya'!"

His words jarred the breath out of Moses! "Tell, Doc!" he yelled, to one of the women in the hall. He ran for the door, his legs weak from the fear he felt for Sarah and the baby! He raced to his horse, grabbing up his reins, and bounded into the saddle! It startled the horse, and he instantly reared-up, nearly unseating Moses! "Easy, boy, easy!" he said, yanking at the reins! Then, he turned the horse toward home, digging his heels into its sides, racing as fast as he could to get to Sarah!

Sarah took a deep breath, shaking with fear, as pain after pain tore through her body! She felt ravaged by it! Beads of sweat stood out upon her forehead. "Oh, Mother," she whispered aloud, knowing her mother was long dead, and she was alone. She was more afraid than she had ever been before: afraid for the baby in her, and afraid for herself! She wondered if she was dying? No one had ever told her the pains would be so bad. No one had ever told her she would feel like she was ripping apart! She grasped the blanket as another pain began. Her body tightened, trying to push the child from within her. She clenched her teeth, a scream rising from her lips, as she felt the full force of it! It seemed *forever* till it ended, and she was so afraid that something was wrong! She wiped the tears from her eyes, telling herself that everything would be all right! Telling herself that Moses would come soon and everything would be all right! She took a deep breath, relaxing a bit. It was short-lived, however, as another pain began. She had to grit her teeth, her fingers digging into the blanket, gasping! Was it coming breech, she wondered, like Melinda Rose's Danny had?

It was then that the *feelings* came...not feelings of more pain, but feelings of...she didn't know how to describe them. Suddenly, she felt calm. At peace. As though she knew, *beyond a doubt,* that all was well, and she and the baby would be all right! She wasn't sure if she heard the whispered words of comfort, or felt them, but she listened, and felt soothed. "It'll be all right, my daughter. This is how it is when a baby comes. Don't be afraid!" She knew the voice was that of her mother, and tears filled her eyes. Then, to her surprise, she distinctly heard another voice:

"Remember how the Indian women have their babies, Sarie. Don't be afraid. We're right here with you." She wondered later if her eyes had been closed, or opened, when she heard them speak: her mother, and Old John. She had *no doubt* she had heard them, *both* of them, and knew she was no longer alone! Some would doubt, if she told them what she had heard. Some would say she had a *huge* imagination. Still others, would think she had been out of her mind, because of the pain. But, she *knew* the truth. She had *no* doubts, *whatsoever*! Her mother and John had been with her, had comforted her. She had heard them... in the room, in her mind, or in her heart! And it was then, that she heard the pounding of hooves, and knew that Moses had arrived.

Moses flung himself off Midnight, racing for the cabin, and to Sarah's side! She grasped his hand, clenching her teeth, willing herself not to scream as still another pain tore at her! She pushed, moaning softly as it coursed through her. She heard Moses say something to comfort her as she continued to push. Then the contraction eased and she lay back, her hair damp with sweat. She tried to smile at him, hoping to assure him all was okay, but still another pain—worse than the last—tore through her, and she gasped, pushing for all she was worth! She felt her body tear, then, and liquid gushed from within her, but she could not stop pushing! It felt as though this contraction was going to go on forever, and she writhed in pain, knowing she was weakening. Then suddenly, she felt the baby slip from within her, into Moses' waiting hands! She began to cry, not from pain, but from joy and relief!

She watched the expression of awe on Moses' face as he held the tiny child. Then he got to his feet, and lay the crying baby in her waiting arms. He looked at her, a look so filled with joy and love, that she felt more tears come.

"We've got ourselves a little boy, darlin'," he said, his voice choked with emotion, "a little boy," he repeated. He wiped a hand across his eyes, a smile as big as all the world upon his face! "I *love you,* Sarah Gentry! I love you, darlin'!" he exclaimed. Then he tied and cut the cord, grinning happily as the baby's cries—loud and strong—filled the cabin. He gently washed the tiny infant, then wrapped him in a small blanket. Sarah watched him, smiling contentedly, before she closed her eyes and rested. The baby quieted, warmed by the blanket, as Moses got a clean cloth and water and began to tend to Sarah. When he finished doing all that was necessary, he kissed her tenderly, telling her again how very much he loved her. Then, picking up the baby, he walked over to the large rocker.

Sarah continued to rest. She thought of the "visit"she had had from her mother and Old John, and it warmed her heart. I must tell Moses, she thought, he'll be so pleased. She lay there, lost in thought: When I was young, I longed for a life of adventure and excitement. A life far different from that of my friends. She saw in her mind's eye, the faces of Gray Eagle, Standing Elk, Little Moon, and Howling Wolf. People far different from my own, she thought, but people I grew to love so dearly.

I always hoped for love, too, she thought, for that one *special* love, who would touch my heart and fill my soul! A man who would stand by me through good times and bad. Who—just by *being*—would make my life complete! The face of her husband, Moses, flashed across her mind, smiling that devilish grin she knew so well!

And I've followed my heart, she thought, sometimes unsure and doubting, and yet...I've always believed that if I did my best, God would lead me to *exactly* the place I was *supposed to be.* Images flooded her mind then: the faces of her father and Rosie, Tommy, and John Bruce. John, she thought, dear John! How strange that his life and mine have always been inextricably entwined from the very first moment we met, when I was ten. He was the best friend I ever had, and now, my dear husband's father, and grandfather to our little boy. She smiled, as her thoughts continued: Long ago, I felt like an outcast, never fitting in with my other young friends. And now I have my very own family: Moses and our precious son. She felt a wealth of contentment, and was enjoying this 'time of remembering' as her thoughts continued. I'm truly home where I belong, now.

Truly where I *want* to be! She glanced to where Moses sat, rocking their baby, holding him safely and securely within his strong arms.

"Moses?" she asked. "Have you thought of a name for our little one?"

"What have you got in mind?" he questioned, smiling at her. "I'd like to call him John, after Old John. I'd like to call him...John *Black Hawk* Gentry."

"Johnny Black Hawk," Moses replied. "I like that *just fine*, darlin'!"

And so it was.

THE END.

OTHER BOOKS IN THE OUTCAST SERIES BY SUSAN ILEEN LEPPERT INCLUDE:

Courageous Outcast

Johnny Black Hawk

Red Road Home

www.ingramcontent.com/pod-product-compliance
Lightning Source LLC
Chambersburg PA
CBHW021609120626
46545CB00001B/141